Robert Chambers

The Songs of Scotland Prior to Burns

Robert Chambers

The Songs of Scotland Prior to Burns

ISBN/EAN: 9783337181666

Printed in Europe, USA, Canada, Australia, Japan

Cover: Foto ©Thomas Meinert / pixelio.de

More available books at **www.hansebooks.com**

THE

SONGS OF SCOTLAND

PRIOR TO BURNS.

With the Tunes.

EDITED BY

ROBERT CHAMBERS, LL.D.

W. & R. CHAMBERS,
EDINBURGH AND LONDON.

Edinburgh:
Printed by W. and R. Chambers.

CONTENTS.

Humorous Songs.

Sentimental Songs.

CONTENTS.

CONTENTS.

SEVERAL Vignettes in the present volume, it will be perceived, are copied from the tasteful and characteristic sketches in Ritson, and which are believed to have been executed by David Allan.

INTRODUCTORY HISTORICAL SKETCH.

FOR the heart to break forth in song, whether to express love, merriment, or national and political sentiment, is so natural, that we may safely contemplate song as one of the earliest forms of literary composition in all countries. As far as Scotland is concerned—we find that the death of Alexander III. (1286 A. D.) was bewailed in a popular song; that the Scots had satirical songs on Edward I. and admiring ditties regarding Sir William Wallace; and that the triumph over the English at Bannockburn was hailed in an outburst of rude, but joyful verse. We find various allusions to popular songs in the histories of the fourteenth and fifteenth centuries, and in such poems of those ages as have survived, a whole catalogue of such ditties being given in the comic piece called *Cockilby's Sow*, which appears to have been composed in the middle of the fifteenth century. Only names, however, or at the utmost odd lines and verses of these early canticles, have been preserved; and, on the whole, they give us little insight into the general condition of song literature in those days. The utmost that we can be said to learn from them is, that there *were* songs in Scotland during the Bruce and early Stuart reigns—a fact of which a general knowledge of human nature would have assured us, even had not a trace of such compositions survived.

Another fact—a negative one, but of considerable importance—is revealed to us by the time we arrive at the middle of the sixteenth century. Scotland could then boast of a brilliant series of regular poets, all existing within the preceding eighty years—

Henryson, Douglas, Dunbar, and others ; but amongst all their compositions, there are none strictly of the nature of songs. Such men never thought of composing songs ; that is, lyrical compositions to be sung to music by the people. The People appear to have been in all but comparatively recent times the makers of their own songs. The occasion was the inspiration. A peasant felt the charms of his mistress, and a song upon that subject came as naturally from him as the sighs he expired. A droll, or a romantic, or a tragic occurrence, drew general attention, and was irresistibly crystallised into verse, through the medium of some mind that was poetical without knowing what poetry was. A crisis took place in the national affairs, and it somehow found expression through the same channel. It was beneath the poets of culture, the *bishop* Gavin Douglas, the *priests* Kennedy, Henryson, and Dunbar, to contemplate anything so natural and familiar as a subject for their muses.

And such continued to be in a great measure the case for a long time after the middle of the sixteenth century ; for when we examine the writings of Montgomery and Drummond, of Hume and Wedderburn, the poets of the reigns of James VI. and Charles I., we discover nothing strictly describable as a popular Scottish song.[1] The composing of such lyrics still mainly rested with the unpretending multitude, as it had always hitherto done. It is only to be admitted, exceptionally, that *probably* the song of *Tak your Auld Cloak about ye*, and perhaps one or two others, had been written about the reign of Mary, and, as we may infer from their good literary style, by bards of education and refinement, albeit too proud to acknowledge a contribution to the anthology of the vulgar. In the whole of the long series of poems collected into the Bannatyne Manuscript, anno 1568, it is remarkable that there are but two pieces—*The Wooing of Jenny and Jock*, and *Fient a Crum of thee she faws*—which have ever been accepted into collections of Scottish songs.

---

[1] It will be found that a composition of the nature of a song, but of a formal kind, by Montgomery, has been introduced in this collection.

The long era of the religious struggles brings before us but one fact in respect of our national minstrelsy—namely, that it was looked upon as a thing low, clandestine, and sinful : the clergy treated it as simply one of the bad habits of the people. Of this we have a curious illustration in a *Buke of Godly Sangs*, which was first printed in 1599, and a second time with additions in 1621, being an assemblage of dull religious lyrics, many of them composed to the tunes of the vulgar songs of the day, with a view to superseding these, 'for the avoidance of sin and harlotrie.' In this indirect and most unexpected manner, we become aware that there was then a popular song called *John, come Kiss me now;* a lullaby styled *Ba-lu-la-lu;* a song commencing with the significant inquiry, 'Who is at my window ? who, who ?' another, styled from its refrain, 'Hey, the day now daws,' &c. Of the success of this attempt to induce the people to chant the institutes of Calvinism, as an improvement upon such subjects as bonny lasses, good ale, and country merry-makings, history does not inform us.

There was indeed an obvious distinction to be made between the *words* and the *tunes;* as, while the former might be coarse, puerile, or otherwise disqualified for decent society, the attractions of the music were in no such way alloyed. It has hence resulted that we have a manuscript so early as the reign of Charles I., containing a large selection of the national airs, while no such collection of the songs appears to have been thought of till some generations later. The manuscript in question appears to have been the lute-book of a lady of the family of Skene of Hallyards, so eminent in the law in the reigns of James VI. and Charles I. It contains eighty-five tunes, many of which were dances, as the titles *Brangle, Currant,* &c., suggest, while others were obviously the airs to which the popular songs of the era were sung. Of the latter, however, but a few can be recognised as identical with airs still popular, and these for the most part are much altered, and have undergone a change of name. Only two airs still popular—namely, *The Flowers of the Forest,* and *Bonnie Dundee*—appear under the same, or nearly the same names, and with little difference of strain, in the Skene Manuscript.[1]

As far as the literature of the subject is concerned, it fully appears to have pursued a life of contempt till after the Restoration, when what Ritson calls the golden age of song commenced in England. The earliest glimpses we have of it on the horizon of the parlour or concert-room, occur in the reigns of Charles II. and James II. It is not in Scotland, however, that it first emerges among the polite, but in England. It fell to the lot of those who supplied music and song to the court and its connected circles in London, to perceive that there was some merit in the songs which passed from mouth to mouth amongst the people of Scotland. They accordingly began to write new verses for the Scotch tunes, and to compose new tunes and songs in what was called 'the Scotch manner:' some of the latter, strange to say, made their way back to Scotland, and were accepted there as true Scotch productions. The famous Thomas Durfey was an active labourer in this field, as appears from his well-known collection styled *Wit and Mirth;* and the Roxburghe Collection of broadside ballads in the British Museum, shews that Grub Street contributed a large quota to the stock of what may be called Anglo-Scottish songs.

When Scotland herself began, after the Revolution, to rise above her religious troubles, and to pay some attention to secular matters, the upper class, and especially that section of it which inclined to Episcopacy and Jacobitism, became also aware that their country possessed an inheritance of some value in her popular songs and melodies.[2] There remained, indeed,

---

[1] The tunes in the Skene Manuscript were printed with a learned dissertation by William Dauney, Esq. Edinburgh, 4to, 1838.

[2] The earliest published collection of Scottish music appears to have been Henry Playford's, which is dated 1700, being for the violin and flute. In the list, which embraces thirty-nine tunes, many of them dances, we recognise what may be presumed to be still existing favourites in, *I love my Love in secret ; Good-night, and God be with you ; Gingling Geordie ; Stir her up and haud her gaun ; Bessie Bell ; Wap at the*

the serious objection that the upland Muse was of upland manners and upland dress. Although the ladies and gentlemen of that day were not by any means what we should now call overrefined, still they were on a different level from the lads and lasses of the farmer's hall. It became necessary for the reception of the melodies, many of which were of the highest beauty, that they should be adapted to songs of a pure, or comparatively pure character. Accordingly, the era of Anne and George I. is marked by a large fresh growth of Scottish song, mostly by persons of condition, as Robert Crawford, William Hamilton of Gilbertfield, Lady Grizel Baillie, &c.—but, in a greater measure, by Allan Ramsay, who further promoted the cause by his collection of songs styled *The Tea-table Miscellany*, which began to be published in 1724. Under this new flush of song literature, the old popular ditties fell like weeds before a garden culture, to the loss, no doubt, of much we should now wish to possess, for its power of illustrating the history of the national intellect, but as undoubtedly to the benefit of the public taste and morality. Then it was that such polite society as assembled for the winter in Edinburgh permitted, for the first time, of the singing of Scotch songs at their tea-parties, or other meetings, with the accompaniment, it might be, of the spinnet or lute, but more generally without any such aid, and still more rarely with a second or third voice. Allan Ramsay assisted to make this a favourite amusement by publishing, in connection with his *Tea-table Miscellany*, a small collection of Scottish airs, the title-page of which, representing a lady at the spinnet and a gentleman with a violoncello, is here reproduced as a sort of glimpse of the musical enjoyments of the period. Nearly about the same time, an instructed musician, named William Thomson, produced a handsome

---

Widow, my Laddie ; If Love is the cause of my Mourning ; The Birks of Abergeldie ; For old long syne, my Jo ; Widow, gin thou be waking ; Alas, my heart, that we should sunder ; The Lass of Livingstone ; The Deil stick the Minister.—See *Additional Illustrations to Johnson's Museum*, by Mr D. Laing, xc.

assemblage of the best Scotch songs with the music, under the title of *Orpheus Caledonius*, the first volume of which was dedicated to the Queen, and the second to the Duchess of Hamilton.

Lady playing on Spinet, with Violoncello Accompaniment.—From a volume entitled *Music for Tea-table Miscellany*, published by Allan Ramsay.

During the sixty years following upon the publication of *The Tea-table Miscellany*, the repeated editions of that collection and the appearance of several others, particularly the ample one of Mr David Herd, attested the continued esteem of all classes for the national songs of Scotland. In that time, we find many capital songs produced, some of them by persons of elevated station; as, for example, Sir Gilbert Elliot, Miss Jean Elliot, and Lady Anne Lindsay. Others expressing the feelings of a portion of the community for the cause of the Stuart family, were thrown into the general stock, and not a little to its enrichment, as, somehow, what stood ill with the parliamentary senate of Great

Britain contrived to make a tolerably fair appearance in the court of Apollo. We find in the productions of this era much effective poetry, free from all objections in point of good taste and morality; but no one can read Mr Herd's volumes (1776) without acknowledging that there was still a great infusion of the rude, and even the licentious, in the class of songs familiar to the common people.

It is also to be observed, that during this middle part of the eighteenth century, considerable additions were made to the national stock of melodies. The popularity which the original rustic airs had acquired in the time of Ramsay, caused a number of airs in the same style to be composed by instructed musicians; amongst whom none was more notable than James Oswald, originally a teacher of music, successively at Dunfermline and in Edinburgh, but who, about 1741, settled as a music-publisher in London, where he attained the appointment of church-composer to George III. During the same epoch, several ample collections of the Scottish melodies were published; one in twelve small volumes by Oswald himself.

It remained for ROBERT BURNS to arise and purge away what dross remained in the national song. At the time of his appearance in Edinburgh (1787) a worthy tradesman named Johnson, who practised a style of music-engraving by punch or stamp-marking, had commenced a collection of the national songs and airs, under the title of the *Scots Musical Museum.* The project caught the fancy of Burns, and he threw himself into it with characteristic ardour. He contributed songs of his own. He gathered others heretofore inedited. He furnished purified and improved versions of many homely ditties. He noted down many airs also hitherto unknown to paper. He induced others to assist him. At the same time, a respectable musician, Mr Stephen Clark, adjusted the airs and fitted them with accompaniments. The final result was, that Johnson's *Museum* became all but an exhaustive collection of the Scotch songs and their melodies, the entire number comprehended being *six hundred,* whereof a hundred and seventy-nine were furnished by Burns, generally with at the least some brightening touch from his masterly hand. It remained only to be regretted, that a considerable number of songs unfit for decorous society was permitted to mingle with the general mass. A new edition of this work was published by Messrs Blackwood in 1838, with an ample supplement of prose notes by the late Mr William Stenhouse and Mr David Laing—the former a type of all that is faithless and inaccurate in editorship, the latter precisely the reverse. It is on the whole a valuable book, and one not to be dispensed with by any one who desires a minute acquaintance with the subject.

The present Volume is intended to embody the whole of the Pre-Burnsian songs of Scotland that possess merit and are presentable, along with the music ; each accompanied by its own history, as far as that can be ascertained. It is meant as historical in its general scope and arrangement, and may be sufficient, perhaps, to satisfy all ordinary inquirers into the subject, as a department of the national literature. It is also hoped that the collection may be serviceable amongst those who have not consented to the entire banishment of our national airs from the drawing-room.

Historical Songs.

THE FLOWERS OF THE FOREST.

I 've heard the lilt - ing at our yowe milk - ing,

Lass - es a - lilt - ing be - fore the dawn of day;

But now they 're moan-ing on il - ka green loan-ing—The

Flowers of the Fo - rest are a' wede a - way.

Such is the early form of this melody, as preserved in the Skene Manuscript (see *Introduction*). The first and fourth lines of the verse set to it, are the remains of an old ballad, for which probably it was the appropriate air, and of which Sir Walter Scott caught up one other fragment, presenting, he remarked,[1] a simple and affecting image to the mind :

> [Now] I ride single on my saddle,
> For the flowers of the forest are a' wede away.

It seems to relate to some depopulating blow sustained by the district commonly called the Forest—namely, Selkirkshire. Such an incident we readily discover in Scottish history, in the overthrow of the army of James IV. at Flodden, September 1513.

In the last century, there lived in Edinburgh an unmarried lady of family, who is remembered as the chief ornament of her circle, through her talents, intelligence, and good sense—Miss Jean Elliot of Minto. Her father was Sir Gilbert Elliot of Minto, Lord Justice-clerk of Scotland, the able son of an able father, who rose in high state employments under King William, with whom he had returned from an unmerited exile, sustained under the misgovernment of the Stuarts. A son of the Justice-clerk, bearing his own name, was also a man of eminent talents, which he did not disdain occasionally to exercise in penning verses. It is stated that Miss Jeanie, who was born in 1727, shewed such lively faculties in her girlhood, that even then her father would employ her to read his law-papers to him, and declared that he profited by the shrewdness of her remarks. One day, having a conversation with her on the Battle of Flodden, he offered a bet that she would not compose a ballad on that subject ;[2] and thus it came to pass that she took up the fragments of the old lost ballad, and restored them, as it were, to life in the following composition :

---

[1] *Minstrelsy of the Scottish Border*, iii. 128.
[2] Mr D. Laing's Notes on Stenhouse, Johnson's *Museum*, i. *131.

I 've heard the lilting at our yowe-milking,
    Lasses a-lilting before the dawn of day;
But now they are moaning on ilka green loaning—
    The Flowers of the Forest are a' wede away.

At buchts, in the morning, nae blythe lads are scorning,
    The lasses are lonely, and dowie, and wae;
Nae daffin', nae gabbin', but sighing and sabbing,
    Ilk ane lifts her leglen and hies her away.

In hairst, at the shearing, nae youths now are jeering,
    The bandsters are lyart, and runkled, and gray;
At fair, or at preaching, nae wooing, nae fleeching—
    The Flowers of the Forest are a' wede away.

At e'en, at the gloaming, nae swankies are roaming,
    'Bout stacks wi' the lasses at bogle to play;
But ilk ane sits drearie, lamenting her dearie—
    The Flowers of the Forest are a' wede away.

Dule and wae for the order, sent our lads to the Border!
    The English, for ance, by guile wan the day;
The Flowers of the Forest, that foucht aye the foremost,
    The prime o' our land, are cauld in the clay.

We hear nae mair lilting at our yowe-milking,
    Women and bairns are heartless and wae;
Sighing and moaning on ilka green loaning—
    The Flowers of the Forest are a' wede away.

Miss Elliot died at her brother Admiral Elliot's house of Mount Teviot, Roxburghshire, on the 29th March 1805. It cannot apparently be ascertained that she wrote any other song or poem; but the probability, of course, is, that she did not restrict herself to this one happy effusion.

Contemporary with Miss Elliot, there lived in Edinburgh another lady of family, possessed like her of most attractive social qualities, and a frequent and ready writer of verses. Born Alison Rutherford of Fernylee, Selkirkshire, she married, in 1731, Mr Patrick Cockburn, advocate, whom she long survived. She was also familiar with the old ballad of *The Flowers of the Forest*, and some years, it is believed, before Miss Elliot's song was written, composed one to the same tune, and with the same burden, not referring to Flodden, but to a crisis of a monetary nature, when seven good lairds of the Forest were reduced to insolvency, in consequence of imprudent speculations. Mrs Cockburn's song was as follows:

I 've seen the smil-ing of Fortune be-guil-ing, I 've felt all its fa-vours and found its de-cay; Sweet was its bless-ing, kind its ca-ress-ing, But now it is fled, fled far a-way! I 've seen the fo-rest a-dor-ned the fore-most, With

flow - ers of the fair - est, most plea - sant and gay; Sae

bon-ny was their bloom-ing! their scent the air per - fu - ming! But

now they are wi - ther - ed and weed-ed a - way.

I've seen the smiling of fortune beguiling,
　I've felt all its favours and found its decay;
Sweet was its blessing, kind its caressing,
　But now it is fled—fled far away!

I've seen the forest adorned the foremost
　With flowers of the fairest, most pleasant and gay;
Sae bonnie was their blooming! their scent the air per-
　fuming!
But now they are withered and weeded away.

I've seen the morning with gold the hills adorning,
　And loud tempest storming before the mid-day.
I've seen Tweed's silver streams, shining in the sunny beams,
　Grow drumly and dark as he rowed on his way.

Oh, fickle Fortune, why this cruel sporting?
　Oh, why still perplex us, poor sons of a day?
Nae mair your smiles can cheer me, nae mair your frowns
　can fear me;
　For the Flowers of the Forest are withered away.

LAMENT OF THE BORDER WIDOW.

My love built me a bonnie bower, And clad it a' wi' li-ly flow'r; A braw-er bouir ye ne'er did see, Than my true lov-er built for me.

My love built me a bonnie bower,
And clad it a' wi' lily flower;
A brawer bouir ye ne'er did see,
Than my true lover built for me.

There cam a man at mid-day hour,
He heard my song and he saw my bouir—
And he brocht armed men that nicht,
And brake my bouir and slew my knicht.

He slew my knicht, to me sae dear,
And burnt my bouir and drave my gear.
My servants a' for life did flee,
And left me in extremitie.

I sew'd his sheet and made my maen;
I watch'd his corpse, myself alane;
I watch'd by nicht and I watch'd by day;
No living creature came that way.

I bore his body on my back,
And whyles I went and whyles I sat ;
I digg'd a grave and laid him in,
And happ'd him wi' the sod sae green.

But think na ye my heart was sair,
When I laid the moul' on his yellow hair ;
Oh, think na ye my heart was wae,
When I turn'd about, away to gae ?

The man lives not I 'll love again,
Since that my comely knicht is slain.
Wi' ae lock of his yellow hair
I 'll bind my heart for evermair.

Sir Walter Scott published this affecting piece as a 'fragment obtained from recitation in the Forest of Ettrick.' He regarded it as probably relating to the death of Cockburn of Henderland, a freebooter, who was hanged over the gate of his own tower by King James V. in 1529. Its being a genuine relic of antiquity may fairly be a subject of doubt. The resemblance of the poetry to that of Fair Helen of Kirkconnel is worthy of notice.

GILDEROY.

The subject of the following amatory elegy was a man named Patrick Macgregor, but more familiarly *Gillieroy* (the red-haired lad), who, after a desperate course of stouthrief and oppression practised for some years at the head of a band of followers, chiefly in the Highlands of Aberdeenshire, was hanged with his whole party, ten in number, at the Cross of Edinburgh, July 27, 1636. The present ballad, an improvement upon a rude contemporary one, was first printed in Durfey's *Pills to Purge Melancholy*, volume v., 1719. It has been several times printed as the composition of a Sir Alexander Halket, but entirely through a mistake, there being in reality no such person.

O Gilderoy was a bonnie boy ;
   Had roses till his shoon ;
His stockings were of silken soy,
   Wi' garters hanging down :
It was, I ween, a comely sicht,
   To see sae trim a boy ;
He was my joy and heart's delicht,
   My handsome Gilderoy.

Oh, sic twa charming een he had,
   A breath as sweet 's a rose ;
He never wore a Highland plaid,
   But costly silken clothes :

He gain'd the love o' ladies gay,
  Nane e'er to him was coy :
Ah, wae is me ! I mourn the day,
  For my dear Gilderoy.

My Gilderoy and I were born
  Baith in ae town thegither ;
We scant were seven years before
  We 'gan to love each other.
Our daddies and our mammies, they
  Were fill'd with meikle joy,
To think upon the bridal-day
  'Twixt me and Gilderoy.

For Gilderoy, that luve of mine,
  Gude faith, I freely bought
A wedding-sark of Holland fine,
  Wi' silken flowers wrought ;
And he gied me a wedding-ring,
  Which I received with joy :
Nae lad nor lassie e'er could sing
  Like me and Gilderoy.

Wi' meikle joy we spent our prime
  Till we were baith sixteen ;
And aft we pass'd the langsome time
  Amang the leaves sae green :
Aft on the banks we 'd sit us there,
  And sweetly kiss and toy ;
Wi' garlands gay wad deck my hair,
  My handsome Gilderoy.

Oh, that he still had been content
  Wi' me to lead his life !
But, ah, his manfu' heart was bent
  To stir in feats of strife ;

And he in many a venturous deed,
  His courage bauld wad try,
And now this gars my heart to bleed
  For my dear Gilderoy.

And when of me his leave he took,
  The tears they wat mine e'e ;
I gave him a love-parting look,
  My benison gang wi' thee !
God-speed thee weel, mine ain dear heart,
  For gane is all my joy ;
My heart is rent, sith we maun part,
  My handsome Gilderoy.

My Gilderoy, baith far and near,
  Was fear'd in ilka toun,
And bauldly bare away the gear
  Of mony a Lawland loun :
Nane e'er durst meet him hand to hand,
  He was sae brave a boy ;
At length wi' numbers he was ta'en,
  My handsome Gilderoy !

The Queen of Scots possessit nocht,
  That my luve let me want ;
For cow and ewe he to me brocht,
  And e'en when they were scant :
All those did honestly possess,
  He never did annoy,
Who never fail'd to pay their cess
  To my love Gilderoy.

Wae worth the loun that made the laws
  To hang a man for gear !
To reave of life for ox or ass,
  For sheep, or horse, or mear !

Had not their laws been made so strict,
  I ne'er had lost my joy ;
Wi' sorrow ne'er had wat my cheik
  For my dear Gilderoy.

Gif Gilderoy had done amiss,
  He micht have banish'd been ;
Ah, what sair cruelty is this,
  To hang sic handsome men !
To hang the flower o' Scottish land,
  Sae sweit and fair a boy !
Nae lady had sae white a hand
  As thee, my Gilderoy !

Of Gilderoy sae fear'd they were,
  They bound him meikle strong ;
Till Edinburgh they led him there,
  And on a gallows hung :
They hung him high abune the rest,
  He was sae trim a boy ;
There died the youth whom I loo'd best,
  My handsome Gilderoy.

Thus having yielded up his breath,
  I bare his corpse away ;
Wi' tears that trickled for his death,
  I wash'd his comely clay ;
And sicker in a grave sae deep
  I laid the dear-loo'd boy ;
And now for ever maun I weep
  My winsome Gilderoy.

The old *broadside* version of *Gilderoy* ran thus :

> My love he was as brave a man
>   As ever Scotland bred ;
> Descended from a Highland clan,
>   A kateran to his trade.

No woman, then, or womankind,
    Had ever greater joy,
Than we two, when we lodged alone,
    I and my Gilderoy.

First, when I and my love met,
    With joy he did me crown;
He gave me a new petticoat,
    And then a tartan gown, &c.

There is something touching in the conclusion:

And now he is in Edinburgh town;
    'Twas long ere I came there;
They hanged him upon a-hie,
    And he wagg'd in the air.
His relics they were more esteem'd
    Than Hector's were at Troy;
I never love to see the face
    That gazed on Gilderoy!

GENERAL LESLIE'S MARCH TO LONGMARSTON MOOR.

The civil war, deeply as Scotland was involved in it, has handed us down extremely little of song. The genius of Presbyterianism, which enlisted the soldiers, and carried them into the bloodiest struggles, was not in any way kindred to the muse. We do not hear of the covenanting armies having even required the ordinary stimulus of music to accompany their marches. There is, however, one rude legendary piece, which Allan Ramsay has published under the name of *General Leslie's March to Longmarston Moor*, and which may be accepted (though still with some hesitation) as a relic of that terrible era. An air afterwards appeared in Oswald's Second Collection, under the name of *Lesley's March*. Song and air are both repeated here, not as likely to be of any use for parlour singing, but as historical curiosities.

March, march ! why the deil dinna ye march ?
    Stand to your arms, my lads ; fight in good order.
Front about, ye musketeers all,
    Till ye come to the English border.
Stand till 't and fight like men,
    True gospel to maintain ;
The parliament 's blythe to see us a-coming—
    [The bishops, a popish breed,
    When you have crossed the Tweed,
Will faint to hear your sanctified drumming.[1]]

March, march ! &c.
    When to the kirk we come,
    We 'll purge it ilka room,

---

[1] The lines within brackets are modern.

Frae popish relics and sic innovations,
　　That a' the world may see,
　　There's nane in the right but we,
Of the [guid] auld Scottish nation.

March, march ! &c.
　　Jenny shall wear the hood,
　　Jockie the sark of God,
And the kist-fu' o' whistles that maks sic a' cleerie,
　　Our pipers braw
　　Shall hae them a'—
[Laud and his crew shall gae tapsal-teerie !]

Whatever come on it, whatever come on it,
Busk up your plaids, my lads, cock up your bonnets !

I'LL NEVER LOVE THEE MORE.

There was a tune prevalent in England in the early part of the seventeenth century, under the name of *I'll never Love thee more*, probably from the refrain or recurring final line of the stanzas of the song to which it was sung, and which song may have been identical with one found in a manuscript volume of songs and ballads, with music, in the handwriting of John Gamble, the composer, dated 1659, which Mr William Chappell[1] states to be now in the possession of Dr Rimbault—beginning thus :

My dear and only love, take heed,
　　How thou thyself expose,
By letting longing lovers feed
　　Upon such looks as those.
I'll marble-wall thee round about,
　　And build without a door ;
But if thy heart do once break out
　　I'll never love thee more.

[1] Popular Music of the Olden Time, i. 380.

That extraordinary genius, the Marquis of Montrose, whom Cardinal du Retz deemed the most like a Plutarchian hero of all his contemporaries, had, in addition to his other brilliant gifts, a power of verse-making, which he exercised on various remarkable occasions—for one, it will be remembered, in addressing the portrait of the martyred Charles the night before his own execution. He appears to have become acquainted with the popular song of *My Dear and only Love, take heed,* and to have been impelled to compose something of the same strain, but addressed to the state for which he made such exertions and such sacrifices, instead of a flesh-and-blood mistress. The result was a piece which has been often reprinted under the name of *Montrose's Lynes;* of which a copy follows, adapted to the English melody :

My dear and on-ly love, I pray That lit-tle world of thee, Be govern'd by no oth-er sway But pu-rest mon-ar-chy; For if con-fu-sion have a part, Which virtuous souls ab-hor, I'll call a syn-od in my heart, And nev-er love thee more.

My dear and only love, I pray
    That little world of thee
Be govern'd by no other sway
    But purest monarchy ;
For if confusion have a part,
    Which virtuous souls abhor,
I 'll call a synod in my heart,
    And never love thee more.

As Alexander I will reign,
    And I will reign alone ;
My thoughts did evermore disdain
    A rival on my throne.
He either fears his fate too much,
    Or his deserts are small,
Who dares not put it to the touch,
    To gain or lose it all.

But I will reign, and govern still,
    And always give the law,
And have each subject at my will,
    And all to stand in awe :
But 'gainst my batt'ries, if I find
    Thou storm, or vex me sore,
As if thou set me as a blind,
    I 'll never love thee more.

And in the empire of thy heart,
    Where I should solely be,
If others do pretend a part,
    Or dare to share with me ;
Or committees if thou erect,
    Or go on such a score,
I 'll smiling mock at thy neglect,
    And never love thee more.

But if no faithless action stain
  Thy love and constant word,
I 'll make thee famous by my pen,
  And glorious by my sword.
I 'll serve thee in such noble ways,
  As ne'er was known before ;
I 'll deck and crown thy head with bays,
  And love thee more and more.[1]

YOU 'RE WELCOME, WHIGS.

At the Revolution of 1689, the Tories—thenceforward named Jacobites—lost power, but acquired wit. From that time, throughout well-nigh a century, while unable to make effective head against a parliament-elected dynasty and liberal principles of government in church and state, they were at least in some favour with the Muses, and were able to assail their conquerors with a continual pelt of paper missiles, not always stupid or simply vindictive. Often, too, their sufferings for the exiled royal family gave scope to a pathos far above what might have otherwise been looked for from the partisans of an expiring idea.

First in the series of their satiric effusions stands a piece which must be allowed to be very bitter and very unjust, but which, after all, is (with the omission of one or two rough stanzas) eligible for preservation, as having more wit than usual in proportion to its gall.

[1] From Watson's *Collection of Scots Poems,* Part iii. 1711.

You're wel-come, Whigs, from Both-well brigs, You're
ma - lice is but zeal, boys; Most
ho - ly sprites, the hy - po - crites, 'Tis
sack ye drink, not ale, boys; I
must a - ver, ye can - not err, In
break - ing God's com - mand, boys; If
ye in - fringe bish - ops or kings, You've
hea - ven in your hand, boys.

You're welcome, Whigs, from Bothwell brigs!
   Your malice is but zeal, boys;
Most holy sprites, the hypocrites,
   'Tis sack ye drink, not ale, boys;

I must aver, ye cannot err,
   In breaking God's command, boys ;
If ye infringe bishops or kings,
   You've heaven in your hand, boys.

Suppose ye cheat, disturb the state,
   And steep the land with blood, boys ;
If secretly your treachery
   Be acted, it is good, boys.
The fiend himsel', in midst of hell,
   The pope with his intrigues, boys,
You'll equalise in forgeries :
   Fair fa' you, pious Whigs, boys.

      *   *   *   *

You lie, you lust, you break your trust,
   And act all kind of evil ;
Your covenant makes you a saint,
   Although you live a devil.
From murders too, as soldiers true,
   You are advanced well, boys ;
You fought like devils, your only rivals,
   When you were at Dunkeld, boys.

King William's hands, with lovely bands,
   You're decking with good speed, boys ;
If you get leave you'll reach his sleeve,
   And then have at his head, boys.
You're welcome, Jack, we'll join a plack,
   To drink your last confusion,
That grace and truth you may possess
   Once more without delusion.[1]

---

[1] This severe tirade upon the Presbyterians, from several allusions,
seems to have been written between the years 1690 and 1700.

THE BATTLE OF KILLIECRANKIE.

While Scotland was in the crisis of the Revolution settlement, an effort was made in behalf of the expatriated king by the Viscount Dundee (better known by his patrimonial name of Claverhouse or Claverse), who had great influence among the Highland clans, and easily gathered a few thousands of them together. An encounter took place between him and General Mackay at Killiecrankie, July 17, 1689, when the brave Dundee was victorious, but fell by a bullet-shot towards the close of the action. In the following probably contemporary ballad, the chief attention is drawn to the mode of fighting, and the sentiments and expressions of the mountaineer soldiery.

Clav-erse and his High-land-men Came down up-on the raw, man; Who, be-ing stout, gave mo-ny a shout; The lads be-gan to claw, then. Wi' sword and targe in-to their hand, Wi' which they were na slaw, man; Wi' mo-ny a fear-fu' heavy sigh, The lads be-gan to claw, then.

Claverse and his Highlandmen
  Came down upon the raw, man ;
Who, being stout, gave mony a shout ;
  The lads began to claw, then.
Wi' sword and targe into their hand,
  Wi' which they were na slaw, man ;
Wi' mony a fearfu' heavy sigh,
  The lads began to claw, then.

Ower bush, ower bank, ower ditch, ower stank,
  She flang amang them a', man ;
The butter-box[1] gat mony knocks ;
  Their riggings paid for a', then.
They got their paiks wi' sudden straiks,
  Which, to their grief they saw, man ;
Wi' clinkum-clankum ower their crowns,
  The lads began to fa', then.

Her[2] leap'd about, her skipp'd about,
  And flang amang them a', man ;
The English blades got broken heads,
  Their crowns were cleaved in twa, then ;
The durk and dour made their last hour,
  And proved their final fa', man ;
They thocht the devil had been there,
  That play'd them sic a pa', man.

---

[1] Butter-box ; slang word for a Dutchman, on account of the great quantity of butter they eat.—GROSE. In Mackay's little army there were several Dutch regiments.

[2] The Highlanders have only one pronoun, and as it happens to resemble the English word *her*, it has caused the Lowlanders to have a general impression that they mistake the feminine for the masculine gender. It has even become a sort of nickname for them, as in the present case, and in a subsequent verse, where it is extended to— *Her-nain-sell.*

The Solemn League and Covenant
  Cam whigging up the hill, man ;
Thocht Highland trews durst not refuse
  For to subscribe their bill, then :
In Willie's name, they thocht nae ane
  Durst stop their course at a', man ;
But Her-nain-sell, wi' mony a knock,
  Cried, Furich, Whigs, awa', man.

Sir Evan Dhu,[1] and his men true,
  Cam linking up the brink, man ;
The Hogan Dutch, they feared such,
  They bred a horrid stink, then.
The true MacLean, and his fierce men,
  Cam in amang them a', man ;
Nane durst withstand his heavy hand ;
  A' fled and ran awa', then.

Och on a righ ! och on a righ !
  Why should she lose King Shames, man ?
Och rig in di ! och rig in di !
  She shall break a' her banes, then ;
With *furichinich,* and stay a while,
  And speak a word or twa, man ;
She 's gie ye a straik out ower the neck,
  Before ye win awa', then.

Oh, fie for shame, ye 're three for ane !
  Her-nain-sell's won the day, man.
King Shames' red-coats should be hung up,
  Because they ran awa', then.[2]

---

[1] Sir Evan Cameron of Lochiel.

[2] The author appears here to allude to the general conduct of King James's army in the crisis of the Revolution.

Had they bent their bows like Highland trews,
    And made as lang a stay, man,
They'd saved their king, that sacred thing,
    And Willie'd run awa', then.[1]

A professor Kennedy (qu. Kerr?), of Aberdeen, is stated by James Hogg to have produced a Latin ballad on the Battle of Killiecrankie, being in some degree a paraphrase of this rough vernacular song, but including references to heroes of the cavalier party not here adverted to. It begins as follows:

    Gramius notabilis coegerat montanos,
    Qui clypeis et gladiis fugarunt Anglicanos:
    Fugerunt Vallicolæ, atque Puritani;
    Cacavere Batavi et Cameroniani.[2]

THE BRAES OF KILLIECRANKIE.

There is a second popular ballad on the Battle of Killiecrankie, of much more comic expression than the preceding. It has been given with its melody in Johnson's *Museum*, but with some improvements from the hand of Burns.

Where hae ye been sae braw, lad? Where hae ye been sae bran-kie, O? Where hae ye been sae braw, lad? Cam ye by Kil-lie-cran-kie, O? An

---

[1] From Herd's Collection, 1776.
[2] Of this clever production Sir Walter Scott, in his turn, wrote a versified translation, which was printed in *Chambers's Journal*, First Series, No. 48.

ye had been where I hae been, Ye wad-na been sae can-tie, O; An ye had seen what I hae seen, On th' braes o' Kil - lie - crank - ie, O.

Where hae ye been sae braw, lad ?
   Where hae ye been sae brankie, O ?
Where hae ye been sae braw, lad ?
   Cam ye by Killiecrankie, O ?
     An ye had been where I hae been,
     Ye wadna been sae cantie, O ;
     An ye had seen what I hae seen
      On the braes o' Killiecrankie, O.

I've faught at land, I've faught at sea ;
   At hame I faught my auntie, O ;
But I met the deevil and Dundee,
   On the braes o' Killiecrankie, O !

The bauld Pitcur fell in a fur,
   And Claverse gat a clankie, O ;
Or I had fed an Athole gled,
   On the braes o' Killiecrankie, O.

SUCH A PARCEL OF ROGUES IN A NATION!

This song embodies pretty fairly the anti-union feeling of Scotland, which was essentially a Jacobite feeling, though partaken of by many who were not Jacobites, and echoed by a vast proportion of the populace, while in reality, for anything that has yet appeared, the sober good sense of the country was willing to see the long-contemplated junction effected. The usual charge of corruption against the majority of the Scottish parliament is also here embodied; a charge, however, which, it is but fair to say, never has been borne out by clear evidence.

Fare - well to a' our Scot - tish fame, Farewell our an - cient glo - ry; Fare - well ev'n to the
Scot - tish name, Sae famed in an - cient sto - ry! Now
Sark rins o'er the Sol - way Sands, and Tweed rins to the
o - cean, To mark where England's pro - vince stands: Such a
par - cel of rogues in a na - tion!

Farewell to a' our Scottish fame,
    Farewell our ancient glory ;
Farewell ev'n to the Scottish name,
    Sae famed in ancient story !
Now Sark rins ower the Solway sands,
    And Tweed rins to the ocean,
To mark where England's province stands :
    Such a parcel of rogues in a nation !

What force or guile could not subdue,
    Through many warlike ages,
Is wrought now by a coward few,
    For hireling traitors' wages.
The English steel we could disdain,
    Secure in valour's station ;
But English gold has been our bane :
    Such a parcel of rogues in a nation !

I would, ere I had seen the day,
    That treason thus could sell us,
My auld gray head had lain in clay,
    Wi' Bruce and loyal Wallace !
But pith and power, to my last hour
    I 'll make this declaration,
We 're bought and sold for English gold :
    Such a parcel of rogues in a nation !

THE WEE, WEE GERMAN LAIRDIE.

The Scottish Jacobites affected to consider the line chosen in
the act of succession as one of very poor account among European
sovereignties. George, the elector of Hanover, was, in their
esteem, but a small squire, in comparison with the old race of
monarchs whom he superseded. A song pouring unsparing
derision upon him under the name of *The Wee, Wee German*

Lairdie, and couched, it must be admitted, in vigorous poetical language, appeared in Cromek's *Reliques of Nithsdale and Galloway Song*, 1810, with a note stating that it was one version out of several which the editor had heard sung. This was transferred, with some verbal alterations, to Hogg's *Jacobite Relics*, with an additional verse at the end, part of which the editor said was from an older collection. Cromek—the victim of the singular impostures of Allan Cunningham—and James Hogg, are but fallacious authorities to rest upon. No matter. The song has obtained a deserved popularity, and may be here repeated, along with the air supplied by Hogg.

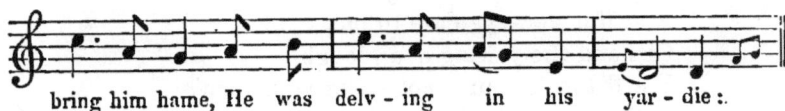

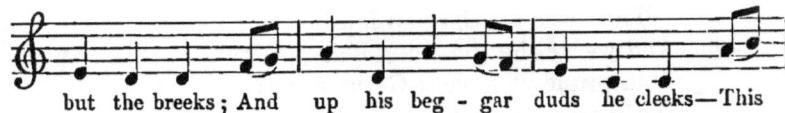

Wha the deil hae we got-ten for a king, But a wee, wee Ger-man lair - die? And, when we gaed to bring him hame, He was delv - ing in his yar - die: Sheughing kail, and lay - ing leeks, But the hose, and but the breeks; And up his beg - gar duds he cleeks—This wee, wee Ger - man lair - die.

Wha the deil hae we gotten for a king,
    But a wee, wee German lairdie ?
And, when we gaed to bring him hame,
    He was delving in his yardie :
Sheughing kail, and laying leeks,
But[1] the hose, and but the breeks ;
And up his beggar duds he cleeks—
    This wee, wee German lairdie.

And he's clapt down in our guidman's chair,
    The wee, wee German lairdie ;
And he's brought fouth o' foreign trash,
    And dibbled them in his yardie.
He's pu'd the rose o' English loons,
And broken the harp o' Irish clowns ;
But our thistle taps will jag his thumbs—
    This wee, wee German lairdie.

Come up amang our Highland hills,
    Thou wee, wee German lairdie,
And see how the Stuarts' lang-kail thrive
    They dibbled in our yardie :
And if a stock ye dare to pu',
Or haud the yoking o' a plough,
We'll break your sceptre o'er your mou',
    Thou wee bit German lairdie.

Our hills are steep, our glens are deep,
    Nae fitting for a yardie ;
And our Norland thistles winna pu',
    Thou wee bit German lairdie :
And we've the trenching blades o' weir,
Wad prune ye o' your German gear—
We'll pass ye 'neath the claymore's shear,
    Thou feckless German lairdie !

[1] Without.

Auld Scotland, thou'rt ower cauld a hole
　　For nursin' siccan vermin ;
But the very dogs o' England's court
　　They bark and howl in German.
Then keep thy dibble in thy ain hand,
　　Thy spade but and thy yardie ;
For wha the deil now claims your land,
　　But a wee, wee German lairdie ?

THE PIPER O' DUNDEE.

Dundee, as the winter haunt of the Forfarshire gentry, was, in 1715, as remarkable for its Jacobite prepossessions as it has since been for the meritorious industry which in sixty years has quadrupled its population. So much may be said in partial explanation of an enigmatical song, called *The Piper o' Dundee*, which seems to hint at a private meeting of the Jacobite party in preparation for the rising under the Earl of Marr. It can only be added, that if Carnegie of Finhaven was the person meant by the piper of Dundee, he proved a roguey indeed, as he afterwards deserted his party—not to speak of his proving the best runner from the field of Sheriff-muir.

The pip - er came to our town, To
our town, to our town, The pip - er came to
our town, And he played bon - ni - lie. He

D

played a spring the laird to please, A spring brent new frae

yont the seas; And then he gae his bags a wheeze, And

played a - nith - er key. And was - na he a

ro - guey, a ro - guey, a ro - guey, And

was - na he a roguey, The pi - per o' Dun - dee.

The piper came to our town,
To our town, to our town,
The piper came to our town,
    And he played bonnilie.
He played a spring the laird to please,
A spring brent new frae yont the seas ;
And then he ga'e his bags a wheeze,
    And played anither key.
       And wasna he a roguey,
       A roguey, a roguey,
       And wasna he a roguey,
         The piper o' Dundee ?

He played 'The welcome ower the main,'
And ' Ye 'se be fou and I 'se be fain,'
And 'Auld Stuarts back again,'
    Wi' muckle mirth and glee.

He played 'The Kirk,' he played 'The Quier,'
'The Mullin Dhu' and 'Chevalier,'
And 'Lang awa', but welcome here,'
    Sae sweet, sae bonnilie.

It's some gat swords, and some gat nane,
And some were dancing mad their lane,
And mony a vow o' weir was taen
    That night at Amulrie!
There was Tullibardine and Burleigh,
And Struan, Keith, and Ogilvie,
And brave Carnegie, wha but he,
    The piper o' Dundee?

CARLE, AN THE KING COME!

This song, in its first form, probably originated in the days of the Commonwealth, when the Restoration was a subject of daily prayers to the loyalists. Ramsay afterwards introduced a version of his own in *The Gentle Shepherd*, beginning, 'Peggy, now the king's come.' The copy here given is that improved by Burns for Johnson's *Museum;* the second stanza is believed to be wholly his.

Car - le, an the king come, Carle, an the king come,

Thou shalt dance and I will sing, Car - le an the

king come. An some - bo - dy were come a - gain, Then

some - bo - dy maun   cross the main; And   ev' - ry man shall

hae   his ain, O   Car - le,   an   the   king come.

> Carle, an the king come,
> Carle, an the king come,
> Thou shalt dance and I will sing,
> Carle, an the king come.
> An somebody were come again,
> Then somebody maun cross the main ;
> And every man shall hae his ain,
> Carle, an the king come.

> I trow we swappit for the worse ;
> We ga'e the boot and better horse ;
> And that we 'll tell them at the corse,
> Carle, an the king come.

> Cogie, an the king come,
> Cogie, an the king come,
> I 'se be fou and thou 'se be toom,
> Cogie, an the king come.

When George IV. was about to land in Scotland, Sir Walter Scott got his old music-master, Alister Campbell, to play over the air of *Carle, an the King come;* and when he had got its strain into his head (which Alister told me a few days after was no easy matter), he scribbled a long series of verses anticipating the doings of the royal visit, with the burden of 'Carle, now the king's come,' and had it printed on ballad-paper for sale in the streets.

THE AULD STUARTS BACK AGAIN.

This song, remarkable for its intense bitterness towards the Whig party, appears to have been composed at a moment of high hope among the friends of the Stuarts, when the principal chiefs were understood to be assembling in Braemar, as for a Highland hunting, but in reality to arrange for an insurrection of the clans.

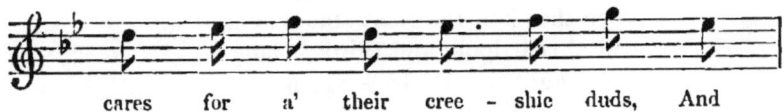

The auld Stu - arts back a - gain! The

auld Stu - arts back a - gain! Let

how - let Whigs do what they can, The

Stu - arts will be back a - gain. Wha

cares for a' their cree - shic duds, And

a' Kil - mar - nock's sow - en suds? We'll

wauk   their   hides,   and   fyle   their   fuds,   And

bring   the   Stu - arts   back   a - gain.

The auld Stuarts back again !
The auld Stuarts back again !
Let howlet Whigs do what they can,
   The Stuarts will be back again.
Wha cares for a' their creeshie duds,
And a' Kilmarnock's sowen suds ?
We 'll wauk their hides, and fyle their fuds,
   And bring the Stuarts back again.

There's Ayr, and Irvine, wi' the rest,
And a' the cronies o' the west ;
Lord ! sic a scaw'd and scabbit nest,
   And *they 'll* set up their crack again !
But wad they come, or daur they come,
Afore the bagpipe and the drum,
We 'll either gar them a' sing dumb,
   Or 'Auld Stuarts back again.'

Give ear unto this loyal sang,
A' ye that ken the richt frae wrang,
And a' that look, and think it lang,
   For auld Stuarts back again :
Were ye wi' me to chase the rae,
Out ower the hills and far away,
And saw the lords come there that day,
   To bring the Stuarts back again :

There ye might see the noble Marr,
Wi' Athole, Huntly, and Traquair,
Seaforth, Kilsyth, and Auldublair,
   And mony mae, what reck, again.
Then what are a' their westlin' crews ?
We 'll gar the tailors tack again :
Can they forstand the tartan trews,
   And 'Auld Stuarts back again ?'

THE HIGHLAND MUSTER-ROLL, 1715.

The following was probably a contemporary ballad, though it did not get into print for nearly a century after. It appeared in the sixth volume of Johnson's *Museum*, published in 1803. The bustling, hurrying tide of names, and the mirthful hopefulness expressed by the bard, are very amusing.

Chorus.

Lit - tle wat ye wha 's coming, Lit - tle wat ye wha's coming,

Lit - tle wat ye wha 's coming ; Jock and Tam and a''s coming !

Dun - can 's com - ing, Don - ald 's com - ing,

Co - lin 's com - ing, Ron - ald 's com - ing,

Dou - gald 's com - ing, Lauch - lan's com - ing,

Al - is - ter and a' 's com - ing!

Little wat ye wha 's coming,
Little wat ye wha 's coming,
Little wat ye wha 's coming;
Jock and Tam and a' 's coming!

Duncan 's coming, Donald 's coming,
Colin 's coming, Ronald 's coming,
Dougal 's coming, Lauchlan 's coming,
Alister and a' 's coming!

Little wat ye wha 's coming,
Little wat ye wha 's coming,
Little wat ye wha 's coming;
Jock and Tam and a' 's coming!

Borland and his men 's coming,
The Camerons and Maclean 's coming,
The Gordons and Macgregor 's coming,
A' the Duniewastles coming!

Little wat ye wha 's coming,
Little wat ye wha 's coming,
Little wat ye wha 's coming;
MacGilvray o' Drumglass is coming!

Winton's coming, Nithsdale's coming,
Carnwath's coming, Kenmure's coming,
Derwentwater and Foster's coming,
Withrington and Nairn's coming![1]

    Little wat ye wha's coming,
    Little wat ye wha's coming,
    Little wat ye wha's coming;
    Blythe Cowhill[2] and a''s coming!

The Laird o' Macintosh is coming,
Macrabie and Macdonald's coming,
The Mackenzies and Macphersons coming,
A' the wild MacCraws coming!

    Little wat ye wha's coming,
    Little wat ye wha's coming,
    Little wat ye wha's coming;
    Donald Gun and a''s coming!

They gloom, they glowr, they look sae big,
At ilka stroke they'll fell a Whig;
They'll fright the fuds of the Pockpuds;[3]
For mony a buttock bare's coming.

    Little wat ye wha's coming,
    Little wat ye wha's coming,
    Little wat ye wha's coming;
    Jock and Tam and a''s coming!

[1] Lowland and English partisans.
[2] A gentleman of Dumfriesshire.
[3] The English, from a supposition of their being great eaters, were often called the *Pock-puddings* by the abstemious Scotch.

KENMURE'S ON AND AWA', WILLIE.

Ken - mure's on and a - wa', Wil - lie,
Ken-mure's on and a - wa'! And Kenmure's lord 's the
brav - est lord, That ev - er Gal - lo - way saw. Success to Ken - mure's band, Willie, Suc - cess to Ken - mure's
band; There 's no a heart that fears a Whig, That
rides by Ken - mure's hand.

Kenmure 's on and awa', Willie,
    Kenmure 's on and awa' !
And Kenmure 's lord 's the bravest lord,
    That ever Galloway saw.
Success to Kenmure's band, Willie,
    Success to Kenmure's band ;
There 's no a heart that fears a Whig,
    That rides by Kenmure's band.

  Here's Kenmure's health in wine, Willie,
   Here's Kenmure's health in wine ;
  There ne'er was a coward o' Kenmure's bluid,
   Nor yet o' Kenmure's line.
  O Kenmure's lads are men, Willie,
   O Kenmure's lads are men ;
  Their hearts and swords are metal true,
   And that their foes shall ken.

  They 'll live or die wi' fame, Willie,
   They 'll live or die wi' fame ;
  But soon, wi' sounding victorie,
   May Kenmure's lord come hame !
  Here's him that's far awa', Willie,
   Here's him that's far awa' ;
  And here's the flower that I lo'e best,
   The rose that's like the snaw !

We receive this song as Burns sent it to Johnson's *Museum:* most probably, it received at least some touches from his hand. In a set printed in Cromek's *Remains of Nithsdale and Galloway Song*, and since reprinted in several collections, there are three additional and very execrable verses, palpably spurious. William Gordon, Viscount of Kenmure, rode forth to join the insurgent standard in 1715, at the head of two hundred mounted tenants, in the highest hopes of success to the Stuart cause. Joining the English branch of the rebels, he was taken prisoner at Preston, was carried in ignominious circumstances to London, and there tried, condemned, and (February 24, 1716) beheaded. By extraordinary efforts on the part of his widow, the estate was preserved to the family, and his grandson, John Gordon of Kenmure, entertained Burns at the ancient family seat in 1793. The title was restored in the person of this gentleman in 1824, but it has since become dormant.

THE BATTLE OF SHERIFF-MUIR.

The meeting between the clans under the Earl of Marr, and the royal forces under the Duke of Argyle, at Sheriff-muir, near Dunblane, on the 13th of November 1715, with its wavering proceedings and uncertain issue, as also the particular behaviour of many of the chief persons on both sides, are all cleverly and clearly described in the following contemporary song, the writer of which appears to have enjoyed the poor conduct of both parties with great impartiality. The air to which he composed his verses is one styled *John Paterson's Mare rides foremost*, being that of a rough ballad descriptive of the confused horse-race which used to take place at all country bridals long ago, between the home of the bride's father and that of her husband; of which ballad a specimen follows :

> The black and the brown
> Cam nearest the town,
> But Paterson's mare she came foremost ;
> The dun and the gray
> Kept farthest away,
> But Paterson's mare she came foremost.
> Fy, whip her in, whip her out,
> Six shillings in a clout,
> O'er the kirk-style and away wi' her !

One can discern a deep comic sense in the poet's adoption of such a strain for the description of a battle which was to decide the fate of dynasties, but only shewed the miserable effects of inferior discipline and generalship.

There's some say that we wan, And some say that they wan, And some say that nane wan at

a', man; But ae thing I'm sure, that

at Sher - iff - muir A bat - tle there was, that I

saw, man; And we ran, and they ran; and

they ran, and we ran; And we ran, and they ran a-

wa', man; And we ran, and they ran, and

they ran, and we ran; But Flor - ence ran fast - est of

a', man. Ar - gyle and Bel - ha - ven, not

like fright - ed Le - ven, Which Rothes and Had - ding - ton

saw, man; For they all, with Wight - man, advanced on the right, man, While others took flight, be - ing

raw, man. And we ran, and they ran, &c.

There's some say that we wan, and some say that they wan,
   And some say that nane wan at a', man ;
But ae thing I'm sure, that at Sheriff-muir
   A battle there was, that I saw, man ;
      And we ran, and they ran ; and they ran, and we ran ;
      And we ran, and they ran awa', man.

Brave Argyle and Belhaven,[1] not like frighted Leven,[2]
   Which Rothes [3] and Haddington [4] saw, man ;
For they all, with Wightman,[5] advanced on the right, man,
   While others took flight, being raw, man.

Lord Roxburgh [6] was there, in order to share
   With Douglas,[7] who stood not in awe, man,
Volunteerly to ramble with Lord Loudoun Campbell ;[8]
   Brave Ilay [9] did suffer for a', man.

   [1] [2] [3] [4] Lord Belhaven, the Earl of Leven, and the Earls of Rothes and
Haddington, who all bore arms as volunteers in the royal army.
   [5] Major-general Joseph Wightman, who commanded the centre of the
royal army.
   [6] John, first Duke of Roxburgh, a loyal volunteer.
   [7] Archibald, Duke of Douglas, who commanded a body of his vassals in
the royal army.
   [8] Hugh Campbell, third Earl of Loudoun, of the royal army.
   [9] The Earl of Ilay, brother to the Duke of Argyle. He came up to the
field only a few hours before the battle, and had the misfortune to be
wounded.

Sir John Shaw,[1] that great knight, with broadsword most bright,
    On horseback he briskly did charge, man ;
A hero that's bold, none could him withhold,
    He stoutly encountered the targemen.

For the cowardly Whittam,[2] for fear they should cut him,
    Seeing glittering broadswords with a pa', man,
And that in such thrang, made Baird aid-du-camp,
    And from the brave clans ran awa', man.

The great Colonel Dow gaed foremost, I trow,
    When Whittam's dragoons ran awa', man ;
Except Sandy Baird, and Naughton, the laird,
    Their horse shewed their heels to them a', man.

Brave Marr and Panmure[3] were firm, I am sure ;
    The latter was kidnapped awa', man ;
But with brisk men about, brave Harry[4] retook
    His brother, and laughed at them a', man.

Grave Marshall[5] and Lithgow,[6] and Glengary's[7] pith, too,
    Assisted by brave Logie A'mon',[8]
And Gordons the bright, sae boldly did fight,
    The red-coats took flight and awa', man.

[1] Sir John Shaw of Greenock, an officer in the troop of volunteers, noted for his keen Whiggish spirit.

[2] Major-general Whitham, who commanded the left wing of the king's army.

[3] James, Earl of Panmure.

[4] The Honourable Harry Maule of Kellie, brother to the foregoing, whom he recaptured after the engagement.

[5] [6] The Earls of Marischal and Linlithgow.

[7] The chief of Glengary.

[8] Thomas Drummond of Logie Almond.

Strathmore[1] and Clanronald[2] cried still, 'Advance, Donald!'
  Till both of these heroes did fa', man ;
For there was sic hashing, and broadswords a-clashing.
  Brave Forfar[3] himsel got a claw, man.

Lord Perth[4] stood the storm, Seaforth[5] but lukewarm,
  Kilsyth[6] and Strathallan[7] not slaw, man ;
And Hamilton[8] pled the men were not bred,
  For he had no fancy to fa', man.

Brave, generous Southesk,[9] Tullibardine[10] was brisk,
  Whose father, indeed, would not draw, man,
Into the same yoke, which served for a cloak,
  To keep the estate 'twixt them twa, man.

Lord Rollo,[11] not feared, Kintore[12] and his beard,
  Pitsligo[13] and Ogilvie[14] a', man,
And brothers Balfours, they stood the first stours ;
  Clackmannan[15] and Burleigh[16] did claw, man.

[1] The Earl of Strathmore, killed in the battle.
[2] The chief of Clanranald.
[3] The Earl of Forfar—on the king's side—wounded in the engagement.
[4] James, Lord Drummond, eldest son of the Earl of Perth, was lieutenant-general of horse under Marr, and behaved with great gallantry.
[5] William Mackenzie, fifth Earl of Seaforth.
[6] The Viscount Kilsyth.   [7] The Viscount Strathallan.
[8] Lieutenant-general George Hamilton, commanding under the Earl of Marr.
[9] James, fifth Earl of Southesk.
[10] The Marquis of Tullibardine, eldest son of the Duke of Athole.
[11] Lord Rollo.   [12] The Earl of Kintore.
[13] Lord Pitsligo.   [14] Lord Ogilvie, son of the Earl of Airly.
[15] Bruce, Laird of Clackmannan—the husband, I believe, of the old lady who knighted Robert Burns with the sword of Bruce, at Clackmannan Tower.
[16] Lord Burleigh. He was an excitable person—almost a madman—and at this time a condemned criminal, having murdered a schoolmaster for marrying a country girl he was in love with.

But Cleppan [1] acted pretty, and Strowan,[2] the witty,
   A poet that pleases us a', man ;
For mine is but rhyme, in respect of what's fine,
   Or what he is able to draw, man.

For Huntly [3] and Sinclair,[4] they baith played the tinkler,
   With consciences black like a craw, man ;
Some Angus and Fife men, they ran for their life, man,
   And ne'er a Lot's wife there at a', man !

Then Lawrie, the traitor, who betrayed his master,
   His king, and his country, and a', man,
Pretending Marr might give order to fight
   To the right of the army awa', man ;

Then Lawrie, for fear of what he might hear,
   Took Drummond's best horse, and awa', man ;
'Stead of going to Perth, he crossed the Forth,
   Alongst Stirling Bridge, and awa', man.

To London he pressed, and there he addressed,
   That he behaved best o' them a', man ;
And there, without strife, got settled for life,
   A hundred a year to his fa', man.

In Borrowstounness, he rides with disgrace,
   Till his neck stand in need of a draw, man ;
And then in a tether, he'll swing from a ladder,
   And go off the stage with a pa', man.[5]

[1] Major William Clephane.
[2] Alexander Robertson of Struan, chief of the Robertsons.
[3] Alexander, Marquis of Huntly, afterwards Duke of Gordon.
[4] The Master of Sinclair.
[5] These four stanzas seem to refer to a circumstance reported at the time ; namely, that a person had left the Duke of Argyle's army, and joined the Earl of Marr's, before the battle, intending to act as a spy; and that, being employed by Marr to inform the left wing that the right was victorious, he gave a contrary statement, and, after seeing them retire accordingly, went back again to the royal army.

Rob Roy[1] stood watch on a hill, for to catch
　　The booty, for ought that I saw, man ;
For he ne'er advanced from the place he was stanced,
　　Till no more to do there at a', man.

So we all took the flight, and Mowbray the wright,
　　But Lethem, the smith, was a braw man,
For he took the gout, which truly was wit,
　　By judging it time to withdraw, man.

And trumpet M'Lean, whose breeks were not clean,
　　Through misfortune he happened to fa', man ;
By saving his neck, his trumpet did break,
　　Came aff without music at a', man.

So there such a race was, as ne'er in that place was,
　　And as little chase was at a', man ;
From other they ran, without touk of drum,
　　They did not make use of a pa', man.

Whether we ran, or they ran, or we wan, or they wan,
　　Or if there was winning at a', man,
There's no man can tell, save our brave generall,
　　Wha first began running awa', man,

Wi' the Earl o' Seaforth, and the Cock o' the North ;[2]
　　But Florence ran fastest ava, man,
Save the Laird o' Finhaven,[3] who swore to be even
　　Wi' any general or peer o' them a', man.
　　　　And we ran, and they ran ; and they ran, and we ran ;
　　　　And we ran, and they ran awa', man.[4]

---

[1] The celebrated Rob Roy. This redoubted hero was prevented, by mixed motives, from joining either party : he could not fight against the Earl of Marr, consistently with his conscience, nor could he oppose the Duke of Argyle, without forfeiting the protection of a powerful friend.

[2] An honorary popular title of the Duke of Gordon.

[3] Carnegie of Finhaven.

[4] From Herd's Collection, 1776, except the sixth and the two last verses, which are added from the *Jacobite Relics*, although they contain a contradiction regarding the conduct of the Earl of Marr.

UP AND WAUR THEM A', WILLIE.

This is one of the contemporary popular songs on the Battle of Sheriff-muir : in style of composition, it bears a marked resemblance to *The Battle of Killiecrankie*. The earliest collection in which it appears is Herd's. The air possesses a liveliness that has made it a great favourite in Scotland. When William, Duke of Cumberland, came to Edinburgh to put himself at the head of the government troops for the suppression of the rebellion (January 1746), the music bells of St Giles's Kirk played *Up and Waur them a', Willie.*

Up and waur them a', Wil - lie!

Up and waur them a', Wil - lie!

Lairds and lords cam there be - deen, And

vow gin they were braw, Wil - lie! When

we went to the braes o' Marr, And

to the wea - pon - shaw, Wil - lie, With

true de - sign to stand our ground, And

chase our faes a - wa', Wil - lie!

Up and waur them a', Wil - lie!

Up and waur them a', Wil - lie!

Lairds and lords cam there be - deen, And

vow gin they were braw, Wil - lie!

When we went to the braes o' Marr,
   And to the weaponshaw, Willie,
With true design to stand our ground,
   And chase our faes awa', Willie,
Lairds and lords cam there bedeen,
   And vow gin they were braw, Willie!
     Up and waur them a', Willie!
     Up and waur them a', Willie!

But when our standard was set up,
   Sae fierce the wind did blaw, Willie,
The royal nit upon the tap
   Down to the ground did fa', Willie.

Then second-sichted Sandy said,
  We'd do nae guid at a', Willie.[1]
    Up and waur, &c.

But when the army joined at Perth,
  The bravest e'er ye saw, Willie,
We didna doubt the rogues to rout,
  Restore our king and a', Willie ;
Pipers played frae richt to left,
  ' Fy, furich, Whigs, awa' !' Willie.
    Up and waur, &c.

But when we marched to Sherra-muir,
  And there the rebels saw, Willie,
Brave Argyle attacked our right,
  Our flank and front and a', Willie.
Traitor Huntly soon gave way,
  Seaforth, St Clair, and a', Willie.
    Up and waur, &c.

But brave Glengary, on our right,
  The rebels' left did claw, Willie.
He there the greatest slaughter made
  That ever Donald saw, Willie.
And Whittam turned about for fear,
  And fast did rin awa', Willie.
    Up and waur, &c.

He had ca'd us a Highland mob,
  Said he wad slay us a', Willie ;
But we chased him back to Stirling brig,
  Dragoons, and foot, and a', Willie !
At length we rallied on a hill,
  And briskly up did draw, Willie.
    Up and waur, &c.

[1] A historical fact.

But when Argyle did view our line,
  And them in order saw, Willie,
He straught gaed to Dunblane again,
  And back his left did draw, Willie ;
And we to Auchterarder gaed,
  To wait a better fa', Willie.
      Up and waur, &c.

Now if ye spier wha wan the day,
  I 've telled ye what I saw, Willie ;
We baith did fight, and baith did beat,
  And baith did rin awa', Willie.
So there 's my canty Highland sang
  About the thing I saw, Willie.
      Up and waur them a', Willie,
      Up and waur them a', Willie.

It will be readily observed that the air of *There 's nae Luck about the House* is merely a slightly modified version of *Up and Waur them a', Willie.*

———

THE CAMPBELLS ARE COMING.

The Campbells are com - in', O - ho, O - ho, The
Campbells are com - in', O - ho, O - ho, The
Campbells are com - in' to bon - nie Loch - le - ven, The

Campbells are com - in', O - ho, O - ho! Upon the Lo - monds I lay, I lay, Upon the Lo - monds I lay, I lay, I
look - it down to bon - nie Loch - le - ven, And
saw three perch - es play, play.

The Campbells are comin', Oho, Oho,
The Campbells are comin', Oho, Oho,
The Campbells are comin' to bonnie Lochleven,
The Campbells are comin', Oho, Oho!

Upon the Lomonds I lay, I lay,
Upon the Lomonds I lay, I lay,
I lookit down to bonnie Lochleven,
And saw three perches play, play.

Great Argyle he goes before,
He maks his cannons and guns to roar;
Wi' sound o' trumpet, fife, and drum,
The Campbells are comin', Oho, Oho!

The Campbells they are a' in arms,
Their loyal faith and truth to shew,
Wi' banners rattlin' in the wind,
The Campbells are comin', Oho, Oho !

The tune has in this case preserved a rather foolish and not
very intelligible song : it has long been considered' as the
Campbells' March. Most probably the verses took their rise in
some of the movements connected with the insurrection of
1715.

AWA', WHIGS, AWA' !

A - wa', Whigs, a - wa'! A - wa', Whigs, a -
wa'! Ye 're but a pack o' trait - or loons, Ye 'll
do nae guid at a'! Our thris - tles flourished
fresh and fair, And bon - nie bloomed our ros - es; But
Whigs cam like a frost in June, And
wi - thered a' our pos - ies

Awa', Whigs, awa' !
Awa', Whigs, awa' !
Ye 're but a pack o' traitor loons,
Ye 'll do nae guid at a' !

Our thristles flourished fresh and fair,
And bonnie bloomed our roses ;
But Whigs came like a frost in June,
And withered a' our posies !

Our sad decay in kirk and state
Surpasses my descriving ;
The Whigs came o'er us for a curse,
And we have done wi' thriving.

[Our ancient crown 's fa'n i' the dust,
Deil blind them wi' the stour o't !
And write their names in his black beuk,
Wha ga'e the Whigs the power o't !

Grim Vengeance lang has ta'en a nap,
But we may see him wauken :
Gude help the day, when royal heads
Are hunted like a maukin !]

The air here given to this lively effusion is one to which the
editor has been accustomed to hear it sung in the house of a
Perthshire Jacobite family, and which has been included by
George Thomson in his collection, with a slight alteration.　In
Johnson's *Museum*, the song is set to a tune wholly different,
and very much less suitable, which Mr Stenhouse believed
to be of considerable age, there being an old copy of it in
his possession, under the title of *Oh, Silly Soul, Alace !* He
also deemed it the progenitor of the popular tune called *What
Ails this Heart o' Mine ?* and of *My Dearie, an Thou Die.*

The two verses here given within brackets, were added by
Burns.

TO DAUNTON ME.

To daun - ton me, to daun - ton me, Ken
ye the things that would daun - ton me? O
eigh - ty eight and eigh - ty nine, And a' the drea - ry
years sin' syne, With cess, and press, and Pres - by - trie, Guid
faith these had like to hae daun - toned me!

To daunton me, to daunton me,
Ken ye the things that would daunton me?[1]
O eighty-eight and eighty-nine,
And a' the dreary years sin' syne,
With cess, and press, and Presbytrie,
Guid faith these had like to hae dauntoned me!

[1] In playing the tune, and in the singing of some of the other songs adapted to it, it is necessary to repeat the first part.

But to wanton me, to wanton me,
Do you ken the things that would wanton me?
To see guid corn upon the rigs,
And a gallows hie to hang the Whigs,
And the right restored where the right should be,
O these are the things that would wanton me!

To wanton me, to wanton me,
Ken you what maist would wanton me?
To see King James at Edinburgh cross,
Wi' fifty thousand foot and horse,
And the usurper forced to flee,
O this is what maist would wanton me.

These verses, according to Mr Stenhouse, appear in *A Collection of Loyal Songs, Poems,* &c., printed in 1750. Three other Jacobite songs to the same tune appear in Mr Hogg's Collection. Burns also composed a song in which a young woman, wooed by an old man, sings :

> The bluid-red rose at Yule may blaw,
> The summer lilies bloom in snaw,
> The frost may freeze the deepest sea,
> But an auld man shall never daunton me. &c.

THIS IS NO MY AIN HOUSE.

There was an old nursery-song in Scotland, of which the following copy has been preserved by Mr Stenhouse :

> O this is no my ain house,
> My ain house, my ain house,
> O this is no my ain house,
>   I ken by the riggin' o't.
> For bread and cheese are my door-cheeks,
> Are my door-cheeks, are my door-cheeks,
> For bread and cheese are my door-cheeks,
>   And pancakes the riggin' o't.

O this is no my ain wean,
My ain wean, my ain wean,
O this is no my ain wean,
    I ken by the greetie[1] o't.
I 'll tak the curchie aff my head,
Aff my head, aff my head,
I 'll tak the curchie aff my head,
    And row't about the feetie o't.

When the Scottish Jacobite contemplated the changed condition of his country under a parliament-appointed dynasty, he recalled the refrain of this grandam's ditty, and metaphorising the state as his house, broke out in a political song, representing the whole of its architectural features as changed for the worse, and above all the daddy—the auld guidman—driven out of his chair in the hall, to give place to a foreign intruder.

O this is no my ain house, I
ken by the big - gin' o't, For
bow kail thrave at my door cheek, And
this - tles on the rig - gin' o't. A
car - le cam wi' lack o' grace, Wi'

[1] Style of weeping.

un - co gear and un - co face, And

sin' he claimed my dad - dy's place, I

dow - na bide the trig - gin' o't.

O this is no my ain house,
I ken by the biggin' o't,
For bow-kail thrave at my door-cheek,
 And thristles on the riggin' o't.

A carle cam wi' lack o' grace,
Wi' unco gear and unco face,
And sin' he claimed my daddy's place,
 I downa bide the triggin' o't.

Wi' rowth o' kin and rowth o' reek,
My daddy's door it wadna steek,
But bread and cheese were his door-cheek,
 And girdle-cakes the riggin' o't.

My daddy bag his housie weel,
By dint o' head and dint o' heel,
By dint o' arm and dint o' steel,
 And muckle weary priggin' o't.

Then, was it dink or was it douce,
For ony cringin' foreign goose,
To claucht my daddy's wee bit house,
 And spoil the hamely triggin' o't?

> Say, was it foul or was it fair,
> To come a hunder miles and mair,
> For to ding out my daddy's heir,[1]
> And dash him wi' the whiggin' o't?

Ramsay and Burns were also impelled, by the charm of the melody, to compose sentimental songs to it ; but regarding these there is no occasion at present to speak.

An earlier and simpler, but much inferior set of the air, is given by Mr Stenhouse from 'Mrs Crockat's Book, written in 1709.' In Johnson's *Museum*, the song is presented in connection with an air entirely different, which is commonly recognised under the name of *Deil Stick the Minister*, being the proper melody of a song so called, too primitive in its style of ideas for modern society. The old hard laird of Dumbiedykes, it will be recollected (*Heart of Midlothian*, chap. viii.), 'soughed awa in an attempt to sing *Deil Stick the Minister*.' As this classic circumstance may have given the reader an interest in the subject, the melody is here repeated, with the first verses of *This is no my ain House*, set to it.

O this is no my ain house, I ken by the big-gin' o't, For bow-kail thrave at my door-cheek, And thris-tles on the rig-gin' o't. A car-le cam wi'

---

[1] Variation—

    To ding my daddie frae his chair.

lack o' grace, Wi' un - co gear and un - co face, And

sin' he claimed my dad - dy's place, I dow - na bide the

trig - gin' o't.

HERE'S TO THE KING, SIR.

Burns entertained a great admiration for a simple old air which passed by the name of *Tuttie Taittie*, but which, up to his time, had never been printed. He said in a letter to Mr George Thomson: 'I am delighted with many little melodies which the learned musician despises as silly and insipid. I do not know whether the old air, *Hey Tuttie Taittie*, may rank among this number; but well I know that with Fraser's haut-boy it has often filled my eyes with tears. There is a tradition which I have met with in many places of Scotland, that it was Robert Bruce's march at the Battle of Bannockburn.' The patriotic enthusiasm of Burns led him afterwards to compose his noble ode, entitled *Bruce's Address to his Troops at Bannock-burn*, to this tune; which necessarily has given it a high celebrity and importance in our codex of national music.

There is, of course, little importance to be attached to such a tradition as that mentioned by Burns. It may, indeed, be questioned if there be a possibility of transmitting such a fact for five hundred years by tradition. All that we know with any certainty of the history of *Tuttie Taittie* is, that it was the spirited air of a certain Jacobite song, which, from a historical

allusion in one of its verses, may be presumed to have been
composed about the year 1718.

Here's to the king, sir, Ye ken wha I mean, sir,

And to ev'-ry hon-est man, That will do 't a-gain!

Fill, fill your bum-pers high, Drain, drain your glass-es dry,

Out up-on him, fye! oh, fye! That win-na do 't a-gain!

Here's to the king, sir,
Ye ken wha I mean, sir,
And to every honest man,
   That will do 't again !

   Fill, fill your bumpers high,
   Drain, drain your glasses dry,
   Out upon him, fye ! oh, fye !
   That winna do 't again !

Here's to the chieftains
Of the Scots Highland clans !
They hae done it mair than anes,
   And will do 't again.

When you hear the trumpet sound
Tuttie taittie to the drum,
Up your swords, and down your guns,
   And to the rogues again !

Here's to the king of Swede,
Fresh laurels crown his head !
Fye on every sneaking blade,
    That winna do 't again !

But to mak things right now,
He that drinks maun fight too,
To shew his heart's upright too,
    And that he 'll do 't again !

Sometimes the following verse was added :

Weel may we a' be,
Ill may we never see,
Here's to the king
    And the guid companie !

The song conveys with energy that amounts to poetry the first reviving feelings of hope in the Jacobite party after the defeat they experienced in 1715—1716. It was about 1718 that Charles XII. of Sweden conceived the project of making an inroad upon England in connection with the adherents of the House of Stuart.

THE BLACK BIRD.

This song, which first appeared in the *Tea-table Miscellany*, is a favourable example of the allegorical poetry under which the Jacobites used to veil their treasonable sentiments. The allegory in this case is curious enough. The *Black Bird* was one of the nicknames of the Chevalier de St George, being suggested by his complexion, which was so excessively dark as to form a striking contrast with the light fair countenance of his unfortunate son Charles. Ramsay, though said to have been a Jacobite, was so extremely cautious, that his admission of such a song into his collection is somewhat surprising ; for, though its ostensible meaning be the most innocent in the world, the

F

allegory is by no means so well managed as to conceal altogether
the real meaning, while the decussation of the word blackbird
into two words almost entirely neutralises it. It would appear
that the black complexion of the personage in question was a
matter of notoriety, and was much harped upon by his party;
as in a ring, now in the possession of a Jacobite family in Forfarshire, there is a small parcel of his raven locks, with this
flattering proverbial inscription: 'The black man's the brauest.'

Up - on a fair morn - ing, for soft re - cre -
a - tion, I heard a fair la - dy was mak - ing her
moan, With sigh - ing and sob - bing, and sad la - men -
ta - tion, Aye say - ing, My black bird most roy - al is
flown. My thoughts they de - ceive me, re - flec - tions do
grieve me, And I am o'er - burden'd wi' sad mis - e -
rie; Yet if death should blind me, as true love in -

clines me, My black bird I 'll seek out where-

ev - er he be.

Upon a fair morning, for soft recreation,
   I heard a fair lady was making her moan,
With sighing and sobbing, and sad lamentation,
   Aye saying, My black bird most royal is flown.
My thoughts they deceive me, reflections do grieve me,
   And I am o'erburden'd wi' sad miscrie ;
Yet if death should blind me, as true love inclines me,
   My black bird I 'll seek out wherever he be.

Once into fair England my black bird did flourish ;
   He was the flower that in it did spring ;
Prime ladies of honour his person did nourish,
   Because he was the true son of a king :
But since that false fortune, which still is uncertain,
   Has caused this parting between him and me,
His name I 'll advance in Spain and in France,
   And seek out my black bird wherever he be.

The birds of the forest are all met together ;
   The turtle has chosen to dwell with the dove ;
And I am resolved, in foul or fair weather,
   Once in the spring to seek out my love.
He 's all my heart's treasure, my joy and my pleasure ;
   And justly, my love, my heart follows thee,
Who art constant and kind, and courageous of mind ;—
   All bliss on my black bird, wherever he be !

In England my black bird and I were together,
  Where he was still noble and generous of heart.
Ah ! woe to the time that first he went thither !
  Alas ! he was forced from thence to depart !
In Scotland he 's deem'd, and highly esteem'd ;
  In England he seemeth a stranger to be ;
Yet his fame shall remain in France and in Spain ;—
  All bliss to my black bird, wherever he be !

What if the fowler my black bird has taken !
  Then sighing and sobbing will be all my tune ;
But if he is safe I 'll not be forsaken,
  And hope yet to see him in May or in June.
For him, through the fire, through mud and through mire,
  I 'll go ; for I love him to such a degree,
Who is constant and kind, and noble of mind,
  Deserving all blessings, wherever he be !

It is not the ocean can fright me with danger,
  Nor that like a pilgrim I wander forlorn ;
I may meet with friendship from one is a stranger,
  More than of one that in Britain is born.
I pray Heaven, so spacious, to Britain be gracious,
  Though some there be odious to both him and me.
Yet joy and renown, and laurels shall crown
  My black bird with honour, wherever he be.

THE WHITE COCKADE.

My love was born in A - ber - deen, The bonniest lad that
e'er was seen, But now he maks my heart full sad, He 's

ta'en the field wi' his white cockade. O he's a rantin'
rov - in' blade, O he's a brisk and bonnie lad, Be -
tide what may, my heart is glad To see my lad wi' his
white cockade!

My love was born in Aberdeen,
The bonniest lad that e'er was seen,
But now he maks my heart full sad,
He's ta'en the field wi' his white cockade.
   O he's a rantin' rovin' blade,
   O he's a brisk and bonnie lad,
   Betide what may, my heart is glad
   To see my lad wi' his white cockade![1]

I'll sell my rock, I'll sell my reel,
My rippling-kaim and spinning-wheel,
To buy my lad a tartan plaid,
A braid sword, durk, and a white cockade.

[1] Variation in Herd's Collection :

   'Betide what will, I'll get me ready,
   And follow the lad wi' the tartan plaidie.'

I 'll sell my rokelay and my tow,
My guid gray mare and hackit cow,
That every loyal Buchan lad,
May tak' the field wi' his white cockade.[1]

JOHNIE COPE.

The sad mismanagement of Sir John Cope, as commander of the little government army at first opposed to Prince Charles Stuart, September 1745, formed a subject of triumphant scorn to the Jacobites, and indeed of general derision. The feeling of the hour was embodied in a rustic song to a tune called *Fy to the Hills in the Morning,* which was at once taken up as a general favourite, and has ever since so remained, as it probably will for a long time to come.

Cope sent a let-ter frae Dun-bar:— O, Charlie, meet me an ye daur, And I 'll learn you the art o' war, If you 'll meet me in the morn-ing. Hey, Johnie Cope, are ye wauking yet? Or are your drums a-

[1] A version of this song, slightly different from the above, appears in Herd's Collection. We have here mainly followed Hogg.

beat - ing yet? If ye were wauk - ing,

I wad wait To go to the coals i' the morning.

Cope sent a letter frae Dunbar :—
O, Charlie, meet me an ye daur,
And I'll learn you the art o' war,
    If you'll meet me in the morning.
      Hey, Johnie Cope, are ye wauking yet ?
      Or are your drums a-beating yet ?
      If ye were wauking, I wad wait
        To go to the coals i' the morning.[1]

When Charlie look'd the letter upon,
He drew his sword the scabbard from :
Come follow me, my merry merry men,
    And we'll meet Cope in the morning.

Now, Johnie, be as good's your word :
Come let us try both fire and sword ;
And dinna rin away like a frighted bird,
    That's chased frae its nest in the morning.[2]

[1] The battle-ground lies in the midst of a coal-field from which Edinburgh had for centuries been supplied with most of the fuel it required.

[2] It is curious to find in this droll Scotch song an image which had been previously used by Euripides, in the mouth of Polyxena when called from the tent by the voice of her mother Hecuba :

        ὥστ' ὄρνιν,
   θάμβει τῷδ' ἐξέπταξας.

'I come   *   *   *   *
Like a poor bird affrighted from its nest.'

When Johnie Cope he heard of this,
He thought it wadna be amiss,
To hae a horse in readiness
    To flee awa' in the morning.

Fy now, Johnie, get up and rin,
The Highland bagpipes mak a din ;
It is best to sleep in a hale skin,
    For 'twill be a bluidy morning.

When Johnie Cope to Berwick came,
They speer'd at him, Where's a' your men ?
The deil confound me gin I ken,
    For I left them a' i' the morning.

Now, Johnie, troth ye are na blate
To come wi' the news o' your ain defeat,
And leave your men in sic a strait
    Sae early in the morning.

Oh ! faith, quo' Johnie, I got a fleg
Wi' their claymores and philabegs ;
If I face them again, deil break my legs—
    So I wish you a guid-morning.[1]

TRANENT MUIR.

Another clever rustic song was composed on the Battle of
Preston, to the tune of *Killiecrankie*, and circulated at the
time on a broadside. A certain rough force, both in the
description and the wit, has insured its preservation. Its author

---

[1] Poor Sir John Cope was, perhaps, rather severely judged regarding
his Scotch command in 1745. At least we must admit that he was
unfortunate in having so many raw dragoons to handle at Preston. It
is said that his face brightened in London a few months afterwards, when
a second general (Hawley) gave way before the Highland army. Sir
John died Knight of the Bath, Colonel of the 7th Dragoons, and a
Lieutenant-general, 28th July 1760.

was a farmer who dwelt near the field of battle, and had the misfortune, as he tells us, to be robbed after it by one of the victors. He was Adam Skirving, of the farm of Garleton, between Haddington and Gosford, who died in 1803, at the age of eighty-four, and is buried in the parish fold of Athelstaneford, where the poets Blair and Home were successively ministers. He was noted as a man of sharp and ready wit, but not much addicted to verse-making; a great lover of the sports of curling and golfing; upright in his dealings, a foe to all shams and impostures; generally a favourite. His eldest son Archibald acquired celebrity as a portrait-painter in crayons, and was personally for many a day notable in Edinburgh for a few innocent eccentricities.

The Che - va - lier, being void of fear, Did march up Bir - slie brae, man, And through Tranent, ere he did stent, As fast as he could gae, man; While Gen - e - ral Cope did taunt and mock, Wi' mo - ny a loud huz - za, man; But ere next morn proclaim'd the cock, We heard a - nith - er craw, man.

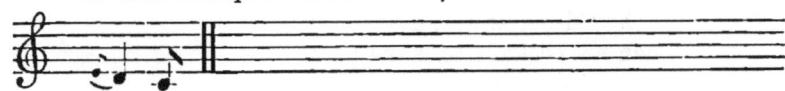

The Chevalier, being void of fear,
    Did march up Birslie brae, man,
And through Tranent, ere he did stent,
    As fast as he could gae, man ;
While General Cope did taunt and mock,
    Wi' mony a loud huzza, man ;
But ere next morn proclaim'd the cock,
    We heard anither craw, man.

The brave Lochiel, as I heard tell,
    Led Camerons on in cluds, man ;
The morning fair, and clear the air,
    They lowsed with devilish thuds, man :
Down guns they threw, and swords they drew,
    And soon did chase them aff, man ;
On Seaton Crafts they bufft their chafts,
    And gart them rin like daft, man.

The bluff dragoons swore, Blood and 'oons,
    They 'd make the rebels run, man ;
And yet they flee when them they see,
    And winna fire a gun, man.
They turned their back, their foot they brak,
    Such terror seized them a', man,
Some wet their cheeks, some fyled their breeks,
    And some for fear did fa', man.

The volunteers pricked up their ears,
    And wow gin they were croose, man ;
But when the bairns saw 't turn to earn'st,
    They were not worth a louse, man :
Maist feck gaed hame—O, fy for shame !
    They 'd better stay'd awa', man,
Than wi' cockade to make parade,
    And do nae good at a', man.

Menteith the great, where Hersell sate,
    Un'wares d'd ding her ower, man ;
Yet wadna stand to bear a hand,
    But aff fou fast did scour, man :
Ower Soutra Hill, ere he stood still,
    Before he tasted meat, man :
Troth, he may brag of his swift nag,
    That bare him aff sae fleet, man.

And Simson keen, to clear the een
    Of rebels far in wrang, man,
Did never strive wi' pistols five,
    But gallop'd wi' the thrang, man :
He turn'd his back, and in a crack
    Was cleanly out of sight, man ;
And thought it best ; it was nae jest·
    Wi' Highlanders to fight, man.

'Mangst a' the gang, nane bade the bang
    But twa, and ane was tane, man ;
For Campbell rade, but Myrie staid,
    And sair he paid the kain, man :
Fell skelps he got, was waur than shot,
    Frae the sharp-edged claymore, man ;
Frae many a spout came running out
    His reeking-het red gore, man.

But Gard'ner brave did still behave
    Like to a hero bright, man ;
His courage true, like him were few,
    That still despised flight, man :
For king and laws, and country's cause,
    In honour's bed he lay, man ;
His life, but not his courage, fled,
    While he had breath to draw, man.

And Major Bowle, that worthy soul,
    Was brought down to the ground, man ;
His horse being shot, it was his lot
    For to get mony a wound, man.
Lieutenant Smith, of Irish birth,
    Frae whom he call'd for aid, man,
Being full of dread, lap ower his head,
    And wadna be gainsaid, man.

He made sic haste, sae spurr'd his beast,
    'Twas little there he saw, man ;
To Berwick rade, and safely said,
    The Scots were rebels a', man.
But let that end, for weel 'tis kend
    His use and wont to lie, man ;
The Teague is naught, he never fought,
    When he had room to flee, man.[1]

And Cadell drest, amang the rest,
    With gun and good claymore, man,
On gelding gray, he rode that way,
    With pistols set before, man :
The cause was good, he'd spend his blood,
    Before that he would yield, man ;
But the night before, he left the cor',
    And never took the field, man.

---

[1] 'It is reported that, after the publication of the ballad, [Lieutenant Smith] sent Mr Skirving a challenge to meet him at Haddington, and answer for his conduct in treating him with such opprobrium. "Gang awa' back," said Mr Skirving to the messenger, "and tell Mr Smith I have nae leisure to gae to Haddington ; but if he likes to come here, I 'll tak a look o' him, and if I think I can fecht him, I 'll fecht him ; and if no— I 'll just do as he did at Preston—I 'll rin awa'." '—Stenhouse's *Notes to Johnson.*

But gallant Roger, like a soger,
   Stood and bravely fought, man ;
I'm wae to tell, at last he fell,
   But mae down wi' him brought, man :
At point of death, wi' his last breath
   (Some standing round in ring, man),
On's back lying flat, he waved his hat,
   And cry'd, God save the king, man.

Some Highland rogues, like hungry dogs,
   Neglecting to pursue, man,
About they faced, and in great haste
   Upon the booty flew, man ;
And they, as gain for all their pain,
   Are deck'd wi' spoils of war, man ;
Fu' bauld can tell how her nainsell
   Was ne'er sae pra pefore, man.

At the thorn-tree, which you may see
   Bewest the Meadow-mill, man,
There mony slain lay on the plain,
   The clans pursuing still, man.
Sic unco hacks, and deadly whacks,
   I never saw the like, man ;
Lost hands and heads cost them their deads,
   That fell near Preston-dyke, man.

That afternoon, when a' was done,
   I gaed to see the fray, man ;
But had I wist what after past,
   I'd better staid away, man :
In Seaton Sands, wi' nimble hands,
   They pick'd my pockets bare, man ;
But I wish ne'er to drie sic fear,
   For a' the sum and mair, man.

CHARLIE IS MY DARLING.

Chorus.

And Char - lie is my dar - ling, My dar - ling, my

dar - ling, And Char - lie is my dar - ling, The

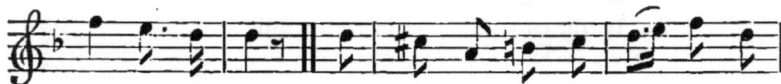

Young Che - va - lier. 'Twas on a Mon - day morning, Right

ear - ly in the year, That Char - lie cam to

our town, The Young Che - va - lier. And Char - lie is my

dar - ling, My dar - ling, my dar - ling, And

Char - lie is my dar - ling, The Young Che - va - lier.

'Twas on a Monday morning,
　　Right early in the year,
That Charlie cam to our town,
　　The Young Chevalier.
　　　　And Charlie is my darling,
　　　　My darling, my darling,
　　　　And Charlie is my darling,
　　　　The Young Chevalier.

As he cam walking up the street,
　　The pipes played loud and clear ;
And young and auld cam out to greet
　　The Young Chevalier.

O up yon heathery mountain,
　　And down yon scroggy glen,
We daurna gang a-milking,
　　For Charlie and his men.

This song, in a somewhat different version, was first published in Johnson's *Museum*, and it is probably of not much older date.

LEWIE GORDON.

One of the most favourite songs of the Jacobites in the latter days of the party, was *Lewie Gordon*, referring primarily to that noted partisan of the cause, but mainly a longing reminiscence of the prince himself, as he had appeared in Highland guise throughout his romantic expedition. Lord Lewis, a younger son of the second Duke of Gordon, raised two battalions for the prince, and gained some reputation by routing a large party of loyal volunteers under Macleod of Macleod at Inverury, December 23, 1745. After Culloden, he escaped to France, whence he was not destined ever to return 'hame,' as he died at Montreuil in 1754.

Lewie Gordon is a variety of the south-country air of *Tarry Woo,* which will reappear in a subsequent part of this collection. It is vaguely stated by James Hogg that this song

Lord Lewis Gordon.

was a composition of the eccentric Alexander Geddes, who originally was the Catholic priest at Shenval, in the Enzie, Banffshire.

O send Lew-ie Gor-don hame, And the lad I daur-na name;

Tho' his back be at the wa', Here's to him that's far a-wa'.

Chorus.

Och-on, my Highlandman! O my bon-nie Highlandman!

Weel would I my true love ken, A-

mang ten thou-sand High-land-men.

O send Lewie Gordon hame,
And the lad I daurna name ;
Though his back be at the wa',
Here's to him that's far awa'.
 Ochon, my Highlandman !
 O my bonnie Highlandman !
 Weel would I my true love ken,
 Amang ten thousand Highlandmen.

O ! to see his tartan trews,
Bonnet blue, and laigh-heel'd shoes,
Philabeg aboon his knee !
That's the lad that I'll gang wi'.

G

This lovely youth of whom I sing,
Is fitted for to be a king ;
On his breast he wears a star :
You'd tak him for the god of war.

O ! to see this princely one
Seated on a royal throne !
Disasters a' would disappear ;
Then begins the jub'lee year.

YOU'RE WELCOME, CHARLIE STUART.

Under the general feeling of irritation left in Scotland by the behaviour of the victorious army of Cumberland, a warm welcome was given, beyond Jacobite circles, to a song which then came into circulation, being set to a tune called *Miss Stewart's Reel.*

You're wel-come, Char-lie Stu-art, You're welcome, Char-lie Stuart, You're welcome, Char-lie Stuart, There's none so right as thou art! Had I the pow'r as I've the will, I'd make thee fam-ous by my quill, Thy foes I'd scat-ter, take, and kill, Frae Billingsgate to Du-art.

You're welcome, Charlie Stuart,
You're welcome, Charlie Stuart,
You're welcome, Charlie Stuart,
There's none so right as thou art!

Had I the power as I've the will,
I'd make thee famous by my quill,
Thy foes I'd scatter, take, and kill,
Frae Billingsgate to Duart.

Thy sympathising complaisance,
Made thee believe intriguing France;
But woe is me for thy mischance,
Which saddens every true heart.

Had'st thou Culloden battle won,
Poor Scotland had not been undone,
Nor butchered been with sword and gun
By Lockhart and such cowards.

Kind Providence, to thee a friend,
A lovely maid did timely send,
To save thee from a fearful end,
Thou charming Charlie Stuart!

Great glorious prince, we firmly pray,
That she and we may see the day,
When Britons all with joy shall say,
You're welcome, Charlie Stuart.

Though Cumberland, the tyrant proud,
Doth thirst and hunger after blood,
Just Heaven will preserve the good,
To fight for Charlie Stuart.[1]

Upon the anniversary of the Battle of Culloden in 1749, some military officers attending the theatre in the Canongate,

[1] There are three verses more, of inferior merit.

Edinburgh, called to the musicians for the tune of *Culloden;* whereupon the audience, in resentment, demanded *You're Welcome, Charlie Stuart,* and had their request complied with. A riot, ending in the complete humiliation of the officers, was the consequence.

LADY KEITH'S LAMENT.

The following song appears in Hogg's Collection, without any indication of its origin. Its very beauty as a pathetic effusion provokes a suspicion of its genuineness; and, indeed, it bears all the marks of having proceeded from Hogg's own pen. The air is a variety of *The Boyne Water.*

I may sit in my wee croo house, At the
rock and the reel to toil fu' drea - ry;
I may think on the day that's gane, And
sigh and sab till I grow wea - ry.
I ne'er could brook, I ne'er could brook, A

for - eign loon to own or flat - ter; But

I will sing a ran - tin' sang, That

day our king comes o'er the wa - ter.

I may sit in my wee croo house,
    At the rock and the reel to toil fu' dreary ;
I may think on the day that 's gane,
    And sigh and sab till I grow weary.
I ne'er could brook, I ne'er could brook,
    A foreign loon to own or flatter ;
But I will sing a rantin' sang,
    That day our king comes ower the water.

O gin I live to see the day,
    That I hae begg'd, and begg'd frae Heaven,
I 'll fling my rock and reel away,
    And dance and sing frae morn till even :
For there is ane I winna name,
    That comes the beingin' byke to scatter ;
And I 'll put on my bridal-gown,
    That day our king comes ower the water.

I hae seen the guid auld day,
    The day o' pride and chieftain's glory,
When royal Stuarts bare the sway,
    And ne'er heard tell o' Whig nor Tory.

Though lyart be my locks and gray,
    And eild has crook'd me down—what matter !
I'll dance and sing ae other day,
    The day our king comes ower the water.

A curse on dull and drawling Whig,
    The whining, ranting, low deceiver,
Wi' heart sae black, and look sae big,
    And canting tongue o' clish-ma-claver !
My father was a guid lord's son,
    My mother was an earl's daughter ;
And I'll be Lady Keith again,
    That day our king comes ower the water.

OVER THE WATER TO CHARLIE.

Come boat me o'er, Come row me o'er, Come

boat me o'er to Char-lie ; I'll gie John Ross an-

o-ther baw-bee To fer-ry me o'er to Char-lie.

We'll o'er the wa-ter and o'er the sea, We'll

o'er the wa-ter to Char-lie; Come weal, come woe, we'll
gather and go, And live and die wi' Char-lie.

Come boat me o'er, come row me o'er,
    Come boat me o'er to Charlie;
I'll gie John Ross another bawbee
    To ferry me o'er to Charlie.
        We'll o'er the water and o'er the sea,
        We'll o'er the water to Charlie;
        Come weal, come woe, we'll gather and go,
        And live and die wi' Charlie.

Weel, weel, I lo'e my Charlie's name,
    Though some there be that abhor him;
But oh to see Auld Nick gaun hame,
    And Charlie's foes before him!

I swear by moon and stars sae bright,
    And the sun that glances early,
If I had twenty thousand lives,
    I'd risk them a' for Charlie!

I once had sons, I now hae nane,
    I bred them, toiling sairly;
And I wad bear them a' again,
    And lose them a' for Charlie!

This song probably took its rise about the time when a section
of the people of Scotland acted with such sad results upon its
sentiment. In coming to us, however, through the hands of
Burns and Hogg, it has doubtless sustained some changes. The
tune appeared in the fourth volume of Oswald's *Pocket Companion*.

THE SOUTERS O' SELKIRK.

At some time, probably in the earlier half of the eighteenth century, the souters or shoemakers of Selkirk—a town noted for that craft—had a competition at football with certain men of the Merse, retainers of the Earl of Hume. The souters won, and their victory was celebrated in a boisterous song and air, the latter of which is sure of permanent preservation.

(It's) up wi' the sou-ters o' Sel-kirk, And

down wi' the Earl of Hume; But up wi'

il - ka braw cal - lant That sews the sing - le soled

shoon. (It's) fy up - on yel - low and yel - low, And

fy up - on yel - low and green, But up wi' the

true blue and scar - let, And up wi' the

sing - le soled shoon.

Up wi' the souters o' Selkirk,
  And down wi' the Earl of Hume ;
But up wi' ilka braw callant
  That sews the single-soled shoon.
    Fy upon yellow and yellow,
      And fy upon yellow and green,
    But up wi' the true blue and scarlet,
      And up wi' the single-soled shoon.

Up wi' the lads o' the Forest,
  That ne'er to the Southron wad yield ;
But deil scoup o' Hume and his menyie,
  That stood sae abeigh on the field.

Fy on the green and the yellow,[1]
  The craw-hearted loons o' the Merse ;
But here's to the souters o' Selkirk,
  The elshin, the lingle, and birse.

Then up wi' the souters o' Selkirk,
  For they are baith trusty and leal ;
And up wi' the lads o' the Forest,
  And down wi' the Merse to the deil !

The allusions made to the brave conduct of the souters of
Selkirk, and the disaffection popularly but unjustly ascribed to
the Lord Hume, at the Battle of Flodden, have led to a supposition that this song relates purely to that conflict. The above
account, however, which is that given by the Rev. Mr Robertson
in his Statistical Account of Selkirk, seems to be the only one
entitled to any respect. In the song, it must be admitted, there
is little poetry or common sense ; but the air is one of great
merit.

[1] The livery of the Hume family.

Humorous Songs.

THE WOOING OF JENNY AND JOCK.

THIS very curious song dates not later than the regency of Moray, as it is inserted in the Bannatyne Manuscript, 1568. In the present copy, which was directly transcribed from the MS., the spelling is modernised, but no other changes are made. The vanity of the mother-in-law, which leads her to give a catalogue of her daughter's worldly goods and chattels, and draws from the wooer an equally minute inventory of his possessions, may be considered fortunate for us, as we are thus furnished with an exhaustive picture of the 'guids and gear' of a Scotch yeoman of the sixteenth century.

Ro-bin's Jock cam to woo our Jen-ny, On our feast-even when we were fou; She brank-it fast and made her bon-ny, And said, Jock, come ye for to woo?

Robin's Jock cam to woo our Jenny,
On our feast-even when we were fou ;
She brankit-fast and made her bonny,
And said, Jock, come ye for to woo ?
She burneist her, baith breist and brow,
And made her clear as ony clock ;
Then spak her dame, and said, I trow,
Ye come to woo our Jenny, Jock.

Jock said, Forsuith, I yearn full fain
To loot [1] my heid, and sit down by you :
Than spak her mother, and said again,
My bairn has tocher-guid [2] to gie you.
Te-hee, quoth Jenny, Keek, keek, I see you !
Mother, yon man maks you a mock :
I shrew thee, leear ! full leese me you,
I come to woo your Jenny, quoth Jock.

My bairn, she says, has of her awin
Ane guse, ane gryce, [3] ane cock, ane hen,
Ane calf, ane hog, ane foot-braid sawin, [4]
Ane kirn, ane pin, that ye weel ken ;
Ane pig, [5] ane pot, ane raip there ben,
Ane fork, ane flaik, ane reel, ane rock,
Dishes and dublers nine or ten :
Come ye to woo our Jenny, Jock ?

Ane blanket, and ane wecht also,
Ane shool, ane sheet, and ane lang flail,
Ane ark, [6] ane amry, [7] and ladles two,
Ane milk-syth, with ane swine-tail,

---

[1] Stoop.   [2] Portion.   [3] Young pig.
[4] Corn sufficient to sow a foot-breadth.   [5] Pipkin.
[6] Large chest for meal.   [7] Cupboard.

Ane rusty whittle to sheer the kail,
Ane wheel, ane mell the beir to knock,
Ane cog, ane card wanting ane nail ;
Come ye to woo our Jenny, Jock ?

Ane furm, ane furlot, ane pot, ane peck,
Ane tub, ane barrow, with ane wheelband,
Ane turse, ane trouch, and ane meal-sack,
Ane spurtle braid, and ane elwand.
Jock took Jenny by the hand,
And cried ane feast, and slew ane cock,
And made a brydal up-o-land ;
Now have I gotten Jenny, quoth Jock.

Now, dame, I have your bairn married,
Suppose ye mak it never sae teuch ;
I lat you wit she's nocht miscarried,
It is weel kenned I have eneuch :
Ane crookit gleyd[1] fell in ane heuch,
Ane spade, ane spit, ane spur, ane sock ;
Withouten oxen I have a pleuch,
To gang together Jenny and Jock.

I have ane helter, ane eik, ane heck,
Ane cord, ane creel, and als ane cradle,
Five fidder[2] of rags to stuff ane jack,
Ane auld pannel of ane laid saddle,
Ane pepper pock, made of a paidel,[3]
Ane spounge, ane spindle wanting ane knock,
Twa lusty lips to lick ane ladle,
To gang together Jenny and Jock.

Ane bregham,[4] and twa brooches fine,
Weel buckled with a bridle reinyie,[5]
Ane serk made of the Lincum twine,
Ane gay green cloak that will not steinzie ;[6]

---

[1] An old horse.   [2] A certain amount by weight.
[3] A leather bag for pedler's wares.   [4] Horse-collar.   [5] Rein.   [6] Stain.

And yet, for mister, I will not feinyie,
Five hundred flaes now in a flock,
Call ye nocht that ane jolly menyie,
To gae together Jenny and Jock ?

Ane treen trencher, ane ramhorn spune,
Twa bits of barkit blasnit leather,
All graith that gaes to hobble shoon,[1]
Ane thrawcrook to twine ane tether,
Ane bridle, ane girth, and ane swyne blethe ,
Ane masken-vat, ane fettered lock,
Ane sheep weel keepit frae ill weather,
To gang together Jenny and Jock.

Tak thae for my part of the feast,
It is weel known I am weel bodin ;[2]
Ye may not say my part is least.
The wife said, Speed ; the kail are sodden,
And als the laverock is fuft[3] and lodden,
When ye have done tak hame the broche.
The roast was teuch, sae were they bodin ;[4]
Syne gaed together Jenny and Jock.

TAK YOUR AULD CLOAK ABOUT YE.

To all appearance, this song is in much the same style as the preceding ; and what seems further to justify its being assigned to the sixteenth century, is the quotation of a passage apparently from it by Iago in *Othello*, with only the change of King Robert into King Stephen. We cannot, however, trace the song further back than the *Tea-table Miscellany* of Ramsay, 1724.

[1] Hob-nailed shoes.
[2] Furnished.
[3] The lark on the spit is fully done.
[4] So they had foretold.

It is needless to remark how the humour of the matrimonial dialogue has rendered the song one of the most favourite with the entire nation. The air, which suits the verses remarkably well, was considered by Mr Stenhouse as most probably coeval with it.

In win - ter, when the rain rain'd cauld, And

frost and snaw on il - ka hill, And Boreas, wi' his

blasts sae bauld, Was threat'nin' a' our kye to kill: Then

Bell, my wife, who lo'es na strife, She said to me richt

has - ti - lie, Get up, guidman, save Crummie's life, And

tak your auld cloak a - bout ye.

In winter, when the rain rain'd cauld,
And frost and snaw on ilka hill,
And Boreas, wi' his blasts sae bauld,
Was threat'nin' a' our kye to kill:

H

Then Bell, my wife, who lo'es na strife,
 She said to me richt hastilie,
Get up, guidman, save Crummie's life,
 And tak your auld cloak about ye.[1]

My Crummie is a usefu' cow,
 And she is come of a good kin';
Aft has she wet the bairns's mou',
 And I am laith that she should tyne;
Get up, guidman, it is fu' time,
 The sun shines frae the lift sae hie;
Sloth never made a gracious end;
 Gae, tak your auld cloak about ye.

My cloak was ance a guid gray cloak,
 When it was fitting for my wear;
But now it's scantly worth a groat,
 For I have worn 't this thretty year:
Let's spend the gear that we hae won,
 We little ken the day we 'll die;
Then I 'll be proud, since I have sworn
 To hae a new cloak about me.

In days when our King Robert rang,
 His trews they cost but half-a-croun;
He said they were a groat ower dear,
 And ca'd the tailor thief and loon:
He was the king that wore a croun,
 And thou's the man of laigh degree:
It's pride puts a' the country doun;
 Sae tak thy auld cloak about ye.

[1] In singing this song, a mistake is very generally made in the empha-
sising of the final line of the verses, which ought to be

  'And tak your auld cloak about ye.'

Ilka land has its ain lauch,
  Ilk kind o' corn has its ain hool ;
I think the world is a' gane wrang,
  When ilka wife her man wad rule :
Do ye no see Rob, Jock, and Hab,
  As they are girded gallantlie,
While I sit hurklin i' the asse ?—
  I 'll hae a new cloak about me.

Guidman, I wat it 's thretty year
  Sin' we did ane anither ken ;
And we hae had atween us twa
  Of lads and bonnie lasses ten :
Now they are women grown and men,
  I wish and pray weel may they be ;
If you would prove a guid husband,
  E'en tak your auld cloak about ye.

Bell, my wife, she lo'es na strife,
  But she would guide me, if she can ;
And, to maintain an easy life,
  I aft maun yield, though I 'm guidman :
Nocht 's to be gain'd at woman's hand,
  Unless ye gie her a' the plea ;
Then I 'll leave aff where I began,
  And tak my auld cloak about me.

DAME, DO THE THING WHILK I DESIRE.

This song, which bears a remarkable resemblance in its style
of humour and composition to *Tak your Auld Cloak about Ye*, is
given by Ritson in his *Scottish Songs*, 1794, from a manuscript
of Charles I.'s time in the British Museum (*Bib. Sloan*, 1489).

Get up, guidwife, don on your claise,
    And to the market mak you boune :
'Tis lang time sin' your neebors rase ;
    They're weel-nigh gotten into the toune.
    See ye don on your better goune,
And gar the lasse big on the fyre.
    Dame, do not look as ye wad frowne,
But doe the thing whilk I desyre.

I spier what haste ye hae, guidman !
    Your mother staid till ye war born ;
Wad ye be at the tother can,
    To scoure your throat sae sune this morne ?
    Guid faith, I haud it but a scorne,
That ye suld with my rising mell ;[1]
    For when ye have baith said and sworne,
I 'll do but what I like mysell.

Guidwife, we maun needs have a care,
    Sae lang's we wonne in neebors' rawe,
O' neeborheid to tak a share,
    And rise up when the cocks does crawe ;
    For I have heard an auld said sawe,
' They that rise the last big on the fyre.'
    What wind or weather so ever blaw,
Dame, do the thing whilk I desyre.

Nay, what do ye talk of neeborheid ?
    Gif I lig in my bed till noone,
By nae man's shins I bake my breid,
    And ye need not reck what I have done.
    Nay, look to the clooting o' your shoone,
And with my rising do not mell ;
    For, gin ye lig baith sheets abune,
I 'll do but what I will mysell.

---

[1] Meddle.

Guidwife, ye maun needs tak a care
    To save the geare that we hae won ;
Or lay away baith plow and car,
    And hang up Ring[1] when a' is done.
    Then may our bairns a-begging run,
To seek their mister[2] in the myre.
    Sae fair a thread as we hae won !
Dame, do the thing whilk I require.

Guidman, ye may weel a-begging gang,
    Ye seem sae weel to bear the pocke :
Ye may as weel gang sune as syne,
    To seek your meat amang guid folke.
    In ilka house ye'll get a locke,[3]
When ye come whar your gossips dwell.
    Nay, lo you luik sae like a gowke,
I'll do but what I list mysell.

Guidwife, you promised, when we were wed,
    That ye wad me truly obey ;
Mess John can witness what you said,
    And I'll go fetch him in this day :
    And, gif that haly man will say,
Ye'se do the thing that I desyre,
    Then sall we sune end up this fray,
And ye sall do what I require.

I nowther care for John nor Jacke—
    I'll tak my pleasure at my ease ;
I care not what you say a placke—
    Ye may go fetch him gin ye please.
    And, gin ye want ane of a mease,
Ye may e'en gae fetch the deil frae helle ;
    I wad you wad let your japin cease,
For I'll do but what I like mysell.

---

[1] The dog.   [2] Supposed to signify money, or means of livelihood.
[3] Handful.

Well, sin' it will nae better be,
  I 'll tak my share or a' be gane :
The warst card in my hand sall flee,
  And, i' faith, I wait I can shifte for ane.
I 'll sell the plow, and lay to wadd the waine,
And the greatest spender sall beare the bell :
  And then, when all the guids are gane,
Dame, do the thing ye list yoursell.

EVER ALAKE MY AULD GUIDMAN.[1]

This is a third song, of apparently old date, upon the humours involved in matrimonial altercations. It appeared in the *Tea-table Miscellany*, marked as a song of unknown antiquity.

Late in an even - ing forth I went, A

lit - tle before the sun gaed down; And there I chanced, by

ac - ci - dent, To light on a bat - tle new be - gun.

A man and his wife were faun in strife; I

can - na weel tell ye how it began ; But aye she wail'd her

[1] Anglicè—*My first husband.*

wretch - ed   life, And   cried,   Ev - er   a - lake my

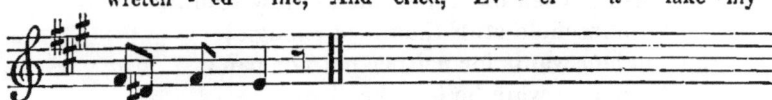

auld   guid - man!

Late in an evening forth I went,
    A little before the sun gaed down ;
And there I chanced, by accident,
    To light on a battle new begun.
A man and his wife were faun in strife ;
    I canna weel tell how it began ;
But aye she wail'd her wretched life,
    And cried, Ever alake my auld guidman !

HE.

The auld guidman that thou tells of,
    The country kens where he was born,
Was but a puir silly vagabond,
    And ilka ane leuch him to scorn ;
For he did spend and mak an end
    Of gear that his forefathers wan ;
He gart the puir stand frae the door :
    Sae tell nae mair of thy auld guidman.

SHE.

My heart, alake, is like to break,
    When I think on my winsome John ;
His blinking een, and gait sae free,
    Was naething like thee, thou dozent drone.
His rosy face and flaxen hair,
    And skin as white as ony swan,
Was large and tall, and comely withal ;
    And thou 'lt never be like my auld guidman.

HE.

Why dost thou pleen ? I thee mainteen ;
  For meal and maut thou disna want ;
But thy wild bees I canna please,
  Now when our gear 'gins to grow scant.
Of household stuff thou hast enough ;
  Thou wants for neither pot nor pan ;
Of siclike ware he left thee bare :
  Sae tell me nae mair of thy auld guidman.

SHE.

Yes, I may tell, and fret mysell,
  To think on the blythe days I had,
When he and I thegither lay
  In arms, into a weel-made bed.
But now I sigh, and may be sad ;
  Thy courage is cauld, thy colour wan ;
Thou faulds thy feet, and fa's asleep :
  And thou 'lt never be like my auld guidman.

Then coming was the nicht sae dark,
  And gane was a' the licht of day ;
The carle was fear'd to miss his mark,
  And therefore wad nae langer stay.
Then up he gat, and he ran his way ;
  I trow the wife the day she wan ;
And aye the owerword o' the fray
  Was, Ever alake my auld guidman !

I HAE LAID THREE HERRING IN SAUT.

I hae laid three herrin' in saut—
  Lass, gin ye 'll tak me, tell me now ;
I hae brew'n three pickles o' maut,
  And I canna come ilka day to woo—
    To woo, to woo, to lilt and to woo,
    And I canna come ilka day to woo.

I hae a wee calf that wad fain be a cow—
Lass, gin ye'll tak me, tell me now ;
I hae a gryce that wad fain be a sow,
And I canna come ilka day to woo—
To woo, to woo, to lilt and to woo,
And I canna come ilka day to woo.

*　　　*　　　*　　　*

This song appears as a fragment in Herd's Collection, 1776 ; but for the origin of the ditty we have to go back to an early period of the sixteenth century. The people who heard the sermons of Cranmer and Latimer in England, and of Knox in Scotland, were familiar with a droll canticle on the idea of a lover professing to make a great show of small possessions to his sweetheart, and telling her that his time was too valuable to allow of his wooing her every day. The English song about the time of Henry VIII. opened thus :

Joan, quoth John, when will this be ?
Tell me, when wilt thou marry me,
My corn, and eke my calf and rents,
My lands and all my tenements :
Say, Joan, quoth John, what wilt thou do ?
I cannot come every day to woo.[1]

Some ages later, what appears as the entire song, but probably a good deal modified, was presented in musical publications : as follows, for example, in *Pills to Purge Melancholy*, 1698.

I've corn and hay in the barn hard by,
And three fat hogs pent up in the stye,
I have a mare and she is coal-black,
I ride on her tail to save her back.
　　Then say, my Joan, &c.

---

[1] This little song was printed in Smith's *Musica Antiqua* (1812) as from a manuscript of the above-mentioned reign. The above copy is as it appears more correctly in Rimbault's *Little Book of Songs and Ballads*.

I have a cheese upon the shelf,
And I cannot eat it all myself;
I have three good marks that lie in a rag,
In the nook of the chimney instead of a bag.
    Then say, my Joan, &c.

To marry I would have thy consent,
But, faith, I never could compliment;
I can say nought but 'Hey, go ho,'
Words that belong to the cart and the plough.
    Then say, my Joan, wilt that not do?
    I cannot come every day to woo.

There was also, as early as 1611, a song of seven stanzas, giving the same idea only a little modified, the first verse being:

I have house and land in Kent,
    And if you will love me, love me now;
Twopence-halfpenny is my rent;
    I cannot come every day to woo.[1]

These, it will be observed, are English songs; but there was a Scottish parallel, of which Lord Hailes gave a verse in the notes to his extracts from the Bannatyne Manuscript:

I hae a wee lairdship down in the Merse
    [Lass, gin ye loe me, tell me now],
The nineteenth part of a goose's grass,
And I wonna come ilka day to woo.

The nineteenth part of a goose's grass in the Merse would be a very fair counterpart to the twopence-halfpenny rent in Kent.

In the last century, a new version of *I hae laid Three Herrin' in Saut* was produced by James Tytler, very much in the burlesque style of the old verses. It is given with the air in Johnson's *Musical Museum* as follows:

[1] Melesmata, 1617.

I hae laid a herring in saut—
  Lass, gin ye lo'e me, tell me now ;
I hae brew'd a forpit o' maut,
  And I canna come ilka day to woo:
I hae a calf that will soon be a cow—
  Lass, gin ye lo'e me, tell me now ;
I hae a stook, and I 'll soon hae a mowe,
  And I canna come ilka day to woo :

I hae a house upon yon moor—
  Lass, gin ye lo'e me, tell me now ;
Three sparrows may dance upon the floor,
  And I canna come ilka day to woo :

I hae a but, and I hae a ben—
  Lass, gin ye lo'e me, tell me now ;
A penny to keep, and a penny to spen',
  And I canna come ilka day to woo :

I hae a hen wi' a happitie-leg—
  Lass, gin ye lo'e me, tell me now ;
That ilka day lays me an egg,
  And I canna come ilka day to woo :
I hae a cheese upon my skelf—
  Lass, gin ye lo'e me, tell me now ;
And soon wi' mites 'twill rin itself,
  And I canna come ilka day to woo.

It may be remarked, that the air of *I hae laid a Herrin' in Saut*, as usually sung in Scotland, is a quick and lively one. As is not uncommon, however, it is susceptible of great tenderness when played slow. Burns's pretty pastoral song, *The Bonnie Blinks of Mary's Ee*, has been of late years sung to this tune in slow time.[1]

DONALD COUPER.

We get a very decisive example of the homely simplicity and rustic baldness of the early popular music of Scotland, in an undoubted favourite lively air of at least the age of the Commonwealth—namely, *Donald Couper*—which has been preserved in Playford's *Dancing Master*, published in 1657. That it was a dancing tune in general esteem then and in the reign of Charles II. is proved, first, by its being thus admitted into a contemporary English collection ; and, secondly, by an allusion to it in Cleland's poem on the Highland Host, circa 1679 :

> ' Trumpets sounded, skenes were glancing,
> Some were *Donald Couper* dancing.'

Nor did this wide popularity soon cease, for in Durfey's *Pills to*

---

[1] See Wood's *Songs of Scotland*, ii. 120.

Purge Melancholy, volume v., published in 1719, there is an indecorous song by himself 'to the tune of *Daniel Cooper.*'

If the original verses, as published by Herd, and here placed in connection with Playford's version of the air, had been presented by Playford also, we should have had an equally expressive example of what nearly all our evidence tends to shew, the extreme rusticity, as well as puerility, of the great bulk of our national song poetry before the time when a few men of cultivated talents—Sir William Scott (?), Lieutenant Hamilton (?), Ramsay, Crawford, Mallet, and others—took it up, purified, and elevated it.

The history of our national airs and songs may be said to exhibit a constant process of change upon certain original elements. One air becomes the mother of a fairer daughter, or of a family of fairer daughters. Thus we can readily trace, in the rude *staccato* strains of *Donald Couper*, the basis of the much superior *For a' that, and a' that.* The elements of several of our best existing airs are seen in the variously named melodies of the Skene Manuscript, as some of the roots of our language are visible in Sanscrit.

Don - ald Cou - per and his man, They 've gane to the fair; They 've gane to court a bon - nie lass; But fient a ane was there. Sing hey Don - ald, how Don - ald, Hey Don - ald Cou - per! He 's

gane a - wa' to court a wife, And he 's come hame with-

out her!

Donald Couper and his man,
    They 've gane to the fair ;
They 've gane to court a bonnie lass ;
    But fient a ane was there.
        Sing hey Donald, how Donald,
        Hey Donald Couper !
    He 's gane awa' to court a wife,
    And he 's come hame without her !

But he has gotten an auld wife,
    And she 's come hirplin' hame ;
And she 's faun o'er the buffet stool,
    And brak her rumple bane !

HAUD AWA', BIDE AWA' !

In Playford's *Dancing Master*, 1657, is inserted another of the primitive rustic airs of Scotland, one which is still recognised as *Haud awa' frae me, Donald*, this title being probably a refrain of the original foolish verses for which this was the appropriate music. The air is here reproduced ; but as the original song or rant is lost, we are obliged to adapt to the melody a superior and more modern song, which was published by Herd, being a dialogue between a lover and his mistress, in which a misunderstanding is pleasantly cleared up (here, however, somewhat abridged).

O come a-wa', come a - wa, Come a-wa' wi'
me, Jen-ny; Sic frowns I can-na bear frae ane Whase
smiles ance ravished me, Jen-ny. If you 'll be kind, you'll
nev - er find That ought can al - ter me, Jen-ny; For
you're the mistress of my mind, What - e'er you think of
me, Jen - ny.

DONALD.

O come awa', come awa',
    Come awa' wi' me, Jenny ;
Sic frowns I canna bear frae ane
    Whase smiles ance ravished me, Jenny.
If you 'll be kind, you 'll never find
    That ought can alter me, Jenny ;
For you 're the mistress of my mind,
    Whate'er you think of me, Jenny.

JENNY.

O haud awa', haud awa',
    Haud awa' frae me, Donald ;
Your heart is made o'er large for ane,
    It is not meet for me, Donald.
Some fickle mistress you may find,
    Will jilt as fast as thee, Donald ;
To ilka swain she will prove kind,
    And nae less kind to thee, Donald.

[O] now for ever haud awa',
    Haud awa' frae me, Donald ;
Gae seek a heart that's like your ain,
    And come nae mair to me, Donald.
For I'll reserve mysel for ane,
    For ane that's liker me, Donald ;
If sic a ane I canna find,
    I'll ne'er lo'e man nor thee, Donald !

DONALD.

Then, I'm thy man, and false report
    Has only tauld a lie, Jenny ;
To try thy truth and make us sport,
    The tale was raised by me, Jenny.

JENNY.

When ye prove this, and still can love,
    Then come awa' wi' me, Donald ;
I'm weel content ne'er to repent
    That I hae smiled on thee, Donald.

Another and still more recent song to this tune (published
in Ritson's Collection, 1794) is in a comic vein, exhibiting
some of the peculiarities of the Scottish mountaineer when he
descends to the Lowlands and attempts to enunciate himself
in Anglo-Saxon.

HAUD AWA' FRAE ME, DONALD!

O will ye hae ta tartan plaid,
  Or will ye hae ta ring, matam ?
Or will ye hae ta kiss o' me,
  And dat's a pretty ting, matam ?
    Haud awa', bide awa',
      Haud awa' frae me, Donald ;
    I 'll neither kiss nor hae a ring,
      Nae tartan plaids for me, Donald.

Hur can beshow a petter hough
  Tan him tat wears ta crown, matam ;
Hersel hae pistol and claymore,
  To flee ta Lawland loon, matam.
    Haud awa', bide awa',
      Haud awa' frae me, Donald,
    For a' your houghs and warlike arms
      You 're not a match for me, Donald.

In ta morning, when ye rise,
  Ye 'se get fresh whey for tea, matam ;
Sweet milk and ream as much you please,
  Far cheeper tan Bohea, matam.
    Haud awa', bide awa',
      Haud awa' frae me, Donald,
    I winna quit my morning's tea ;
      Your whey will ne'er agree, Donald.

Faits ye 'se pe ket a siller brootch,
  Far pigger as ta moon, matam ;
Ye 'se ride in curroch 'stead o' coach,
  And wow put ye 'll pe fine, matam.

I

Haud awa', bide awa',
 Haud awa' frae me, Donald ;
For a' your Highland rarities,
 You 're not a match for me, Donald.

What 's tis a way tat ye 'll pe kind
 To a protty man like me, matam !
Sae lang 's claymore pe py my side,
 I 'll never marry thee, matam !
  O come awa', come awa',
   O come awa' wi' me, Donald,
  I wadna quit my Highlandman ;
   Frae Lawlands set me free, Donald.

TIBBIE FOWLER.

The following song, full of Scotch cynical humour, very cleverly expressed, first appeared complete in Johnson's *Museum*, a mere fragment having previously been given by Herd. It probably refers to a real Tibbie Fowler, and tradition at Leith points to the person in a certain Isabella Fowler, who was married to a son of Logan of Restalrig, the conspirator, in the seventeenth century. (Campbell's *History of Leith*, note, p. 314.) A house which is believed to have belonged to the pair, bearing the date 1636, is pointed out in the Sheriff-brae, in Leith.

It happens that tradition here indicates persons who actually existed. That George Logan, son of the conspirator, wedded Isobel Fowler, daughter of Ludowick Fowler of Burncastle, is stated on authentic grounds by Nisbet (*Heraldry*, i. 202). We know not, however, whether Isobel Fowler had previously been the subject of extensive competition among the other sex, or whether she sank into the arms of Logan without a sigh from herself or others. Neither have we any authentic account of the date of the composition. The song does not appear to be in a style earlier than the reign of George I.

'Tib - bie Fow - ler o' the Glen, There's

ower mo - ny woo - ing at her;

Tib - bie Fow - ler o' the Glen, There's

ower mo - ny woo - ing at her.

Chorus.

Woo - in' at her, pu' - in' at her,

Court - in' her, and can - na get her;

Fil - thy elf, it's for her pelf That

a' the lads are woo - in' at her.

Tibbie Fowler o' the Glen,
　There's ower mony wooing at her ;
Tibbie Fowler o' the Glen,
　There's ower mony wooing at her.

Wooin' at her, pu'in' at her,
　　Courtin' her, and canna get her ;
Filthy elf, it 's for her pelf
　　That a' the lads are wooin' at her

Ten cam east, and ten cam west ;
　　Ten cam rowin' ower the water ;
Twa cam down the lang dyke-side :
　　There 's twa-and-thirty wooin' at her.

There 's seven but, and seven ben,
　　Seven in the pantry wi' her ;
Twenty head about the door :
　　There 's ane-and-forty wooin' at her !

She 's got pendles in her lugs ;
　　Cockle-shells wad set her better !
High-heel'd shoon, and siller tags ;
　　And a' the lads are wooin' at her.

Be a lassie e'er sae black,
　　Gin she hae the name o' siller,
Set her up on Tintock tap,
　　The wind will blaw a man till her.

Be a lassie e'er so fair,
　　An she want the penny siller,
A flie may fell her in the air,
　　Before a man be even'd till her.

BONNIE DUNDEE.

There is a long musical genealogy connected with the now industrious and populous town of Dundee. First, in the Skene Manuscript, temp. Car. Primi, there occurs a melody named *Adieu, Dundee,* which is only a simple form of the fine air now recognised as *Bonnie Dundee.* In the latter part of the seventeenth century, the tune, under the name of *Bonnie Dundee,* was known in England, for it appears by that title in an Appendix to one of the editions of Playford's *Dancing Master,* of date 1688. To what verses was it then sung? Possibly to a simple ditty which still retains a certain degree of popularity in Scotland, beginning:

> O whar gat ye that haver-meal bannock?
> Silly blind body, O dinna ye see?
> I gat it frae a brisk sodger laddie,
> Atween St Johnston and Bonnie Dundee.
>
> Oh, gin I saw the dear laddie that gae me 't!
> Aft has he doudled me on o' his knee.
> But now he 's awa', and I dinna ken whar he 's,
> O gin he was back to his minnie and me! [1]

Possibly, however, I feel sorry to say, to a remarkably coarse Grub Street song of licentious sentiment, which is printed in more than one English collection of the early part of the eighteenth century, under the title of *Jockey's Deliverance,* or

[1] In *Notes and Queries,* August 1859, is printed a various version of this song, transmitted by a gentleman styling himself Yemen, who states that he found it among some old family papers:

> O! whar got ye that auld crooked penny?
> For ane o' bricht goud wad ye niffer wi' me?
> Richt fou are baith ends o' my green silken wallet,
> And high are my wa's, ower in Bonnie Dundee.
>
> O! gin I saw the dear laddie that had it,
> Wha, when we were bairnies twa, gied it to me,
> For a' the bricht goud in your green silken wallet
> I never wad niffer my crooked bawbee.
>
> O! whar got ye that auld worsted plaidie?
> A mantle o' satin is fitter for ye.
> I 'll clead ye in satin, and mak ye a lady,
> Gin ye 'd gang wi' me to Bonnie Dundee.
>
> Ye may clead me in satin and mak me a lady,
> And tak me ower heartless to Bonnie Dundee,
> But my heart neither satin nor goud can procure ye,
> I sell 't it lang syne for this crooked bawbee.

the Valiant Escape from Dundee, professedly to be sung ' to an Excellent Tune, called *Bonny Dundee :*' which song begins in a strain giving it the appearance of a parody or imitation of some preceding ballad :

> Where gottest thou the Haver-mill Bonack?
> Blind booby, canst thou not see ?
> I 'se got it out of a Scotchman's wallet, &c.

This song describes the escape of a treacherous and very reckless profligate from Dundee, and has for a refrain :

> Come fill up my cup, come fill up my can,
> Come saddle my horse, and call up my man ;
> Come open the gates and let me go free,
> For I 'se gang no more to Bonnie Dundee.

The last verse is as follows :

> With swords ready drawn they rid to the gate,
> Where being denied a free passage through,
> The Master and Man they fought at that rate,
> That some ran away and others they slew ;
> Thus Jockey the Laird and Sawney the Man,
> They valiantly fought as Highlanders can,
> In spite of the loons, they set themselves free,
> And so bid adieu to Bonnie Dundee.

In illustration of which transaction, there is an engraving representing a hand-to-hand fight at the gate of Dundee—a gate, however, such as it would have been difficult to find in any Scotch town in the seventeenth century.

In order to convey the air of *Bonnie Dundee* to the modern reader, it may be allowable to present the old song as modified by Burns :

O whare did ye get that haver-meal bannock? O, sil-ly auld bo-dy, O, din-na ye see, I

gat it frae a young brisk sodger lad - die, Between St John - ston and Bon - nie Dun - dee. O,
gin I saw the lad - die that gae me 't!
Aft has he dan - dled me on his knee; May
heav - en pro - tect my bon - nie Scots lad - die, And
send him safe hame to his ba - by and me.

O whare did ye get that haver-meal bannock ?
   O, silly auld body, O, dinna ye see,
I gat it frae a young brisk sodger laddie,
   Between St Johnston and Bonnie Dundee.
O, gin I saw the laddie that gae me 't !
   Aft has he dandled me on his knee ;
May heaven protect my bonnie Scots laddie,
   And send him safe hame to his baby and me.

My blessings upon thy sweet wee lippie !
   My blessings upon thy bonnie e'e-bree !
Thy smiles are sae like my blithe sodger laddie,
   Thou 's aye be the dearer and dearer to me !

But I 'll bigg a bowir on yon bonnie banks,
    Where Tay rins wimpling by sae clear ;
And I 'll cleid thee in the tartan sae fine,
    And mak thee a man like thy daddie sae dear.

RATTLIN' ROARIN' WILLIE.

O rattlin' roar-in' Wil-lie, O he held to the fair, And
for to sell his fid-dle, And buy some oth-er ware. But,
part-ing wi' his fid-dle, The saut tear blin't his e'e; And
ratt-lin' roar-in' Wil-lie, Ye 're wel-come hame to me.

O rattlin' roarin' Willie,
    O he held to the fair,
And for to sell his fiddle,
    And buy some other ware.
But, parting wi' his fiddle,
    The saut tear blin't his e'e ;
And rattlin' roarin' Willie,
    Ye 're welcome hame to me.

O, Willie, come sell your fiddle,
  O sell your fiddle sae fine ;
O, Willie, come sell your fiddle,
  And buy a pint o' wine.
If I should sell my fiddle
  The warld wad think I was mad,
For mony a rantin' day
  My fiddle and I hae had.

This song, which seems to have appeared for the first time in Johnson's *Musical Museum*, 1788, has little intelligence in it—little more than rant—and yet, from the hint it gives of a mirthful *insouciant* character, and a certain pathos regarding the fiddle—with which the hero has so come to intercommunicate himself, that he speaks as if it had been a living thing which partook of his merriment—we should not like to part with it. So also had felt Robert Burns, who communicated it to the *Museum*, along with the original air. The bard, on coming to Edinburgh, found his way to a certain club of good fellows taking to themselves the name of the Crochallan Fencibles, from the name of a Highland song wherewith their host, Daniel Douglas, used to regale them. Among these merry men, the face of one named Willie Dunbar—in daylight, a respectable 'writer' (that is, solicitor)—shone out with extraordinary lustre, seeming to the rustic bard a perfect realisation of the Rantin' Roarin' Willie of the old song. Hereupon the muse of Kyle broke out in an additional stanza, descriptive of Dunbar's appearance in the presidentship of the Crochallan Fencibles :

As I cam by Crochallan,
  I cannily keekit ben :
Rattlin' roarin' Willie
  Was sittin' at yon board-en',
Sittin' at yon board-en',
  Amang guid companie ;
Rattlin' roarin' Willie,
  Ye 're welcome hame to me !

Burns felt peculiarly sorry, on leaving Edinburgh, for his

parting with Willie Dunbar, and wrote to him: '1 have a strong fancy that, in some future eccentric planet, the comet of happier systems than any with which astronomy is yet acquainted, you and I, among the harum-scarum sons of imagination and whim, with a hearty shake of a hand, a metaphor, and a laugh, shall recognise old acquaintance.'

After these particulars, it is curious to learn that the simple little ballad relating to Rattlin' Roarin' Willie and his fiddle must have been kept alive on the breath of tradition for a century before the days of Burns. *Rantin' Roarin' Willie* is mentioned as a *tune* in the *Tea-table Miscellany*, 1724, being in all likelihood that of the song which Burns preserved. We learn, however, from Sir Walter Scott that Rattlin' (or Rantin') Roarin' Willie was a real person, of whom it may be assumed that he probably lived in the seventeenth century, being a musician well known on the Border, and who, having the misfortune to murder a brother in trade who passed by the name of *Sweet Milk*, was executed at Jedburgh. One cannot suppose that so gay a man as Willie could commit deliberate murder. We may charitably surmise that the act was one of manslaughter or chance-medley only, in the course of one of those tavern brawls which used to be attended occasionally with bloody results in an age when all men wore weapons, and were continually getting into conditions under which a reckless use of them became nearly unavoidable. A contemporary ballad jested with the unfortunate minstrel on his condemnation to an ignominious death, saying:

> Drink maun be dear wi' Willie,
> When Sweet Milk gars him die.

There is another snatch of traditionary song to the tune of *Rattlin' Roarin' Willie*, which presents the hero in an amatory light:

> Rattlin' roarin' Willie,
> Where have ye been sae late?
> I 've been to see my Peggy,
> Sae weel as I ken the gate!

> Sae weel as I ken the gate,
> And the tirlin' o' the pin;
> And, gang I late or ear',
> She 'll rise and let me in![1]

In Halliwell's *Nursery Rhymes*, we find a fragment of *Rattlin'
Roarin' Willie* reduced to a nursery ditty.[2]

AS I CAME IN BY FISHERRAW.

Herd's Collection, 1776, gives us a short rustic song, alluding
to an unfortunate love affair in humble life, of which all that
is presentable is as follows:

> As I came in by Fisherraw,
> Musselburgh was near me;
> I threw my mussel-pock aside,
> And courted wi' my dearie.
> Up stairs, down stairs,
> Timmer stairs fear me;
> I thought it lang to lie my lane,
> When I'm sae near my dearie.

The editor assigns to it as a tune *Jenny Dang the Weaver*. It
appears to be one of the old simple country songs which Allan
Ramsay well-intendingly endeavoured to supersede with purer,
if not better verses, for he gives in his *Tea-table Miscellany* a
song of his own, beginning

> O mither dear, I 'gin to fear,
> Though I 'm baith blithe and bonnie—

as to the tune of *Jenny Beguiled the Webster*, and with an indication of the auld chorus, as he phrases it, 'Up stairs, down
stairs,' &c.

There is reason to believe that the old song and air existed
from a time a good way back in the seventeenth century, for
in a poetical tract published in London in 1686, under the title

---

[1] Communicated to the editor in 1831 by Mr James Hendry, Keith,
Aberdeenshire.

[2] See also *Notes and Queries*, second series, v. 186.

of *A Joco-Serious Discourse, in Two Dialogues between a North-
umberland Gentleman and his Tenant, a Scotchman, by George
Stuart,* the said tenant is represented as singing the first verse
of one of his native songs as follows :

> This Janet is a bonnie lass,
> This Janet is my dearie ;
> What then need I lig by mysel,
> And Janet's bed sae near me ?

which, however, the gentleman does not allow him to continue,
such a strain being, he says, unfit to celebrate the coronation
of their majesties (James II. and his queen). The tenant, thus
interrupted, strikes up a more fitting strain as follows :

The this-tle is the heal-ing plant: What
then need I to fear me? For my guid health I
ne'er can want, The this-tle grows so near me : It
cures con-vul-sions (in the state), It helps a' these are
aguish; And rag-ing fevers it will 'bate, Al-
be-it they were plaguish.

The thistle is the healing plant :
   What then need I to fear me ?
For my guid health I ne'er can want,
   The thistle grows so near me :
It cures convulsions (in the state),
   It helps a' these are aguish ;
And raging fevers it will 'bate
   Albeit they were plaguish.

Wha canna luve the thistle weel
   Are oddly gi'en to folly ;
Take thou of it, and thou 'll ne'er feel
   Disease of melancholy :
Against the rickets it is guid,
   The ligaments it looses,
And purifies corrupted blood,
   Sae never spare thy doses.

But this tune, it will be observed, is different from that now recognised as *Jenny Dang the Weaver.*

THE AULD MAN'S MARE'S DEAD.

The auld man's mare's dead, The poor man's mare's dead, The auld man's mare's dead, A mile a-boon Dun-dee. She was cut lug-git, painch lip-pit, Steel wam-ed, stain-cher fit-tit,

Chan - ler chafted, lang neckit, And yet the brute did die ! The

auld man's mare's dead, The   poor   man's mare's dead, The

auld man's mare's dead, A   mile   a - boon Dun - dee.

The auld man's mare's dead,
The poor man's mare's dead,
The auld man's mare's dead,
   A mile aboon Dundee.

She was cut-luggit, painch-lippit,
Steel-wamed, staincher-fittit,
Chanler-chafted, lang-neckit,
   And yet the brute did die !
      The auld man's mare's dead, &c.

Her lunyie banes were knags and neuks,
She had the cleeks, the cauld, the crooks,
The jawpish, and the wanton yeuks,
   And the howks aboon her e'e.
      The auld man's mare's dead, &c.

My master rade me to the town,
He tied me to a staincher round,
He took a chappin till himsel,
   But fient a drap gae me.
      The auld man's mare's dead, &c.

The auld man's mare 's dead,
The poor man's mare 's dead,
The peats and turrs and a' to lead,
    And yet the jade did die !

This rich specimen of rustic Scotch humour appears to have been the composition of one Patie Birnie, who practised the art of a violer at the burgh of Kinghorn in the early part of the last

Patie Birnie.

century, and upon whom, in 1721, Allan Ramsay composed a humorous elegy, stating many biographical and characteristic

particulars. Patie is described as having been at the Battle of
Bothwell Bridge, probably as one of the militia of his native
county of Fife ; but, Horace-like, he ran away, and never stopped
till he came to Edinburgh. He was ready-witted, with a strong
instinct for the advancement of his professional objects, told a
story well, and never was at a loss. Hearing of company at the
inn, Patie would push in with his fiddle, and seldom failed to
secure a paying auditory. Sometimes a dwarf, named Stocks,
would dance on a table to the strains of the violer, and the two
would thus keep up the merriment for the greater part of a
night. A portrait of Patie, done by Aikman, has been handed
down, and exhibits a face mingling cleverness, drollery, roguery,
and impudence in harmonious proportions. As to the authorship of the song, we can only infer it from the language of
Ramsay, while describing the violer's deportment towards inn
company :

> —— Soon his face wad mak you fain,
> When he did sough,
> 'O wiltu, wiltu, do 't again,'
> And graned and leuch.

> This sang he made frae his ain head,
> And eke ' *The auld man's mare she's dead,*
> *And peats and turrs and a' to lead* '—
> O fye upon her !
> A bonnie auld thing this, indeed,
> An 't like your honour.

> After ilk tune he took a sowp, &c.

CAULD KAIL IN ABERDEEN.

The favourite air, *Cauld Kail in Aberdeen*, does not appear in
any collection before that of Johnson (volume ii., published in
1788), where it was associated with an erotic effusion of Alexander
fourth Duke of Gordon. It would appear, however, that the

melody took its origin early in the last century, and most probably in connection with a rude country ditty, which ran as follows:

> Cauld kail in Aberdeen,
> And castocks in Stra'bogie!
> But yet I fear they'll cook o'er soon,
> And never warm the cogie.

> * * * *

> Wow, Aberdeen, what did you mean,
> Sae young a maid to woo, sir!
> I'm sure it was nae [joke] to her,
> Whate'er it was to you, sir. &c.[1]

It would appear that these verses relate to some incident in the life of the first Earl of Aberdeen, who died in 1720, at the age of eighty-three, after being some years a widower. If this conjecture be right, the cauld kail of Aberdeen was no mess connected with the ancient city, but a metaphorical allusion to the faded love-fervours of an aged nobleman, who, spite of years, was presuming to pay his addresses to a young lady.

There's cauld kail in A - ber - deen, And cas - tocks in Stra-

bo - gie, Where il - ka man maun hae his lass, But

I maun hae my co - gie. I maun hae my

co - gie, sirs, I can - na want my co - gie; I

[1] The entire song was published in Herd, 1776.

J

wad - na gie the three-gir'd cog For a' the queans in

Bo - gie.

There's cauld kail in Aberdeen,
And castocks in Strabogie,
Where ilka man maun hae his lass,
But I maun hae my cogie.
I maun hae my cogie, sirs,
I canna want my cogie ;
I wadna gie the three-gir'd cog
For a' the queans in Bogie.

There's Johnie Smith has got a wife,
Wha scrimps him o' his cogie ;
If she were mine, upon my life,
I'd douk her in a bogie.

Mr Stenhouse states that this song (which extends to two more verses, but of indifferent humour as well as morality) was published in Dale's *Collection of Songs*, before the days of Burns.

THE BLYTHSOME BRIDAL.

The Blythsome Bridal is an extraordinary picture of humble life, as presented in a Scotch village in the seventeenth century. Its enumeration of oddly characterised men and women, all with appropriate nicknames, is only to be equalled by its list of the rough viands and dainties with which they were to be regaled. Over all is an air of intense hearty good-humour and love of merriment, that leaves us almost bewildered when we think of the general sombreness of Scottish rustic life, and in particular the zealous efforts of the clergy, by fines and censures, to prevent all dancing and other joyance at weddings. Nothing could prove more expressively how much of 'tipsy jest and jollity' there has always lurked under the sober exterior of Scottish life, or (to change the expression of the idea) how liable our quiet countrymen are to strange outbreakings of vivacious feeling, even to the extent of recklessness and frolic.

Fy let us a' to the brid - al, For there 'll be lilt - in' there; For Jock 's to be mar - ried to Mag - gie, The lass wi' the gowd - en hair. And there 'll be lang - kale and pot - tage, And ban - nocks o' bar - ley meal; And there 'll be good saut her - rin', To re - lish a cogue o' guid yill.

Fy let us a' to the bridal,
   For there 'll be liltin' there ;
For Jock 's to be married to Maggie,
   The lass wi' the gowden hair.
And there 'll be lang-kale and pottage,
   And bannocks o' barley-meal ;
And there 'll be good saut herrin',
   To relish a cogue o' guid yill.
      Fy let us a', &c.

And there 'll be Sandie the souter,
   And Will wi' the mickle mou' ;
And there 'll be Tam the plouter,
   And Andrew the tinkler, I trow.
And there 'll be bow-leggit Robbie,
   Wi' thoomless Katie's guidman ;
And there 'll be blue-cheekit Dallie,
   And Lawrie, the laird o' the land.

And there 'll be sow-libber Patie,
   And plookie-faced Wat o' the mill ;
Capper-nosed Gibbie, and Francie,
   That wins in the howe o' the hill.
And there 'll be Alaster Dougal,
   That splae-fitted Bessie did woo,
And sniffling Lillie and Tibbie,
   And Kirstie, that belly-god sow !

And there 'll be Geordie M'Lowrie,
   And blinkin' daft Barbara and Meg,
And there 'll be blencht Gillie-Wimple,
   And pewter-faced fleeching Joug.
And there 'll be happer-hipped Nancie
   And fairy-faced Jeanie by name,
Gleed Katie and fat-luggit Leesie
   The lass wi' the gowden [kame].

And there 'll be Girnagain Gibbie,
    And his glaikit wife Jeanie Bell,
And mizly-chinned flytin' Geordie,
    The lad that was skipper himsel.
There 'll be a' the lads and the lasses,
    Set down in the mids o' the ha' ;
Wi' sybows, and reefarts, and carlins,
    That are baith sodden and raw.

There 'll be tarten, dragen, and brachen,
    And fouth o' guid gabbocks o' skate,
Powsoudie, and drammock, and crowdie,
    And caller nowt-feet on a plate ;
And there 'll be partans and buckies,
    And speldins and haddocks enew,
And singit sheep-heads and a haggis,
    And scadlips to sup till ye 're fou.

There 'll be guid lapper-milk kebbucks,
    And sowens, and farles, and baps,
Wi' swats and weel-scraped painches,
    And brandy in stoups and in caups ;
And there 'll be meal-kail and castocks,
    Wi' skink to sup till ye rive ;
And roasts to roast on a brander,
    Of flouks that were taken alive.

Scraped haddocks, wilks, dulse and tangle,
    And a mill o' guid sneeshin' to prie ;
When weary wi' eatin' and drinkin',
    We 'll rise up and dance till we dee.
        Fy let us a' to the bridal,
           For there 'll be liltin' there ;
        For Jock 's to be married to Maggie,
           The lass wi' the gowden hair.

This singular piece appeared first in Watson's *Collection of*

Scottish Poems, 1709, and from thence was transferred into the *Tea-table Miscellany* and Thomson's *Orpheus Caledonius*, as it has been into nearly every collection of Scotch songs published since. The authorship is to be considered as doubtful. The song used to be commonly ascribed to Francis Sempill of Beltrees, Renfrewshire, who is believed to have written several other popular songs, and who flourished during the reign of Charles II., dying not long before the year 1685. Sempill was a man of lively talents, a keen cavalier or loyalist, even to the persecution of conventiclers,[1] and in his latter days was reduced by suretyship to a poverty befitting his poetical character. We are to regard him as one of a section of society by whom the spirit of mirth and song was maintained during those days of seriousness verging upon gloom —a protestantism of human nature against the asceticism and self-mortification of the puritanic system. It is remarkable that his father and grandfather were both poets. His grandson, Robert Sempill of Beltrees, who died at Kilbarchan in 1789, at the great age of a hundred and two, seems to have been the authority for attributing to him the authorship of *The Blythsome Bridal.*[2]

Of late years a claim for this honour has been put forward by Mr Mark Napier [3] on behalf of Sir William Scott of Thirlstain, direct male ancestor of the present line of the Lords Napier. It rests on a communication from the late Lord Napier to Mr Mark Napier, of date 15th December 1831, in the following terms: ' Sir William Scott was the author of that well-known Scots song, *Fy, let us a' to the bridal, for there 'll be liltings there*—a better thing than Horace ever wrote. My authority was my father, who told me he had it from *his*, and that he had it from *his*, who was Sir William's son.'

[1] In the Privy Council Record, 13th January 1681, is a petition from Francis Sempill of Beltrees for reward for his services in putting down conventicles.

[2] *The Poems of the Sempills of Beltrees*, edited by James Paterson, Edinburgh, 1849.

[3] *Partition of the Lennox*, Edinburgh, 1835, p. 237.

This claim must be allowed to be not without some support in what we know of Sir William Scott from other sources. He was one of a group of wits, composed of Archibald Pitcairne, David Gregory, Thomas Kincaid, Sir William Bennet of Grubbet, &c., who, living at the beginning of the eighteenth century, and cultivating the muse, though chiefly in the Latin language, might be said to mark the *renaissance* of polite literature in Scotland after the long night of the religious troubles. A volume of their Latin verses, edited by Ruddiman in 1727, shews them all to have been intensely Jacobite, and of course confessors in the protestantism above alluded to. On Sir William, who died on the 8th of October 1725, John Ker, professor of Greek at Aberdeen, writes an elegy, in which he speaks of his deceased friend as :

———Deliciæ novem sororum,
Et *Caledoniæ* decus *Camœnæ ;*

a strong hint that Sir William wrote also in Scots verse. Ruddiman adverts to him in highly flattering terms : 'Sir William Scott of Thirlstain, illustrious in his birth, more illustrious by his virtues, an excellent counsellor and philologist, a judge of all polite letters, and a man to be compared with few in regard to integrity of life and suavity and elegance of manners, deserves to be ranked in the next place to Pitcairne. He composed some very neat and pretty Latin poems, which, as he was a man of consummate modesty, he would never shew except to a very few friends ; nor would he ever, while in life, permit them to see the light by way of publication.' Professor Ker's elegy, besides admitting Sir William's learning and sagacity, speaks strongly of his convivial temper, his wit, and many agreeablenesses ; impressing us with the idea of a most delightful person, notwithstanding an escape of candour on the part of the poet—

Solebat
Meas esse aliquid putare nugas.

One of Sir William's pieces of a macaronic character, exhibits a strain of humour that recalls *The Blythsome Bridal,* and shews that he might have been its author.

AD E——M E——M, EQUITEM, M.D. VILLADELPHINUS[1] FRATER.

Qualis in terris fabulatur Orpheus
Natus Irlandis, ubi nulla wivat
Spidera telam, neque fœda spouttat
    Tædda venenum ;
Dura, Clarshoo modulante, saxa,
Et viros saxo graviores omni,
Et lacus, et bogs, fluviosque, et altas
    Ducere sylvas.
Talis Hiberno similis poetæ
Villadelphinus ego, nec secundus,
Dum mihi possham sonat, aut canoram
    Dextera trumpam :
Asinus semper comes est, et anser,
Vocibus partes modulare promti,
Porcus in stayo facilique bassum
    Murmure grumphat :
Per domum dansant tabulæ, cathedræ,
Fistules, furmæ, simul atque chistæ ;
Rusticam ducit leviterque dansam
    Armo-cathedra.
Tum mihi starkam promit anus aillam,
Ipsa quam broustrix veterem botello
Condidit, frater, datus in theatro
    Cum tibi plausus ;
Tunc mihi notæ redeunt Camœnæ,
Tunc ego possum atque imitare Sappho,
Blackere et nigrum bene, winterano
    Cortice riftans :
Musa Taiguæos mea poetastros,
Judice vel te, superabit omnes,
Ipse Pentlandis licet arrivaret
    Flecnus in agris.

---

[1] Under this mystic appellative lurks a reference to the simple little village of Dolphinton, in Lanarkshire.

SCORNFUL NANCY.

This is one of the songs of unknown age and authorship which appeared in the *Tea-table Miscellany* and *Orpheus Caledonius*. Its *naif* dialogue has secured it a place in every subsequent collection.

Nan - cy's to the green - wood gane, To
hear the gowd - spink chatt'ring; And Wil - lie he has
fol - low'd her, To gain her love by flatt'ring: But,
a' that he could say or do, She geck'd and scorned
at him; And, aye when he be - gan to woo, She
bad him mind wha gat him.

Nancy 's to the greenwood gane,
    To hear the gowdspink chatt'ring ;
And Willie he has follow'd her,
    To gain her love by flatt'ring :
But, a' that he could say or do,
    She geck'd and scorned at him ;
And, aye when he began to woo,
    She bad him mind wha gat him.

What ails ye at my dad, quoth he,
    My minnie or my auntie ?
Wi' crowdy-mowdy[1] they fed me,
    Lang-kale and ranty-tanty :[2]
Wi' bannocks o' guid barley-meal,
    Of thae there was richt plenty,
Wi' chappit stocks fu' butter'd weel,
    And was not that richt dainty ?

Although my father was nae laird,
    'Tis daffin to be vaunty,
He keepit aye a guid kale-yard,
    A ha' house, and a pantry :
A guid blue bonnet on his head,
    An owerlay 'bout his craigie ;[3]
And aye, until the day he dee'd,
    He rade on guid shanks-naigie.[4]

Now wae and wonder on your snout,
    Wad ye hae bonnie Nancy ?
Wad ye compare yoursel to me—
    A docken till a tanzie ?

[1] A mess composed of milk and meal boiled together.
[2] The broad-leafed sorrel, so called, used to be gathered by our frugal ancestresses in spring, and added to the cabbage or kail in the dinner broth.
[3] A cravat about his neck.
[4] A jocular way of stating that he used his limbs in moving about.

I hae a wooer o' my ain,
  They ca' him Souple Sandy ;
And weel I wat his bonnie mou'
  Is sweet like sugar-candy.

Now, Nancy, what need a' this din ?
  Do I no ken this Sandy ?
I 'm sure the chief o' a' his kin
  Was Rab, the beggar-randy :
His minnie Meg, upon her back,
  Bare baith him and his billy ;[1]
Will ye compare a nasty pack
  To me, your winsome Willie ?

My gutcher [2] left a guid braidsword :
  Though it be auld and rusty,
Yet ye may tak it on my word,
  It is baith stout and trusty ;
And if I can but get it drawn,
  Which will be richt uneasy,
I shall lay baith my lugs in pawn,
  That he shall get a heezy.

Then Nancy turn'd her round about,
  And said, Did Sandy hear ye,.
Ye wadna miss to get a clout ;
  I ken he disna fear ye :
Sae haud your tongue, and say nae mair,
  Set somewhere else your fancy ;
For as lang 's Sandy 's to the fore,
  Ye never shall get Nancy.

[1] Brother.   [2] Goodsire or grandfather.

THE COCK-LAIRD.

A cock-laird is a small proprietor. The present song first
appeared in the *Orpheus Caledonius*, but in a rude version, upon
which some improvements were afterwards made, probably by
Ramsay. The style of the verse somewhat reminds us of *Scornful
Nancy*, and also of the song immediately following the present,
as if it were a production of the same pen.

A cock-laird, fou cad-gie, Wi' Jen-nie did meet; He
hawsed, he kiss'd her, And ca'd her his sweet. Wilt
thou gang a-lang wi' me Jen-nie, Jen-nie? Thou'se
be my ain lem-an-jo, Jen-nie, quo' he.

A cock-laird, fou cadgie,
    Wi' Jennie did meet ;
He hawsed, he kiss'd her,
    And ca'd her his sweet.
Wilt thou gang along wi' me,
    Jennie, Jennie ?
Thou 'se be my ain leman-jo,
    Jennie, quo' he.

Gin I gae alang wi' thee,
  Ye maunna fail
To feast me wi' caddels
  And guid hackit kail.
What needs a' this vanity,
  Jennie ? quo' he ;
Is na bannocks and dribly-beards [1]
  Guid meat for thee ?

Gin I gang alang wi' you,
  I maun hae a silk hood,
A kirtle-sark, wyliecoat,
  And a silk snood,
To tie up my hair in
  A cockernonie.
Hout awa', thou 'se gane wud, I trow,
  Jennie ! quo' he.

Gin ye 'd hae me look bonnie,
  And shine like the moon,
I maun hae katlets and patlets,
  And cam'rel-heel'd shoon ;
Wi' craig-claiths and lug-babs, [2]
  And rings twa or three.
Hout, the deil 's in your vanity,
  Jennie ! quo' he.

And I maun hae pinners,
  With pearlins set roun',
A skirt o' the paudy, [3]
  And a waistcoat o' brown.
Awa' wi' sic vanities,
  Jennie, quo' he,
For curches and kirtles
  Are fitter for thee.

---

[1] Cabbage, which beslabber the beard.
[2] Cloths for the throat, and rings for the ears.
[3] Probably paduasoy.

My lairdship can yield me
    As muckle a year,
As haud us in pottage
    And guid knockit bear ;
But, havin' nae tenants,
    Oh, Jennie, Jennie,
To buy ought I ne'er have
    A penny, quo' he.

The borrowstown merchants
    Will sell ye on tick ;
For we maun hae braw things,
    Although they should break :
When broken, frae care
    The fools are set free,
When we mak them lairds
    In the Abbey,[1] quo' she.[2]

MY JO JANET.

This clever song appears in the *Tea-table Miscellany* (1724),
but is probably somewhat older. From the allusion to the
Bass, which we must presume to be the Bass of Inverury—a
noted hillock near that little burgh—and to Aberdeen, one
might justifiably suppose it to have sprung up in that province,
even were there not the pronunciation of ' sheen' for ' shoon' to
substantiate the conjecture. As an expression of Scottish
economic and moral philosophy—the 'saving of all avoid-
able expenses, and the taking down of youthful vanity and

---

[1] That is, oblige them, on account of their debts, to take advantage of
the sanctuary at Holyrood.

[2] The version here given of *The Cock-Laird* is partly from the *Orpheus
Caledonius* (1733) and partly from a more recent copy.

extravagance—the piece is beyond all praise. It is also to be remarked, that the language is choice and the versification perfect—implying an educated mind in the unknown author.

The air is of considerably greater age than the modern song, being identical with one called *Long or ony Old Man,* which appears in the Skene Manuscript, circa 1630.

Sweet sir, for your courtesie, When ye come by the Bass, then,
For the love ye bear to me, Buy me a keek-in' glass, then.
Keek in-to the draw well, Jan-et, Jan-et,
There ye'll see your bon-nie sel, My jo Jan-et.

> Sweet sir, for your courtesie,
>   When ye come by the Bass, then,
> For the love ye bear to me,
>   Buy me a keekin'-glass, then.[1]
>   Keek into the draw-well,
>   Janet, Janet,
>   There ye'll see your bonnie sel,
>   My jo Janet.

[1] A mirror was formerly a rare luxury in rural Scotland. 'In the but-the-house or kitchen there was no allowed looking-glass; but the servant-lasses had a substitute for it, in a full pail of water brought to the light in a clear day, in which the reflection was as distinct as in any mirror. They sometimes had a small Dutch *keeking-glass,* about the size of a playing-card, concealed in their chests, at which they took a stolen glance before going to church.'—Robertson's *Rural Recollections,* 1829.

Keekin' in the draw-well clear,
  What if I fa' in, sir,
Then a' my kin will say and swear,
  I drowned mysel for sin, sir.
    Haud the better by the brae,
      Janet, Janet,
    Haud the better by the brae,
      My jo Janet.

Guid sir, for your courtesie,
  Comin' through Aberdeen, then,
For the love ye bear to me,
  Buy me a pair o' sheen, then.
    Clout the auld, the new are dear,
      Janet, Janet ;
    Ae pair may gain ye half a year,
      My jo Janet.

But, if, dancin' on the green,
  And skippin' like a maukin,
They should see my clouted sheen,
  Of me they will be talkin'.
    Dance aye laigh and late at e'en,
      Janet, Janet.
    Syne their fauts will no be seen,
      My jo Janet.

Kind sir, for your courtesie,
  When ye gae to the Cross, then,
For the love ye bear to me,
  Buy me a pacin' horse, then.
    Pace upon your spinnin'-wheel,
      Janet, Janet,
    Pace upon your spinnin'-wheel,
      My jo Janet.

My spinnin'-wheel is auld and stiff,
   The rock o't winna stand, sir ;
To keep the temper-pin in tiff,
   Employs richt aft my hand, sir.
      Mak the best o't that ye can,
        Janet, Janet,
      Mak the best o't that ye can,
      My jo Janet.

In the Oxford Collection (British Museum) there is a broadside of apparently the time of William III., entitled *Jenny, Jenny, or the False-hearted Knight*, which recites an affair of rustic gallantry, in the usual style, and then represents the lady as putting a series of requests to her lover, all of which are churlishly refused. The dialogue proceeds in the following strain :

    *   *   *   *   *

May't please your kind courtesie,
   To gang under yonders town,
May't please your kind courtesie,
   To buy me a silken gown.
      Mend the old one for a new, quoth he,
        Jenny, Jenny,
      Mend the old for a new, quoth he,
        Jenny, Jenny.

May't please you of kind courtesie,
   To gang into yonder fare [fair],
May't please your kind courtesie,
   To buy me an ambling mare.
      Ride upon thy spinning-wheel, quoth he,
        Jenny, Jenny, &c.

I pray you will not angry be
   Whilst I beg one small boon,
May't please your kind courtesie
   To buy me a pair o' shoon.
      Let [thy next lover] shoe thee, quoth he,
        Jenny, Jenny,
      For thou shalt ne'er be shod by me,
        Jenny, Jenny.
         K

> Once more I beg your kind courtesie,
> To gang to yonders teek,
> And there do so much for me,
> As buy me a seeing kit.
>   Kit even in the well, quoth he,
>   Jenny, Jenny,
>   For there thy beauty thou may'st see,
>   Jenny, Jenny.

Either this is an English original of *My Jo Janet*, or a corrupt English version of an original Scottish *My Jo Janet*. From the evident misunderstanding of the keeking-glass in the last verse quoted, one might be justified in believing the latter to be the case. If so, the Scottish original was probably a rude ballad of the seventeenth century, from which some poet of comparatively cultivated taste had drawn the clever dialogue as we now find it.

ANDRO AND HIS CUTTY GUN.

Ramsay printed this song in his *Tea-table Miscellany*, with some alterations by himself. From its own merits, and those of its lively air, it has always been a great favourite in Scotland, especially as a song for rustic bridal-parties and 'house-heatings.' Burns had a great relish for it, calling it 'a spirited picture of a country ale-house, touched off with all the lightsome gaiety so peculiar to the rural muse of Caledonia.' Adverting to it afterwards in a letter to Mr George Thomson, he says: '*Andro and his Cutty Gun* is the work of a master. By the way, are you not quite vexed to think that those men of genius, for such they were, who composed our fine Scotch lyrics, should be unknown? It has given me many a heart-ache.'

Blithe, blithe and mer - ry was she, Blithe was she but and ben; Weel she loo'd a Haw - ick gill, And leuch to see a tap - pit hen. She took me in, she set me doun, And hecht to keep me law - in' free; But, cun - ning car - line that she was, She gart me birle my baw - bee.

Blithe, blithe and merry was she,
Blithe was she but and ben ;
Weel she loo'd a Hawick gill,[1]
And leuch to see a tappit-hen.[2]
She took me in, she set me doun,
And hecht to keep me lawin'-free ;
But, cunning carline that she was,
She gart me birle my bawbee.
Blithe, blithe, &c.

[1] A Hawick gill, for some unexplained reason, is half-a-mutchkin.
[2] A tappit-hen implies a quart-measure, the term being applied from the resemblance of the knob on the top of the measure to a crested fowl.

We loo'd the liquor weel eneuch ;
　　But, wae's my heart, my cash was done,
Before that I had quench'd my drouth,
　　And laith was I to pawn my shoon.
When we had three times toom'd our stoup,
　　And the neist chappin new begun,
In startit, to heeze up our hope,
　　Young Andro wi' his cutty gun.[1]

The carline brought her kebbuck ben,
　　Wi' girdle-cakes weel-toasted brown ;[2]
Weel does the canny kimmer ken,
　　They gar the scuds gae glibber doun.
We ca'd the bicker aft about,
　　[Nor stirred until we saw the sun,]
And aye the cleanest drinker out
　　Was Andro wi' his cutty gun.

He did like ony mavis sing ;
　　And, as I in his oxter sat,
He ca'd me aye his bonnie thing,
　　And mony a sappy kiss I gat.
I hae been east, I hae been west,
　　I hae been far ayont the sun ;
But the blithest lad that e'er I saw,
　　Was Andro wi' his cutty gun.

[1] Cutty gun, a short fowling-piece.
[2] 'These oatmeal cakes are kneaded out with the knuckles, and toasted over the red embers of wood on a gridiron. They are remarkably fine, and a delicate relish when eaten warm with ale. On winter nights the landlady heats them, and drops them into the quaigh to warm the ale.' —BURNS.

WILLIE WAS A WANTON WAG.

All that is known with certainty of the history of this song, is that it was published in the *Tea-table Miscellany*, with the initials W. W., and reproduced with its lively air in the *Orpheus Caledonius*. As a picture of life-enjoying youth and high animal spirits, it is unsurpassed. There has been a debate about the authorship. It has been set forth, but upon no good authority, that W. W. was William Walkingshaw of that Ilk in Renfrewshire, and Burns had the words 'by Mr Walkingshaw' inserted in the index of Johnson's *Museum*. It appears that there was no William in the family. Mr David Laing expresses his inclination to believe, that by 'W. W.' was meant 'Wanton Willie,' a well-known sobriquet of Lieutenant William Hamilton of Gilbertfield, a friend and correspondent of Allan Ramsay, and who was a copious writer of Scottish verse, though no collection of his poems was ever made. Hamilton died at an advanced age in May 1751.

It will probably appear to most readers a justifiable conjecture, that whoever wrote *Willie was a Wanton Wag*, wrote *Andro and his Cutty Gun* also, if not several other songs giving humorous portraitures of familiar Scottish life, some of which follow.

Wil - lie was a wan - ton wag, The
blith - est lad that e'er I saw: At
brid - als still he bore the brag, And

car - ried aye the gree a - wa'. His

doub - let was of Zet - land shag, And

wow but Wil - lie he was braw; And

at his shou - thers hung a tag That

pleased the lass - es best of a'.

Willie was a wanton wag,
　　The blithest lad that e'er I saw :
At bridals still he bore the brag,
　　And carried aye the gree awa'.
His doublet was of Zetland shag,
　　And wow but Willie he was braw ;
And at his shouthers hung a tag
　　That pleased the lasses best of a'.

He was a man without a clag ;
　　His heart was frank, without a flaw ;
And aye whatever Willie said,
　　It still was hadden as a law.
His boots they were made of the jag,
　　When he went to the weapon-shaw ;
Upon the green nane durst him brag,
　　The fient a ane amang them a'.

And was not Willie weel worth gowd ?
 He wan the love o' grit and sma' ;
For, after he the bride had kiss'd,
 He kiss'd the lasses haill-sale a'.
Sae merrily round the ring they row'd, -
 When by the hand he led them a' ;
And smack on smack on them bestow'd,
 By virtue of a standing law.

And was na Willie a great loun,
 As shyre a lick as e'er was seen ?
When he danced with the lasses round,
 The bridegroom spier'd where he had been.
Quoth Willie, I 've been at the ring ;
 Wi' bobbin', faith, my shanks are sair ;
Gae ca' the bride and maidens in,
 For Willie he dow do na mair.

Then rest ye, Willie, I 'll gae out,
 And for a wee fill up the ring ;
But shame licht on his souple snout !
 He wanted Willie's wanton fling.
Then straight he to the bride did fare,
 Says weel 's me on your bonnie face !
With bobbin' Willie's shanks are sair,
 And I am come to fill his place.

Bridegroom, says she, you 'll spoil the dance,
 And at the ring you 'll aye be lag,
Unless like Willie ye advance ;
 Oh, Willie has a wanton leg !
For wi' 't he learns us a' to steer,
 And foremost aye bears up the ring ;
We will find nae sic dancin' here,
 If we want Willie's wanton fling.

MUIRLAND WILLIE.

This admirable description of rustic courtship appeared in the *Tea-table Miscellany* and *Orpheus Caledonius*, and has never been omitted from any subsequent collection of Scottish songs. The air, which, Mr Stenhouse tells us, is in a collection of 1709 by Mrs Crockat in his possession, is the basis of a popular modern air styled *My Boy Tammie*.

[O] hearken and I will tell you how Young Muirland Willie cam to woo, Tho' he could neither say nor do; The truth I tell to you. But aye he cries, What-e'er be-tide, Mag-gie I'se hae to be my bride. With a fal da dal la lal la la lal la, lal la fa lal la fa lal lal.

Hearken, and I will tell you how
Young Muirland Willie cam to woo,
Though he could neither say nor do ;
    The truth I tell to you.
But aye he cries, Whate'er betide,
Maggie I 'se hae to be my bride.
      With a fal, dal, &c.

On his gray yaud as he did ride,
With durk and pistol by his side,
He prick'd her on with mickle pride,
    With mickle mirth and glee ;[1]
Out ower yon moss, out ower yon muir,
Till he came to her daddie's door.
      With a fal, dal, &c.

Guidman, quoth he, be ye within ?
I 'm come your douchter's luve to win :
I carena for makin' muckle din ;
    What answer gie you me ?—
Now, wooer, quoth he, wad ye licht down,
I 'll gie ye my douchter's luve to win.
      With a fal, dal, &c.

Now, wooer, sin ye are lichtit down,
Where do ye win, or in what toun ?
I think my douchter winna gloom
    On sic a lad as ye.
The wooer he steppit up the house,
And wow but he was wondrous crouse !
      With a fal, dal, &c.

[1] 'This lightsome ballad gives a particular drawing of those ruthless times when thieves were rife, and the lads went a-wooing in their war-like habiliments, not knowing whether they would tilt with lips or lances. Willie's dirk and pistols were buckled on for this uncertain encounter, and not for garnishing and adorning his person.'—BURNS.

I hae three owsen in a pleuch,
Twa guid gaun yauds,[1] and gear eneuch—
The place they ca' it Cadeneugh ;[2]
    I scorn to tell a lie :
Besides I haud, frae the great laird,
A peat-spot and a lang-kale yard.
      With a fal, dal, &c.

The maid put on her kirtle broun ;
It was the brawest in a' the toun ;
I wat on him she did na gloom,
    But blinkit bonnilie.
The lover he stendit up in haste,
And grippit her hard about the waist.
      With a fal, dal, &c.

To win your love, maid, I'm come here ;
I'm young, and hae eneuch o' gear ;
And for mysel ye needna fear,
    Troth, try me when ye like.
He took aff his bannet, and spat in his chew,
He dichtit his gab, and he pried her mou'.
      With a fal, dal, &c.

The maiden blush'd and beingit fu' law :
She hadna will to say him na ;
But to her daddie she left it a',
    As they twa could agree.
The luver he gave her the tither kiss,
Syne ran to her daddie and tellt him this.
      With a fal, dal, &c.

---

[1] Work-horses.

[2] That is, Coldenough, indicating an elevated and exposed situation.
There are many similar names of places in Scotland, as Caldcots, Dead-
for-cald, &c.

Your douchter wadna say me na,
But to yoursel she has left it a',
As we could 'gree between us twa—
 Say what will ye gie me wi' her?
Now, wooer, quoth he, I hae na mickle,
But sic as I hae ye 'se get a pickle.
 With a fal, dal, &c.

A kilnfu' o' corn I 'll gie to thee,
Three soums o' sheep, twa guid milk kye;
Ye 'se hae the waddin'-dinner free;
 Troth, I dow do nae mair.
Content, quoth Willie, a bargain be 't;
I 'm far frae hame; make haste, let 's do 't.
 With a fal, dal, &c.

The bridal-day it came to pass,
With mony a blithesome lad and lass;
But siccan a day there never was,
 Sic mirth was never seen.
This winsome couple straikit hands;
Mess John tied up the marriage-bands.
 With a fal, dal, &c.

And our bride's maidens were na few,
Wi' tap-knots, lug-knots, a' in blue;
Frae tap to tae they were bran new,
 And blinkit bonnilie.
Their toys and mutches were sae clean,
They glanced in our lads's een.
 With a fal, dal, &c.

Sic hirdum-dirdum, and sic din,
Wi' he ower her, and she ower him;
The minstrels they did never blin',
 Wi' mickle mirth and glee;
And aye they bobbit, and aye they beck't,
And aye they reel'd, and aye they set.
 With a fal, dal, &c.

MAGGIE LAUDER.

This very clever song, which first appeared in Herd's Collection, is usually attributed to Francis Sempill of Beltrees, Renfrewshire, who lived and flourished in the middle of the seventeenth century, and died about 1685. The only authority for the statement is the allegation of Sempill's grandchildren, which, however, was equally confident in the case of *She rose and loot me in,* a song now proved to have been by D'Urfey. All that we really know with confidence is, that there was an air called *Moggy Lauther* or *Moggie Lauder* in vogue in England about the beginning of the reign of George II.; that this is introduced in the opera of the *Beggar's Wedding,* second edition, 1729, but under the title of *Moggy Lauther on a Day,*[1] implying a different song from the present; and that the song now so familiar nowhere appears before Herd's Collection. The style of verse, so free and facile, certainly bears little resemblance to any specimens of the muse of Sempill which are not open to dispute. It much more clearly recalls that of *Willie was a Wanton Wag,* and *Muirland Willie.*

Wha wad - na be in love Wi'
bon - nie Mag - gie Lau - der? A
pip - er met her gaun to Fife, And

---

[1] Chappell's *Popular Music of the Olden Time,* p. 620, *note.*

spier'd what was 't they ca'd her: Richt

scorn - ful - ly she an - swer'd him, Be-

gone, you hall - an - shak - er! Jog

on your gate, you blad - der - skate! My

name is Mag - gie Lau - der.

Wha wadna be in love
   Wi' bonnie Maggie Lauder ?
A piper met her gaun to Fife,
   And spier'd what was 't they ca'd her :
Richt scornfully she answer'd him,
   Begone, you hallanshaker ![1]
Jog on your gate, you bladderskate ![2]
   My name is Maggie Lauder.

[1] '*Hallanshaker* is what the old people call a rambling mischievous fellow; one who sods up the burns, ties the doors, and works other pranks of innocent merriment. The *hallan* is a bundle composed of the longest broom, entwisted with willows, placed movable to ward the wind from the door. The partition which divided the spence from the hall was frequently named "the Hallan," being formed of similar materials.' —CROMEK. We are to presume, from this explanation, that one of the pranks of the practical joker in question was to steal in and alarm the evening fireside circle by shaking the hallan.

[2] 'Bladderskate ought to be *Blether-skyte*. " Ye bletherin' loon," " Ye

Maggie ! quoth he ; and, by my bags,
　I'm fidgin' fain to see thee !
Sit doun by me, my bonnie bird ;
　In troth I winna steer thee ;
For I'm a piper to my trade ;
　My name is Rob the Ranter :
The lasses loup as they were daft,
　When I blaw up my chanter.

Piper, quo' Meg, hae ye your bags,
　Or is your drone in order ?
If ye be Rob, I've heard o' you ;
　Live you upo' the Border ?
The lasses a', baith far and near,
　Have heard o' Rob the Ranter ;
I'll shake my foot wi' richt guid will,
　Gif ye'll blaw up your chanter.

Then to his bags he flew wi' speed ;
　About the drone he twisted :
Meg up and wallop'd ower the green ;
　For brawly could she frisk it !
Weel done ! quo' he.　Play up ! quo' she.
　Weel bobb'd ! quo' Rob the Ranter ;
It's worth my while to play, indeed,
　When I hae sic a dancer !

Weel hae ye play'd your part ! quo' Meg ;
　Your cheeks are like the crimson !
There's nane in Scotland plays sae weel,
　Sin' we lost Habbie Simpson.[1]

vile skyte," are terms of familiar reproach still in use, and are innocently
applied to those satiric rogues who have the art of mingling falsehood
with truth with admirable art, annoying with it the sage remarks of the
sober-minded and wise.'—CROMEK.

[1] A celebrated piper at Kilbarchan, Renfrewshire, whose memory and
merits are preserved in an elegy by Robert Sempill.　He flourished about
the middle of the seventeenth century.

I 've lived in Fife, baith maid and wife,
　This ten years and a quarter;
Gin ye should come to Anster Fair,
　Spier ye for Maggie Lauder.

THE GABERLUNYIE MAN.

We owe the preservation of this capital old song to the *Teatable Miscellany*, where it appears with the signature J. It has for many years been usually ascribed to King James V., but upon no authority, and apparently for no other reason but that it relates such a rustic adventure as the fifth James is said to have been addicted to, when he went about in disguise to make himself acquainted with his subjects. In reality, there is not the faintest assimilation of the style of this song to the manner of any of the 'makkers' of the early part of the sixteenth century. Had it been published as a composition of the same pen as *Muirland Willie*, no one would have been surprised.

The　paw-ky　auld carle cam　ower　the lea, Wi'

mo-ny guid-e'ens and　days　to　me, Saying, Guidwife, for your

cour-te-sie, Will ye　lodge a　sil-ly　puir　man?

The　nicht　was　cauld, the　carle was　wat, And

doun a - yont the ingle he sat; My douchter's shouthers he

'gan to clap, And cad - gi - ly rant - ed and sang.

The pawky auld carle cam ower the lee,
Wi' mony guid-e'ens and days to me,
Saying, Guidwife, for your courtesie,
     Will ye lodge a silly puir man?
The nicht was cauld, the carle was wat,
And doun ayont the ingle he sat;
My douchter's shouthers he 'gan to clap,
     And cadgily ranted and sang.

O, wow! quo' he, were I as free
As first when I saw this countrie,
How blithe and merry wad I be,
     And I wad never think lang!
He grew canty, and she grew fain;
But little did her auld minnie ken
What thir slee twa together were sayin',
     When wooing they were sae thrang.

And O! quo' he, an ye were as black
As e'er the croun o' my daddie's hat,
It's I wad lay ye by my back,
     And awa' wi' me ye should gang.
And O! quo' she, an I were as white
As e'er the snaw lay on the dike,
I'd cleid me braw and lady-like,
     And awa' wi' thee I'd gang.

Between the twa was made a plot ;
They rase a wee afore the cock,
And wylily they shot the lock,
   And fast to the bent are they gane.
Up i' the morn the auld wife rase,
And at her leisure put on her claise ;
Syne to the servants' bed she gaes,
   To spier for the silly puir man.

She gaed to the bed where the beggar lay ;
The strae was cauld—he was away ;
She clapped her hands, cried, Waladay !
   For some o' our gear will be gane.
Some ran to coffer, and some to kist ;
But nocht was stown that could be mist.
She danced her lane, cried, Praise be blest,
   I have lodged a leal puir man !

Since naething 's awa', as we can learn,
The kirn 's to kirn, and milk to yirne ;
Gae butt the house, and wauken my bairn,
   And bid her come quickly ben.
The servant gaed where the dauchter lay :
The sheets were cauld—she was away,
And fast to her guidwife 'gan say,
   She 's aff wi' the gaberlunyie man !

Oh, fye gar ride, and fye gar rin,
And haste ye find thae traitors again ;
For she 's be burnt, and he 's be slain,
   The wearifu' gaberlunyie man !
Some rade upo' horse, some ran a-fit,
The wife was wud, and out o' her wit ;
She couldna gang, nor yet could she sit,
   But aye she cursed and she bann'd.

L

Meantime, far hind out ower the lee,
Fu' snug in a glen, where nane could see,
The twa, with kindly sport and glee,
   Cut frae a new cheese a whang.
The prievin' was guid—it pleased them baith ;
To lo'e her for aye he gae her his aith ;
Quo' she, To leave thee I will be laith,
   My winsome gaberlunyie man.

O, kend my minnie I were wi' you,
Ill-faurdly wad she crook her mou' ;
Sic a puir man she 'll never trow,
   After the gaberlunyie man.
My dear, quo' he, ye 're yet ower young,
And ha'na learn'd the beggars' tongue,
To follow me frae toun to toun,
   And carry the gaberlunyie on.

Wi' cauk and keel I 'll win your bread,
And spinles and whorles for them wha need ;
Whilk is a gentle trade indeed,
   To carry the gaberlunyie on.
I 'll bow my leg, and crook my knee,
And draw a black clout ower my e'e ;
A cripple and blind they will ca' me,
   While we 'll be merry and sing.

The Gaberlunyie, and the eight preceding songs, have some
common characters deserving of attention. They are all clever
compositions, verifying themselves as the product, not of rustic,
but of cultivated minds. They display humour both of a rough
and hearty, and of a sly kind. They have all come before the
world anonymously, and for the most part can be traced to the
early part of the eighteenth century—the epoch just preceding
that of Ramsay. Being greatly superior to Ramsay's poetry, it is
the more remarkable that there should be no trace of the authors,

or, shall we say, author, for it is not impossible that they have all come from one source—an EARLIER BURNS, who has chosen to remain for ever unknown.

THE HUMBLE BEGGAR.

In Scotland there lived a hum-ble beg-gar; He had neither house, nor hauld, nor hame; But he was weel liked by il-ka bo-dy, And they gae him sun-kets to raux his wame.

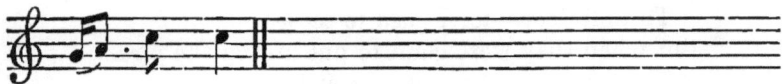

In Scotland there lived a humble beggar ;
    He had neither house, nor hauld, nor hame ;
But he was weel liked by ilka body,
    And they gae him sunkets to raux his wame.
A neivefou o' meal, a handfou o' groats,
    A daud o' a bannock, or pudding-bree,
Cauld parridge, or the lickings of plates,
    Wad make him as blithe as a bodie could be.

A humbler bodie, O, never brake bread,
　For the fient a bit o' pride had he ;
He wad hae ta'en his alms in a bicker,
　Frae gentle, or semple, or poor bodie.
His wallets afore and ahint did hing,
　In as good order as wallets could be.
A lang-kale goolie hung down by his side,
　And a muckle nowte-horn to rout on had he.

It happen'd ill, and it happen'd warse,
　For it happen'd sae that he did die ;
And wha wad ye think were at his lyke-wauk,
　But lads and lasses of high degree.
Some were merry, and some were sad,
　And some were as blithe as blithe could be ;
When up he started, the gruesome carle—
　I rede ye, good folks, beware o' me !

Out scraich'd Kate, who sat in the nook,
　Vow, now, kimmer ! and how do ye ?
He ca'd her waur than witch and limmer,
　And ruggit and tuggit her cockernonie.
They howkit his grave in Douket's kirkyard,
　Twa ell deep—for I gaed to see—
But when they were gaun to put him in the yird,
　The fient a dead nor dead was he.

They brought him down to Douket's kirkyard ;
　He gae a dunt, and the boords did flee ;
And when they gaed to lay him in the grave,
　In fell the coffin, and out lap he !
He cried, I'm cauld ! I'm unco cauld !
　Fu' fast ran they, and fu' fast ran he ;
But he was first hame at his ain ingle-side,
　And he help'd to drink his ain dredgie.

The Humble Beggar appeared first in Herd, and its rich humour and forcible expression have secured it a place in all subsequent collections.

O, AN YE WERE DEAD, GUIDMAN.

O, an ye were dead, guidman, O, an ye were dead, guidman, That I might wair my wi-dow-heid Up-on a rant-ing Highlandman. There's six eggs in the pan, guidman, There's six eggs in the pan, guidman; There's ane to you, and twa to me, And three to our John Highlandman.

Chorus.

O, an ye were dead, guid-man, &c.

O, an ye were dead, guidman,
O, an ye were dead, guidman,
That I might wair my widowheid
Upon a ranting Highlandman.

There's six eggs in the pan, guidman,
There's six eggs in the pan, guidman ;
There's ane to you, and twa to me,
And three to our John Highlandman.

There's beef into the pot, guidman,
There's beef into the pot, guidman ;
The banes to you, the broe to me,
And the beef for our John Highlandman.

There's sax horse in the sta', guidman,
There's sax horse in the sta', guidman ;
There's ane to you, and twa to me,
And three to our John Highlandman.

There's sax kye in the byre, guidman,
There's sax kye in the byre, guidman ;
There's nane o' them yours, but twa o' them mine,
And the lave is our John Highlandman's.

This is one of the old fireside traditionary songs of Scotland,
embodying a reckless humour defiant of session and presbytery,
and shewing what was in the heart of the nation under all
external appearances.   It does not, however, appear in any
collection before Johnson.   It was a favourite with Thomas
Campbell, who used to sing it with much unction and good
effect.

THE BRISK YOUNG LAD.

There   cam   a young man to   my   dad - die's door, My

daddie's   door, my daddie's door; There cam a young man to my

daddie's door, Cam seek - ing me to woo. And

wow! but he was a braw young lad, A brisk young lad, and

a braw young lad; And wow! but he was a

braw young lad, Cam seek - ing me to woo.

There cam a young man to my daddie's door,
My daddie's door, my daddie's door ;
There cam a young man to my daddie's door,
    Cam seeking me to woo.

    And wow ! but he was a braw young lad,
    A brisk young lad, and a braw young lad ;
    And wow ! but he was a braw young lad,
        Cam seeking me to woo.

But I was baking when he came,
When he came, when he came ;
I took him in and gied him a scone,
    To thowe his frozen mou.

I set him in aside the bink ;
I ga'e him bread and ale to drink ;
And ne'er a blithe styme wad he blink,
    Until his wame was fou.

Gae, get you gone, you cauldrife wooer,
Ye sour-looking, cauldrife wooer,
I straightway shewed him to the door,
    Saying, Come nae mair to woo.

There lay a deuk-dub before the door,
Before the door, before the door ;
There lay a deuk-dub before the door,
    And there fell he, I trow.

Out cam the guidman and high he shouted,
Out cam the guidwife and laigh she lootit,
And a' the town neighbours were gathered about it,
    And there lay he, I trow !

Then out cam I, and sneered and smiled,
Ye cam to woo, but ye're a' beguiled,
Ye're faun i' the dirt, and ye're a' befyled,
    We'll hae nae mair o' you !

For the above song, which first appeared in Herd's Collection,
no author has ever been assigned.

OUR GUIDMAN CAM HAME AT E'EN.

O, our guid - man cam hame at e'en, And
hame cam he; And there he saw a rid - ing horse, Where
nae horse should be. Oh, how cam this horse here? And

how can this be? And how cam this horse here, With-

Ad lib. May be spoken.

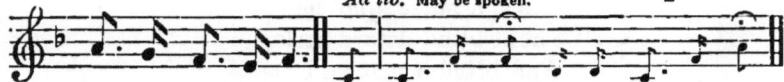

out the leave o' me? A horse! quo' she! Ay, a horse, quo' he.

Ye auld blind dot-ard carle, And blind-er mat ye be! It's

but a bon-nie milk cow, My mith-er sent to me.

A milk cow! quo' he; Ay, a milk cow, quo' she. Weel,

far hae I rid-den, And muckle hae I seen; But a

sad-dle on a milk cow Saw I nev-er nane.

O, our guidman cam hame at e'en,
And hame cam he ;
And there he saw a riding-horse,
Where nae horse should be.

Oh, how cam this horse here ?
 How can this be ?
How cam this horse here,
  Without the leave o' me ?
    A horse ! quo' she !
    Ay, a horse, quo' he.
Ye auld blind dotard carle,
  And blinder mat ye be !
It 's but a bonnie milk-cow,
  My mither sent to me.
    A milk-cow ! quo' he ;
    Ay, a milk-cow, quo' she.
Weel, far hae I ridden,
  And muckle hae I seen ;
But a saddle on a milk-cow
  Saw I never nane.

Our guidman cam hame at e'en,
  And hame cam he ;
He spied a pair o' jack-boots,
  Where nae boots should be.
What 's this now, guidwife ?
  What 's this I see ?
How cam thae boots here,
  Without the leave o' me ?
    Boots ! quo' she ;
    Ay, boots, quo' he.
Ye auld blind dotard carle,
  And blinder mat ye be !
It 's but a pair o' water-stoups,
  The cooper sent to me.
    Water-stoups ! quo' he ;
    Ay, water-stoups, quo' she.
Weel, far hae I ridden,
  And muckle hae I seen ;
But siller-spurs on water-stoups
  Saw I never nane.

Our guidman cam hame at e'en,
  And hame cam he ;
And there he saw a siller sword,
  Where nae sword should be.
What's this now, guidwife ?
  What's this I see ?
O how cam this sword here,
  Without the leave o' me ?
    A sword ! quo' she ;
    Ay, a sword, quo' he.
Ye auld blind dotard carle,
  And blinder mat ye be !
It 's but a parridge-spurtle,
  My minnie sent to me.
    A parridge-spurtle ! quo' he ;
    Ay, a parridge-spurtle, quo' she.
Weel, far hae I ridden,
  And muckle hae I seen ;
But siller-handed parridge-spurtles
  Saw I never nane.

Our guidman cam hame at e'en,
  And hame cam he ;
And there he spied a mickle wig,
  Where nae wig should be.
What's this now, guidwife ?
  What's this I see ?
How cam this wig here,
  Without the leave o' me ?
    A wig ! quo' she ;
    Ay, a wig, quo' he.
Ye auld blind dotard carle,
  And blinder mat ye be !
'Tis naething but a clocken-hen
  My minnie sent to me.
    A clocken-hen ! quo' he ;
    Ay, a clocken-hen, quo' she.

Weel, far hae I ridden,
  And muckle hae I seen,
But pouther on a clocken-hen
  Saw I never nane.

Our guidman cam hame at e'en,
  And hame cam he ;
And there he saw a big coat,
  Where nae coat should be.
How cam this coat here ?
  How can this be ?
How cam this coat here,
  Without the leave o' me ?
    A coat ! quo' she ;
    Ay, a coat, quo' he.
Ye auld blind dotard carle,
  And blinder mat ye be !
It 's but a pair o' blankets
  My minnie sent to me.
    Blankets ! quo' he ;
    Ay, blankets, quo' she.
Weel, far hae I ridden,
  And muckle hae I seen :
But buttons upon blankets
  Saw I never nane !

Ben gaed our guidman,
  And ben gaed he ;
And there he spied a sturdy man
  Where nae man should be.
How cam this man here ?
  How can this be ?
How cam this man here,
  Without the leave o' me ?
    A man ! quo' she ;
    Ay, a man quo' he.

Puir blind body,
  And blinder mat you be!
It's but a new milk-maid
  My mither sent to me.
    A maid! quo' he;
    Ay, a maid, quo' she.
Weel, far hae I ridden,
  And muckle hae I seen,
But lang-bearded milk-maids
  Saw I never nane.

Modern singers modify the last verse as follows:

    A man! quo' she;
    Ay, a man, quo' he.
Oh, hooly, hooly, our guidman,
  And dinna angered be—
It's but our cousin Macintosh,
  Come frae the north countrie!
    Our cousin Macintosh! quo' he;
    Ay, our cousin Macintosh, quo' she.
Ye'll hae us a' hanged, guidwife,
  And that'll be to see;
Ye're hiding rebels in the house,
  Without the leave o' me.

This capital piece of humour appeared first in Herd's Collection.
The air was given in Johnson's *Musical Museum*. It bears all
the marks of a pure Scottish authorship; yet a song on the same
set of ideas has long been known in England. Mr J. H. Dixon
gives a copy from Yorkshire, beginning:

O, I went into the stable, and there for to see,
And there I saw three horses stand by one, by two, and by three;
O, I called to my loving wife, and, Anon, kind sir, quoth she;
O, what do these three horses here, without the leave o' me?
Why, you old fool, blind fool, can't you very well see,
These are three milking cows my mother sent to me!
Odds bobs, well done I, milking cows with saddles on!
  The like was never known!

There is a copy of this English version of the tale in the *Roxburghe Collection,* and therefore probably not later than the seventeenth century.

GET UP AND BAR THE DOOR.

The little comic difficulties of matrimonial life have long been favourite subjects with the Scottish muse; for example, *Tak your Auld Cloak about Ye, Ever Alake my Auld Guidman,* and others in this collection. In the present instance, the humour takes a practical turn, with irresistible effect. The piece, of the authorship of which not the faintest trace survives, appeared in Herd's Collection, and the air was given by Johnson. It is not unworthy of notice that the favourite after-piece of *No Song, No Supper,* contains a scene founded on this song.

It fell about the Martinmas time, And a gay time it was than, O, That our guid-wife had puddins to mak, And she boil'd them in the pan, O.

It fell about the Martinmas time,
    And a gay time it was than, O,
That our guidwife had puddins to mak,
    And she boil'd them in the pan, O.

The wind blew cauld frae south to north,
    It blew into the floor, O ;
Says our guidman to our guidwife,
    Get up and bar the door, O.

My hand is in my hussyfe-skep,
    Guidman, as ye may see, O ;
An it shouldna be barr'd this hunner year,
    It's no be barr'd for me, O.

They made a paction 'tween them twa,
    They made it firm and sure, O,
The first that spak the foremost word
    Should rise and bar the door, O.

Then by there came twa gentlemen,
    At twelve o'clock at nicht, O ;
And they could neither see house nor ha',
    Nor coal nor candle-licht, O.

Now whether is this a rich man's house,
    Or whether is it a puir, O ?
But never a word wad ane o' them speak,
    For the barrin' o' the door, O.

And first they ate the white puddins,
    And syne they ate the black, O ;
And muckle thocht our guidwife to hersel,
    But never a word she spak, O.

Then said the tane unto the tother,
    Hae, man, take ye my knife, O,
Do ye tak aff the auld man's beard,
    And I'll kiss the guidwife, O.

But there's nae water in the house,
　　And what shall we do than, O ?
What ails ye at the puddin' broo,
　　That boils into the pan, O ?

O, up then started our guidman,
　　And an angry man was he, O :
Wad ye kiss my wife before my face,
　　And scaud me wi' puddin' bree, O ?

Then up and startit our guidwife,
　　Gi'ed three skips on the floor, O :
Guidman, ye've spoken the foremost word,
　　Get up and bar the door, O.

TODLIN HAME.

'Perhaps the first bottle-song,' says Burns, 'that ever was composed.' It used to be a great favourite with the merry clubs of Edinburgh, and a gentleman named Balfour so charmed the fraternity of Golfers, by singing it in a characteristic manner, that they had his portrait taken by Raeburn, and hung up in the Golfers' Hall at Leith. The position of the singer, with his thumb turned appropriately down upon the table, and his sly comic look, made this a picture of some value, irrespective of the fame of the artist. The verses appeared in the *Tea-table Miscellany*, and the air in the *Orpheus Caledonius*.

When I hae a saxpence un-der my thoom, Then
I get cred - it in il - ka toun ; But,

aye when I'm poor they bid me gang by, Oh,

Chorus.

pov - er - ty parts guid com-pa - ny ! Tod - lin hame,

tod - lin hame, O couldna my love come tod - lin hame?

When I hae a saxpence under my thoom,
Then I get credit in ilka toun ;
But, aye when I 'm poor they bid me gang by,
Oh, poverty parts guid company !
    Todlin hame, and todlin hame,
    Couldna my love come todlin hame ?

Fair fa' the guidwife and send her guid sale !
She gies us white bannocks to relish her ale ;
Syne, if that her tippeny chance to be sma',
We tak a guid scour o 't, and ca 't awa'.
    Todlin hame, todlin hame,
    As round as a neep come todlin hame.

My kimmer and I lay doun to sleep,
And twa pint-stoups at our bed's feet ;
And aye when we waken'd we drank them dry :—
What think ye o' my wee kimmer and I ?
    Todlin butt, and todlin ben,
    Sae round as my luve comes todlin hame.

M

Leeze me on liquor, my todlin dow,
Ye 're aye sae guid-humour'd when weetin' your mou'!
When sober sae sour, ye 'll fecht wi' a flee,
That 'tis a blithe nicht to the bairns and me,
When todlin hame, todlin hame,
When, round as a neep, ye come todlin hame.

THE MILLER.

This song, which appeared in *The Charmer*, 1751, is usually attributed to Sir John Clerk, of Penicuick, one of the Barons of the Court of Exchequer in Scotland, and a cultivator of matters of taste, including antiquities, during a time when such men were few in the land. He died at a ripe age in 1755.

Mr Stenhouse remarks, that 'the thought expressed in the last two lines, beginning "Who 'd be a king?" appears to be borrowed from a similar idea in the old ballad of *Tarry Woo.*'

O, mer-ry may the maid be That mar-ries the mill-er! For, foul day or fair day, He 's aye bring-ing till her. H'as aye a pen-ny in his pouch, For din-ner or for sup-per; And

gin she please, a guid fat cheese, An' lumps o' yel - low

but - ter.

O, merry may the maid be
　That marries the miller !
For, foul day or fair day,
　He 's aye bringing till her.
H'as aye a penny in his pouch,
　For dinner or for supper ;
And gin she please, a guid fat cheese,
　An' lumps o' yellow butter.

Behind the door stands bags o' meal,
　And in the kist is plenty,
And good hard cakes his mither bakes,
　And bannocks are na scanty.
A good fat sow, a sleeky cow,
　Are standing in the byre ;
Whilst winking puss, wi' mealy mouse,
　Is playing round the fire.

Good signs are these, my mither says,
　And bids me take the miller ;
A miller's wife's a merry wife,
　And he 's aye bringing till her.
For meal or maut she 'll never want,
　Nor ony thing that 's dainty,
And now and then a cackling hen,
　To lay her eggs in plenty.

In winter time, when wind and rain
　　Blow o'er the house and byre,
He sits beside a clean hearthstane,
　　Before a rousing fire ;
O'er foaming ale he tells his tale ;
　　Which rows him o'er fu' happy :
Who 'd be a king, a petty thing,
　　When a miller lives so happy ?

HOOLY AND FAIRLY.

Mr Stenhouse has traced this comical production as far back
as 1751, when it appeared in Yair's *Charmer;* and he adds that
the late Mrs Brown, of Newbattle, had heard the author
(name forgotten) sing it, when residing with her friend Captain
Mason at Eaglesham, Renfrewshire.

Down in yon meadow a cou - ple did tar - ry : The guidwife she drank nae-thing but sack and can - a - ry ; The
guid - man com - plain'd to her friends richt ear - ly—
Oh, gin my wife wad drink hoo - ly and fair - ly !

Hoo - ly   and   fair - ly,   hoo - ly   and   fair - ly,

Oh, gin my wife wad drink hoo - ly and fair - ly!

Doun in yon meadow a couple did tarry :
The guidwife she drank naething but sack and canary ;
The guidman complain'd to her friends richt early—
Oh, gin my wife wad drink hooly[1] and fairly !
 Hooly and fairly, hooly and fairly,
  Oh, gin my wife wad drink hooly and fairly !

First she drank Crummie, and syne she drank Gairie,[2]
And syne she drank my bonnie gray marie,
That carried me through a' the dubs and the lairie—
Oh, gin my wife wad drink hooly and fairly !

She drank her hose, she drank her shoon,
And syne she drank her bonnie new goun ;
She drank her sark that cover'd her rarely—
Oh, gin my wife wad drink hooly and fairly !

Wad she drink but her ain things, I wadna care,
But she drinks my claes that I canna weil spare ;
When I'm wi' my gossips it angers me sairly—
Oh, gin my wife wad drink hooly and fairly !

My Sunday's coat she's laid it in wad,
And the best blue bonnet e'er was on my head ;
At kirk and at mercat I'm cover'd but barely—
Oh, gin my wife wad drink hooly and fairly !

 [1] Moderately.   [2] The two cows.

My bonnie white mittens I wore on my hands,
Wi' her neibour's wife she laid them in pawns ;
My bane-headed staff that I lo'ed sae dearly—
Oh, gin my wife wad drink hooly and fairly !

I never was for wranglin' nor strife,
Nor did I deny her the comforts o' life ;
For when there 's a war, I 'm aye for a parly—
Oh, gin my wife wad drink hooly and fairly !

When there 's ony money she maun keep the purse ;
If I seek but a bawbee she 'll scold and she 'll curse ;
She lives like a queen—I but scrimpit and sparely—
Oh, gin my wife wad drink hooly and fairly !

A pint wi' her cummers I wad her allow ;
But when she sits down, she gets hersel fou,
And when she is fou she is unco camstarie—
Oh, gin my wife wad drink hooly and fairly !

When she comes to the street she roars and she rants,
Has nae fear o' her neibours, nor minds the house wants ;
She rants up some fule-sang, like, Up your heart, Charlie !—
Oh, gin my wife wad drink hooly and fairly !

When she comes hame she lays on the lads,
The lasses she ca's baith [taupies] and jauds,
And ca's mysel an auld cuckle-carlie—
Oh, gin my wife wad drink hooly and fairly !

It is perhaps not unworthy of notice, that the two last verses
have supplied to Scott the humour of a scene in *Waverley*,
where the smith's wife, a tippler and a Jacobite, creates the riot
which ends in the arrest of the hero.

THE LASS OF LIVINGSTONE.

The original ballad of *The Lass of Livingstone* has been doomed for reason good to oblivion, there being nothing of it preserved but a verse beginning,

> The bonnie lass of Livingstone,
> Her name ye ken, her name ye ken.

Ramsay, seeing the impossibility of getting the rustic verses into good company, composed for the air one of his mediocre songs, beginning with this verse:

> Pained with her slighting Jamie's love,
> Bell dropped a tear, Bell dropped a tear;
> The gods descended from above,
> Well pleased to hear, well pleased to hear.

Fortunately, in our wish to convey the air in connection with a song, we are relieved from the dilemma between the original lass and worthy Allan's tear-dropping Bell, by a clever old ditty to this tune,[1] which was taken down some years ago from the singing of an elderly man residing in Peebles.

To hae a wife and rule a wife, Taks a wise man, taks a wise man; But to get a wife to rule a man, O that ye can, O

[1] *The Lass of Livingstone* is the name of one of the tunes in Henry Playford's Collection, 1700.

that ye can. So the wife that 's wise we

aye maun prize, For they 're few, ye ken, they 're

few, ye ken; O Sol - o - mon says ye 'll

no find ane, In hun - dreds ten, in hun - dreds ten.

To hae a wife and rule a wife,
Taks a wise man, taks a wise man;
But to get a wife to rule a man,
O that ye can, O that ye can.
So the wife that's wise we aye maun prize,
For they 're few, ye ken, they 're few, ye ken;
O Solomon says ye 'll no find ane,
In hundreds ten, in hundreds ten.

So he that gets a guid, guid wife,
Gets gear eneuch, gets gear eneuch;
And he that gets an ill, ill wife,
Gets cares eneuch, gets fears eneuch.
A man may spend, and hae to the end,
If his wife be ought, if his wife be ought;
But a man may spare, and aye be bare,
If his wife be nought, if his wife be nought.

We learn from the *Memoirs of Alexander Carlyle*,[1] that the actual bonnie lass of Livingstone was living in that district in

[1] Edinburgh, 1860; p. 97.

1744, by which time she must have reached a mature period of life. Being storm-stayed in November that year on his way to Glasgow, Carlyle spent three days at the little solitary *auberge* of Whitburn, when at length a returning postchaise enabled him to complete his journey. The landlady, whom he characterises as a 'sensible woman,' 'had in her youth been celebrated in a song as "the bonnie lass of Livingstone." The walls and windows,' he adds, 'were all scrawled with poetry ; and I amused myself not a little in composing a satire on my predecessors, which I also inscribed on the walls, to the great delight of my landlady, who shewed it for many years afterwards with vanity to her travellers.'

MY WIFE'S A WANTON WEE THING.

My wife's a wan-ton wee thing, My wife's a wan-ton wee thing, My wife's a wan-ton wee thing; She win-na be guid-ed by me. She play'd the loon ere she was mar-ried, She play'd the loon ere she was mar-ried, She play'd   the   loon   ere   she   was   mar - ried; She'll

do't   a - gain ere she   die!

My wife's a wanton wee thing,
My wife's a wanton wee thing,
My wife's a wanton wee thing ;
    She winna be guided by me.

She play'd the loon ere she was married,
She play'd the loon ere she was married,
She play'd the loon ere she was married ;
    She 'll do 't again ere she die !

She sell'd her coat, and she drank it,
She sell'd her coat, and she drank it,
She row'd hersel in a blanket ;
    She winna be guided by me.

She mind't na when I forbade her,
She mind 't na when I forbade her ;
I took a rung and I claw'd her,
    And a braw guid bairn was she !

Of this somewhat foolish canticle, the first two verses appear in Herd's Collection ; the others are added in Johnson's *Museum*. The air, which is also recognised as a dance, is given in Oswald's *Pocket Companion*.

THE WEARY PUND O' TOW.

So broad a feature of old Scottish life as the use of the spinning-wheel could scarcely have escaped the notice of the native muse. We have several songs on this subject—one, above all, satirising a housewife who neglected her spinning, which appears to have sprung up in the middle of the eighteenth century, as its title and air occur in Oswald's *Caledonian Pocket Companion*. We give this song, as far as it can now be recovered, but preceded by an improved version which Burns supplied to the *Musical Museum*.

The wea - ry pund, The wea - ry pund, The wea - ry pund o' tow, I think my wife will end her life, be - fore she spin the tow! I bought my wife a stane o' lint, As guid as e'er did grow; And a' that she has made o' that Is ae puir pund o' tow.

Chorus.

The wea - ry pund, the, &c.

The weary pund, the weary pund,
    The weary pund o' tow,
I think my wife will end her life,
    Before she spin the tow!

I bought my wife a stane o' lint,
    As guid as e'er did grow ;
And a' that she has made o' that
    Is ae puir pund o' tow.

There sat a bottle in a bole,
    Beyont the ingle low ;
And aye she took the tother sook,
    To drouk the stoury tow.

Quoth I, For shame, ye dirty dame,
    Gae spin your tap o' tow !
She took the rock, and wi' a knock,
    She brak it o'er my pow !

At last her feet, I sang to see 't,
    Gaed foremost o'er the knowe,
And ere I wed another jaud,
    I 'll wallop in a tow.

[OLD VERSION.]

I bought my maiden and my wife
    A half a pund o' tow,
And it will serve them a' their life,
    Let them spin as they dow.
I thought my tow was endit—
    It wasna weel begun !
I think my wife will end her life
    Afore the tow be spun.

I lookit to my yarn-knag,
　　And it grew never mair ;
I lookit to my beef-stand—
　　My heart grew wonder sair ;
I lookit to my meal-boat,
　　And O, but it was howe !
I think my wife will end her life
　　Afore she spin her tow.

But if your wife and my wife
　　Were in a boat thegither,
And yon other man's wife
　　Were in to steer the ruther ;[1]
And if the boat were bottomless,
　　And seven mile to row,
I think they'd ne'er come hame again,
　　To spin the pund o' tow ![2]

[1] Rudder.

[2] Besides the foregoing three stanzas, there is another, which appears
to belong to the same song, but cannot be placed anywhere as a part
of it : probably some intervening stanzas are lost. The delinquent
housewife herself is introduced, endeavouring to borrow linen to make
shirts for her husband, and promising restitution at a period synonymous,
according to all appearance, with the Greek Calends :

　　O weel's us a' on our guidman,
　　　　For he's come hame,
　　Wi' a suit o' new claes ;
　　　　But sarkin he's got nane.
　　Come lend to me some sarkin,
　　　　Wi' a' the haste ye dow,
　　And ye'se be weel pay'd back again,
　　　　When ance I spin my tow.

WOO'D, AND MARRIED, AND A'.

This characteristic old song appeared in Herd's Collection, but had probably been in existence for a considerable time before.

The bride cam out o' the byre, And,

O, as she dight - ed her cheeks! Sirs,

I 'm to be mar - ried the night, And have

neith - er blank - ets nor sheets; Have

neith - er blank - ets nor sheets, Nor

scarce a cov - er - let too; The

bride that has a' thing to bor - row, Has

e'en right muckle a - do. Woo'd, and mar - ried, and a',

Mar - ried, and woo'd, and a'! And

was she nae ve - ry weel off, That was

woo'd, and mar - ried, and a'?

The bride cam out o' the byre,
 And, O, as she dighted her cheeks!
Sirs, I'm to be married the night,
 And have neither blankets nor sheets;
Have neither blankets nor sheets,
 Nor scarce a coverlet too;
The bride that has a' thing to borrow,
 Has e'en right muckle ado.
  Woo'd, and married, and a',
   Married, and woo'd, and a'!
  And was she nae very weel off,
   That was woo'd, and married, and a'?

Out and spake the bride's father,
 As he cam in frae the pleugh;
O, haud your tongue, my dochter,
 And ye 'se get gear eneugh;
The stirk stands i' th' tether,
 And our bra' bawsint yade
Will carry ye hame your corn—
 What wad ye be at, ye jade?

Out and spake the bride's mither,
    What deil needs a' this pride ?
1 had nae a plack in my pouch
    That night I was a bride ;
My gown was linsey-woolsey,
    And ne'er a sark ava ;
And ye hae ribbons and buskins,
    Mae than ane or twa.

    *   *   *   *

Out and spake the bride's brither,
    As he came in wi' the kye ;
Poor Willie wad ne'er hae ta'en ye,
    Had he kent ye as weel as I ;
For ye 're baith proud and saucy,
    And no for a poor man's wife ;
Gin I canna get a better,
    I 'se ne'er tak ane i' my life.

Out and spake the bride's sister
    As she came in frae the byre ;
O gin I were but married,
    It 's a' that I desire :
But we poor folk maun live single,
    And do the best that we can ;
I dinna care what I shou'd want
    If I cou'd get but a man.

At a more recent date, a lady, usually described as 'Mrs Scott of Dumbartonshire,' composed a song to the same tune ; a piece embodying pretty successfully the prudent, pride-humbling philosophy of the Scottish commonalty :

    The grass had nae freedom o' growin'
        As lang as she wasna awa' ;
    Nor in the toun could there be stowin'
        For wooers that wanted to ca'.

Sic boxin', sic brawlin', sic dancin',
  Sic bowin' and shakin' a paw ;
The toun was for ever in brulyies :
  But now the lassie 's awa'.
    Wooed, and married, and a',
      Married, and wooed, and a' ;
    The dandilie toast of the parish,
      She 's wooed, and she 's carried awa.'

But had he a-kenn'd her as I did,
  His wooin' it wad hae been sma' :
She kens neither bakin', nor brewin',
  Nor cardin', nor spinnin' ava ;
But a' her skill lies in her buskin' :
  And, O, if her braws were awa',
She sune wad wear out o' fashion,
  And knit up her huggers wi' straw.

But yesterday I gaed to see her,
  And, O, she was bonnie and braw ;
She cried on her guidman to gie her
  An ell o' red ribbon or twa.
He took, and he set down beside her
  A wheel and a reel for to ca' ;
She cried, Was he that way to guide her ?
  And out at the door and awa'.

The first road she gaed was her mither,
  Wha said, Lassie, how gaes a' ?
Quo' she, Was it for nae ither
  That I was married awa',
But to be set down to a wheelie,
  And at it for ever to ca' ?
And syne to hae 't reel'd by a chieldie
  That 's everly crying to draw.

N

Her mither said till her, Hech, lassie !
  He 's wisest, I fear, o' the twa ;
There 'll be little to put in the tassie,
  Gif ye be sae backward to draw ;
For now ye should work like a tiger,
  And at it baith wallop and ca',
Sae lang 's ye hae youdith and vigour,
  And weanies and debt keep awa'.

Sae swift away hame to your haddin' ;
  The mair fule ye e'er came awa' :
Ye maunna be ilka day gaddin',
  Nor gang sae white-finger'd and braw ;
For now wi' a neebor ye 're yokit,
  And wi' him should cannilie draw ;
Or else ye deserve to be knockit—
  So that 's an answer for a'.

Young luckie thus fand hersel mither'd,
  And wish'd she had ne'er come awa' ;
At length wi' hersel she consider'd,
  That hameward 'twas better to draw,
And e'en tak a chance o' the landin',
  However that matters might fa' :
Folk maunna on freits aye be standin',
  That 's wooed, and married, and a'.[1]

AULD ROB MORRIS.

This song appears in the *Tea-table Miscellany*, 1724, as an old
song with additions. Its air, which is traced to a music-book,
dated 1692, where it appears under the name of *Jock the Laird's
Brother*,[2] has secured it popularity, and induced Burns to compose

[1] From Cromek's *Select Scottish Songs*, 1810.
[2] Laing's *Notes to Stenhouse*, p. 222*.

another song on the basis of the same name, but with a different strain of ideas, by which the present lyric has been in a great measure superseded.

There 's auld Rob Mor - ris, that wons in yon glen, He 's the king o' guid fal - lows, and wale o' auld men; He has four - score o' black sheep, and four - score too; And auld Rob Mor - ris is the man ye maun lo'e.

MOTHER.

There 's auld Rob Morris, that wons in yon glen,
He 's the king o' guid fallows, and wale o' auld men ;
He has fourscore o' black sheep, and fourscore too ;
And auld Rob Morris is the man ye maun lo'e.

DAUGHTER.

Haud your tongue, mother, and let that abee ;
For his eild[1] and my eild can never agree :
They 'll never agree, and that will be seen ;
For he is fourscore, and I 'm but fifteen.

MOTHER.

Haud your tongue, dochter, and lay by your pride,
For he is the bridegroom, and ye 'se be the bride ;
[Ye 'll hae a bein house and right little to do],
Auld Rob Morris is the man ye maun lo'e.

DAUGHTER.

Auld Rob Morris, I ken him fu' weel,
His back sticks out like ony peat-creel ;
He 's out-shinn'd, in-kneed, and ringle-eyed too :
Auld Rob Morris is the man I 'll ne'er lo'e.

MOTHER.

Though auld Rob Morris be an elderly man,
Yet his auld brass will buy you a new pan ;[2]
Then, dochter, ye should na be sae ill to shoe,
For auld Rob Morris is the man ye maun lo'e.

DAUGHTER.

But auld Rob Morris I never will hae,
His back is so stiff, and his beard is grown gray ;
I had rather die than live wi' him a year ;
Sae mair o' Rob Morris I never will hear.

[1] Age.   [2] This expression has become proverbial in Scotland.

GALA WATER.

There is a series of old rustic songs commemorating a 'bonnie lass,' also the 'braw, braw lads,' of Gala Water, and which were sung to a beautiful simple air of one strain. The following is the lyric in praise of the lass:

Bon - nie lass o' Ga - la Wa - ter, Braw, braw lass o'
Ga - la Wa - ter, I could wade the stream sae deep, For
yon braw lass o' Ga - la Wa - ter.

Bonnie lass o' Gala Water,
Braw, braw lass o' Gala Water,
I could wade the stream sae deep,
For yon braw lass o' Gala Water.

Sae fair her hair, sae brent her brow,
Sae bonnie blue her een, and cheerie ;
The mair I kiss her cherry lips,
The mair I wish her for my dearie.
    Bonnie lass, &c.

Ower yonder moss, ower yonder muir,
Through a' yon mossy muirs and heather,
O, I could rin, wi' heart sae licht,
Wi' my dear lassie to forgather !
    Bonnie lass, &c.[1]

[1] Taken down from recitation.

It is otherwise given, as follows, in Herd's Collection, 1776:

> Braw, braw lads of Gala Water,
>   O, braw lads of Gala Water,
> I 'll kilt my coats aboon my knee,
>   And follow my love through the water.

> Sae fair her hair, sae brent her brow,
>   Sae bonnie blue her een, my dearie,
> Sae white her teeth, sae sweet her mou',
>   I aften kiss her till I 'm wearie.

> Ower yon bank, and ower yon brae,
>   Ower yon moss amang the heather,
> I 'll kilt my coats aboon my knee,
>   And follow my love through the water.

There was also a rather incoherent ballad, as follows:

> Out ower yon moss, out ower yon muir,
>   Out ower yon bonnie bush o' heather!
> O all ye lads, whae'er ye be,
>   Shew me the way to Gala Water.
>   Braw, braw lads o' Gala Water,
>   Bonnie lads o' Gala Water;
>   The Lothian lads maun ne'er compare
>   Wi' the braw lads o' Gala Water.

> At Nettlie-flat we will begin,
>   And at Halltree we 'll write a letter;
> We 'll down by the Bower, and take a scour,
>   And drink to the lads o' Gala Water.

> There 's Blindlie and Torwoodlee,
>   And Galashiels is muckle better;
> But young Torsonce he bears the gree
>   Of a' the Pringles o' Gala Water.

Buckham is a bonnie place ;
   But Appletree-leaves is muckle better ;
But Cockleferry bears the gree
   Frae ilka laird on Gala Water.

Lords and lairds came here to woo,
   And gentlemen wi' sword and dagger ;
But the black-eyed lass o' Galashiels
   Wad hae nane but the gree o' Gala Water.

Lothian lads are black wi' reek,
   And Teviotdale lads are little better ;
But she 's kiltit her coats abune her knee,
   And gane wi' the lad o' Gala Water.

Though corn-rigs are guid to see,
   Yet flocks o' sheep are muckle better ;
For oats will shake in a windy day,
   When the lambs will play in Gala Water.

Adieu, sour plooms o' Galashiels,
   Farewell, my father and my mother ;
For I 'll awa' wi' the black herd lad,
   Wha keeps his flocks on Gala Water.
      Braw, braw lads o' Gala Water,
        Bonnie lads o' Gala Water !
      Let them a' say what they will,
        The gree gaes aye to Gala Water.

It is scarcely necessary to remark that Burns put these productions out of their wonted popularity, by his beautiful song to the same air.

THE HIGHLANDMAN'S COMPLAINT.

One of the very old airs of Scotland bore the name of *Clout the Caldron*. Father Hay, in his *Genealogy of the Hayes of Tweeddale*, written about 1690, says that the song of *The Clouting of the Caldron* was written upon a grandfather of Sir John Sinclair of Stevenston, who was 'a famous brewer in Leith, where the Sinclair Society [probably a brewing company] is yet extant.' The liveliness of the air is said to have drawn from the second Bishop Chisholm of Dunblane the declaration that, if he were going to be hanged, he would choose to have *Clout the Caldron* played by the way. The original song being quite too rough for introduction to a tea-table, Allan Ramsay modified it into a strain which he honestly believed to be fit for the society of

> ————ilka lovely British lass,
> Frae Ladies Charlotte, Anne, and Jean,
> Down to ilk bonnie singing Bess,
> Wha dances barefoot on the green—

but which we, in these days, would decidedly condemn to the back of the stable-door at best. Thus all connected with *Clout the Caldron* is put out of court, except the air.

That this may not be lost, it is here given in connection with a song which appears to have been composed for it about the middle of the last century, being a mountaineer's deploration on the changes then introduced into his country, for what was thought to be its improvement, including good roads. This song, commonly entitled *Turnimspike*, was published in Herd's Collection.

Her - sel pe High - land shen - tle - man, Pe

auld as Pothwell Prig, man; And ma-ny al-ter-a-tions seen A-

mang te Lawland Whig, man. Fa la la la, Fa la la la la, Fa

la la la, Fa la la, Fa la la la, Fa la la la, Fa

la la la, Fa la la.

Hersel pe Highland shentleman,
    Pe auld as Pothwell Prig, man ;
And many alterations seen
    Amang te Lawland Whig, man.
        Fa la la la, Fa la la la la, &c.

First when she to te Lawlands came,
    Nainsel was driving cows, man,
There was nae laws to trouble him,
    About te preeks or trews, man.

Nainsel did wear te philabeg,
    Te plaid prick'd on her shouder ;
Te guid claymore hung py her pelt ;
    Her pistol sharged with powder.

But for whereas these cursed preeks,
    Wherewith her legs pe lockit ;
Ohon that ere she saw the day !
    For a' her houghs pe prokit.

Everything in te Highlands now
　　Pe turn'd to alteration ;
Te sodger dwall at our door cheek,
　　And tat pe great vexation.

Scotland pe turn'd a Ningland now,
　　The laws pring in te caudger ;
Nainsel wad dirk him for his deeds,
　　But, oh ! she fears te sodger.

Anither law came after tat,
　　Me never saw the like, man,
They mak a lang road on te crund,
　　And ca' him Turnimspike, man ;

And wow she pe a ponny road,
　　Like Loudon corn-riggs, man,
·Where twa carts may gang on her,
　　And no preak ither's legs, man.

They charge a penny for ilka horse,
　　In troth she'll no be sheaper,
For nought but gaun upon the ground,
　　And they gie her a paper.

They take the horse then py te head,
　　And there they make him stand, man ;
She tell them she had seen the day
　　They had nae sic command, man.

Nae doubt nainsel maun draw her purse,
　　And pay him what him like, man ;
She'll see a shudgement on his toor,
　　That filthy turnimspike, man.

But she'll awa' to te Highland hills,
　　Where deil a ane dare turn her,
And no come near te turnimspike,
　　Unless it pe to purn her.

THE ROCK AND THE WEE PICKLE TOW.

This song, in a somewhat larger form, was written by Alexander Ross, schoolmaster of Lochlee, Forfarshire, author of a dramatic poem, entitled *The Fortunate Shepherdess*, which has not yet been consigned to oblivion. It was published in Herd's Collection. It may be remarked that the air is evidently the basis of a modern Irish melody, entitled *The Land of the West*.

There was an auld wife had a wee pic-kle tow, And

she wad gae try the spinnin' o't; She lout-ed her

doun, and her rock took a - low, And that was a

bad be-gin-nin' o't. She sat and she grat, and she

flat and she flang, And she threw and she blew, and she

wriggled and wrang, And she chok-it and boak-it, and

cried like to mang, A - las, for the drea - ry be-

gin - nin' o't!

There was an auld wife had a wee pickle tow,
    And she wad gae try the spinnin' o't ;
She louted her doun, and her rock took a-low,
    And that was a bad beginnin' o't.
She sat and she grat, and she flat and she flang,
And she threw and she blew, and she wriggled and wrang,
And she chokit and boakit, and cried like to mang,
    Alas, for the dreary beginnin' o't !

I 've wanted a sark for these aught-years-and-ten,
    And this was to be the beginnin' o't ;
But I vow I shall want it for as lang again,
    Or ever I try the spinnin' o't.
For never since ever they ca'd as they ca' me,
Did sic a mishap and mischanter befa' me ;
But ye shall hae leave baith to hang and to draw me,
    The neist time I try the spinnin' o't.

I hae keepit my house now these threescore o' years,
    And aye I kept frae the spinnin' o't ;
But how I was sarkit, foul fa' them that speirs,
    For it minds me upo' the beginnin' o't.
But our women are now-a-days a' grown sae braw,
That ilk ane maun hae a sark, and some hae twa—
The warlds were better where ne'er ane ava
    Had a rag, but ane at the beginnin' o't.

In the days they ca' yore, gin auld fouks [could but get]
  To a surcoat, hough-syde,[1] for the winnin' o't,
Of coat-raips weel cut by the cast o' their [shape],
  They never socht mair o' the spinnin' o't.
A pair o' gray hoggers weil cluikit benew,
Of nae other lit but the hue of the ewe,
With a pair o' rough mullions to scuff through the dew,
  Was the fee they socht at the beginnin' o't.

But we maun hae linen, and that maun hae we,
  And how get we that but by spinnin' o't?
How can we hae face for to seek a great fee,
  Except we can help at the winnin' o't?
And we maun hae pearlins, and mabbies, and cocks,[2]
And some other things that the ladies ca' smocks;
And how get we that, gin we tak na our rocks,
  And pu' what we can at the spinnin' o't?

'Tis needless for us to mak our remarks,
  Frae our mither's miscookin' the spinnin' o't.
She never kenn'd ocht o' the gueed o' the sarks,
  Frae this aback to the beginnin' o't.
Twa-three ell o' plaiden was a' that was socht
By our auld-warld bodies, and that bude be bought;
For in ilka town siccan things wasna wrocht—
  Sae little they kenn'd o' the spinnin' o't!

TULLOCHGORUM.

The author of the following clever song was the Rev. John
Skinner, Episcopal minister at Longmay, Aberdeenshire. He
was a man passing rich with forty pounds a year, who never

[1] Hough-syde; that is, as long in the skirts as to reach the hams.
[2] Varieties of female head-gear.

wanted a smile on his countenance and thankfulness in his heart. Though belonging to a clerical body generally reputed as Jacobites, and though he himself suffered imprisonment during the *Forty-five* on suspicion, it does not appear that Skinner had any strong partisan feelings, except in favour of mirth and social harmony in general. Being one day at the house of a friend named Montgomery, in the village of Ellon, in Aberdeenshire, where a hot dispute raged for some time between two persons of opposite political sentiments, and the lady of the house having called for a song to restore good-humour, Skinner improved on the hint to write a song which has been printed in nearly every subsequent collection—taking as an air the *Reel of Tullochgorum.*

Come gie's a sang, Mont - gom - ery cried, And lay your dis - putes all a - side; What sig - ni - fies 't for folks to chide For what's been done be - fore them? Let Whig and To - ry all a - gree, Whig and To - ry, Whig and To - ry,

Whig and To - ry all a - gree To
drop their Whig - meg - mor - um. Let
Whig and To - ry all a - gree To
spend this night with mirth and glee, And
cheer - fu' sing a - lang wi' me The
reel of Tul - loch - gor - um.

Come gie 's a sang, Montgomery cried,
And lay your disputes all aside ;
What signifies 't for folks to chide
    For what 's been done before them ?
Let Whig and Tory all agree,
Whig and Tory, Whig and Tory,
Let Whig and Tory all agree
    To drop their Whigmegmorum.
Let Whig and Tory all agree
To spend this night with mirth and glee,
And cheerfu' sing alang wi' me
    The reel of Tullochgorum.

O, Tullochgorum 's my delight ;
It gars us a' in ane unite ;
And ony sumph [1] that keeps up spite,
  In conscience I abhor him.
Blithe and merry we 's be a',
Blithe and merry, blithe and merry,
Blithe and merry we 's be a',
  And mak a cheerfu' quorum.
Blithe and merry we 's be a',
As lang as we hae breath to draw,
And dance, till we be like to fa',
  The reel of Tullochgorum.

There need na be sae great a phraise,
Wi' dringing dull Italian lays ;
I wadna gie our ain strathspeys
  For half a hundred score o' 'em.
They 're douff and dowie [2] at the best,
Douff and dowie, douff and dowie,
They 're douff and dowie at the best,
  Wi' a' their variorums.
They 're douff and dowie at the best,
Their allegros, and a' the rest,
They canna please a Highland taste,
  Compared wi' Tullochgorum.

Let warldly minds themselves oppress
Wi' fear of want, and double cess,
And sullen sots themselves distress
  Wi' keeping up decorum.
Shall we sae sour and sulky sit,
Sour and sulky, sour and sulky,
Shall we sae sour and sulky sit,
  Like auld Philosophorums ?

----

[1] Fool.   [2] Stupid and doleful.

Shall we sae sour and sulky sit,
Wi' neither sense, nor mirth, nor wit,
And canna rise to shake a fit
    At the reel of Tullochgorum?

May choicest blessings still attend
Each honest-hearted open friend;
And calm and quiet be his end,
    And a' that's good watch o'er him!
May peace and plenty be his lot,
Peace and plenty, peace and plenty,
May peace and plenty be his lot,
    And dainties, a great store o' 'em!
May peace and plenty be his lot,
Unstain'd by any vicious blot;
And may he never want a groat,
    That's fond o' Tullochgorum.

EWIE WI' THE CROOKIT HORN.

The following is another happy song by the amiable Skinner of Longmay. It seems to refer to some simple domestic incident; yet there was an earlier and still more simple song of the same strain.

O, were I a-ble to re-hearse, My
ew-ie's praise in pro-per verse, I'd sound it out as
loud and fierce as ev-er pip-er's drone could blaw. My

o

ew - ie wi' the   crook - it horn! A' that kenn'd her

would hae sworn, Sic   a   ew - ie ne'er was   born,

Here - a - bouts nor   far   a - wa'.

O, were I able to rehearse,
My ewie's praise in proper verse,
I'd sound it out as loud and fierce
    As ever piper's drone could blaw.
      My ewie wi' the crookit horn!
    A' that kenn'd her would hae sworn,
    Sic a ewie ne'er was born,
      Hereabouts nor far awa'.

She neither needed tar nor keel,
To mark her upon hip or heel;
Her crookit hornie did as weel,
    To ken her by amang them a'.

She never threaten'd scab nor rot,
But keepit aye her ain jog-trot;
Baith to the fauld and to the cot,
    Was never sweir to lead nor ca'.

A better nor a thriftier beast,
Nae honest man need e'er hae wish'd;
For, silly thing, she never miss'd
    To hae ilk year a lamb or twa.

The first she had I ga'e to Jock,
To be to him a kind o' stock ;
And now the laddie has a flock
    Of mair than thretty head and twa.

The neist I ga'e to Jean ; and now
The bairn 's sae braw, has faulds sae fu',
That lads sae thick come her to woo,
    They 're fain to sleep on hay or straw.

Cauld nor hunger never dang her,
Wind or rain could never wrang her ;
Ance she lay an ouk and langer
    Forth aneath a wreath o' snaw.

When other ewies lap the dyke,
And ate the kale for a' the tyke,[1]
My ewie never play'd the like,
    But teesed about the barn wa'.

I lookit aye at even for her,
Lest mischanter should come ower her,
Or the foomart micht devour her,
    Gin the beastie bade awa'.

Yet, last ouk, for a' my keeping
(Wha can tell o't without greeting ?),
A villain cam, when I was sleeping,
    Staw my ewie, horn and a'.

I socht her sair upon the morn,
And down aneath a bush o' thorn,
There I fand her crookit horn,
    But my ewie was awa'.

[1] Notwithstanding the dog.

But gin I had the loon that did it,
I hae sworn as weel as said it,
Although the laird himsel forbid it,
    I sall gie his neck a thraw.

I never met wi' sic a turn :
At e'en I had baith ewe and horn,
Safe steekit up ; but, 'gain the morn,
    Baith ewe and horn were stown awa'.

A' the claes that we hae worn,
Frae her and hers sae aft was shorn ;
The loss o' her we could hae borne,
    Had fair-strae death ta'en her awa'.

O, had she died o' croup or cauld,
As ewies die when they grow auld,
It hadna been, by mony fauld,
    Sae sair a heart to ane o' us a'.

But thus, puir thing, to lose her life,
Beneath a bluidy villain's knife ;
In troth, I fear that our guidwife
    Will never get abune 't ava.

O, all ye bards benorth Kinghorn,
Call up your muses, let them mourn
Our ewie wi' the crookit horn,
    Frae us stown, and fell'd and a' !

The earlier song of the *Ewie wi' the Crooked Horn* thus appears in a manuscript collection in the possession of Mr Thomas Mansfield, accountant, Edinburgh.

Ewie wi' the crooked horn, may you never see the morn ;
Ilka day ye steal my corn, ewie wi' the crooked horn ;
A' the ewes come hame at even, a' the ewes come hame at even,
A' the ewes come hame at even, crooked hornie bides awa'.

Ilka ewie has a lambie, ilka ewie has a lambie,
Ilka ewie has a lambie, crooked hornie she has twa.
Ewie wi' the crooked horn, may you never see the morn,
Ilka day ye steal my corn, ewie wi' the crooked horn.

A' the ewes gie milk eneugh, a' the ewes gie milk eneugh,
A' the ewes gie milk eneugh, but crooked horn gies maist of a'.
Ewie wi' the crooked horn, may you never see the morn,
Ilka day ye steal my corn, ewie wi' the crooked horn.

I'LL GAR OUR GUIDMAN TROW.

I'll gar our guidman trow I'll sell the lad-le, If
he win-na buy to me A bon-nie side sad-dle, To
ride to kirk and brid-al, And round a-bout the town, O;
Stand a-bout, ye fish-er jauds, And gie my gown room!

I'll gar our guidman trow
I'll sell the ladle,
If he winna buy to me
A bonnie side-saddle,
To ride to kirk and bridal,
And round about the town, O ;
Stand about, ye fisher jauds,
And gie my gown room !

I 'll gar our guidman trow
 I 'll tak the fling-strings,
If he winna buy to me
 Twal bonnie gowd rings ;
Ane for ilka finger,
 And twa for ilka thoom ;
Stand about, ye fisher jauds,
 And gie my gown room !

I 'll gar our guidman trow
 That I 'm gaun to die,
If he winna fee to me
 Valets twa or three,
To bear my train up frae the dirt,
 And ush me through the town ;
Stand about, ye fisher jauds,
 And gie my gown room ![1]

GREEN GROW THE RASHES.

Auld Nature swears the lovely dears Her noblest works she
class-es, O; Her 'pren-tice hand she tried on man, And
then she made the lass-es, O. Green grow the

[1] First published in a little collection of old songs, entitled the *Ballad-Book*, which was printed for private distribution, at Edinburgh, under the care of Mr Charles Kirkpatrick Sharpe, in the year 1824.

rash-es, O, Green grow the rash-es, O, The sweet-est hours that
e'er I spent, Were spent a-mang the lass-es, O.

A song of the kind which once passed current amongst innocent people, but would now be utterly condemned by the same
class, has existed from old times, with a refrain beginning—

> Green grow the rashes, O,
> Green grow the rashes, O.

In our wish to convey at least the air, we are driven to the
expedient of presenting it in connection with two of the verses of
a comic song written for the same air by Burns:

> Green grow the rashes, O,
> Green grow the rashes, O,
> The sweetest hours that e'er I spent,
> Were spent amang the lasses, O.
> Auld nature swears the lovely dears
> Her noblest works she classes, O ;
> Her 'prentice hand she tried on man,
> And then she made the lasses, O.

The tune is one of the oldest which have been handed down
to us. A manuscript broadside political song of the reign of
William and Mary, containing the following verse :

> But let them say and do on,
> But let them say and do on,
> Our kirk, that had no head before,
> Has now a he and she one—

is to the tune of *Green Grow the Rashes*.[1] The tune, however,

---

[1] Wodrow Pamphlets, Adv. Lib. Edin.

appears under this name, not only in a manuscript collection of
the reign of Charles II., referred to by Mr Dauney,[1] but in the
Lute-Book of Gordon of Straloch, which was compiled between
1627 and 1629.[2] In the latter collection, it is entitled *A Dance*.

GIN YE MEET A BONNIE LASSIE.

Gin ye meet a bonnie lassie,
  Gie her a kiss and let her gae ;
But gin ye meet a dirty hizzie,
  Fye, gar rub her o'er wi' strae !
    Fye, gar rub her, rub her, rub her,
    Fye, gar rub her o'er wi' strae,
  And gin ye meet a dirty hizzie,
    Fye, gar rub her o'er wi' strae !

This is all that has been preserved of an old song—one of those
for which Ramsay substituted new verses, thereby putting the
old ones out of fashion, and consigning them to oblivion. In
furnishing a new song, which he did by a paraphrase of the
Vides ut alta of Horace, he retained the first of the above verses,
though they do not cohere very well with his own. For the
second, which is only a sort of refrain, we are indebted to the
memory of Burns. The air being one of great merit, Ramsay
also adapted to it one of the songs of his *Gentle Shepherd*, and
Gay introduced it as a melody for one of the songs in his opera
of *Achilles*, which was performed in 1733, after his decease.

The recommendation given in this song as to the treatment
proper for a bonnie lassie, will be generally intelligible, but
scarcely so that pointed out in the case of the dirty hizzie. The
explanation required in the latter case is, that there was an
ancient rustic custom in Scotland of rubbing over with pease-
straw a girl whose lover had proved unfaithful—a jocular kind of
confirmation of the affront.

---

[1] *Ancient Scottish Melodies*, p. 142.　　　　[2] Ibid. p. 369.

Ramsay's entire song to this tune is here subjoined :

And gin ye meet a bon - nie lass - ie,

Gie her a kiss and let her gae; But if ye meet a

dir - ty hiz - zie, Fy, gar rub her ower wi' strae.

Be sure ye din - na quit the grip Of il - ka joy when

ye are young, Be - fore auld age your vi - tals nip, And

lay ye twa fauld ower a rung.

Gin ye meet a bonnie lassie,
  Gie her a kiss and let her gae ;
But if ye meet a dirty hizzie,
  Fy, gar rub her o'er wi' strae.
Be sure ye dinna quit the grip
  Of ilka joy when ye are young,
Before auld age your vitals nip,
  And lay ye twa-fauld ower a rung.

Sweet youth's a blithe and heartsome time :
  Then, lads and lasses, while it's May,
Gae pou the gowan in its prime,
  Before it wither and decay.

Watch the saft minutes o' delight,
　　When Jenny speaks below her breath,
And kisses, layin' a' the wyte
　　On you if she kep ony skaith.

Haith, ye 're ill-bred, she 'll smilin' say,
　　Ye 'll worry me, ye greedy rook ;
Syne frae your arms she 'll rin away,
　　And hide hersel in some dark neuk.
Her lauch will lead ye to the place,
　　Where lies the happiness ye want ;
And plainly tell ye to your face,
　　Nineteen nay-says are hauf a grant.

Now to her heavin' bosom cling,
　　And sweitly tuilyie for a kiss ;
Frae her fair finger whup a ring,
　　As taiken o' a future bliss.
These benisons, I 'm very sure,
　　Are of kind heaven's indulgent grant ;
Then, surly carles, wheesht, forbear
　　To plague us wi' your whinin' cant !

THE MUCKING O' GEORDIE'S BYRE.

The mucking o' Geor-die's byre, And the
sho'eling the gruip sae clean, Has garred me
weet my cheeks, And greet wi' baith my

een. It ne'er was my fath-er's will, Nor yet my

mother's de - sire, That e'er I should fyle my

fing-ers Wi' the mucking o' Geor - die's byre.

The mucking o' Geordie's byre,
　And the sho'eling the gruip [1] sae clean,
Has garred me weet my cheeks,
　And greet wi' baith my een.
　　It ne'er was my father's will,
　　　Nor yet my mother's desire,
　　That e'er I should fyle my fingers
　　　Wi' the mucking o' Geordie's byre.

The mouse is a merry beast,
　The moudiewort [2] wants the een,
But the warld shall ne'er get wit,
　Sae merry as we hae been.

This song, which appeared in Herd's Collection, is supposed to have been composed at a much earlier period on a *mesalliance* formed by a young lady of rank—a baronet's daughter—with a young peasant; and tradition adds that she had subsequently occasion, more than is even usual in such cases, to lament her folly, as her husband used her ill. The air is a favourite, and various other songs have been written for it, but none of much merit.

[1] The sewer of the cow-house.　　　　　[2] The mole.

MY WIFE SHALL HAE HER WILL.

If my dear wife should chance to gang, Wi' me, to Ed'nbro' toun, In-to a shop I will her tak, And buy her a new goun. But if my dear wife should hain the charge, As I ex-pect she will, And if she says, The auld will do, By my word she'll hae her will.

If my dear wife should chance to gang,
    Wi' me, to Ed'nburgh toun,
Into a shop I will her tak,
    And buy her a new goun.

But if my dear wife should hain[1] the charge,
  As I expect she will,
And if she says, The auld will do,
  By my word she 'll hae her will.

If my dear wife should wish to gang,
  To see a neebor or friend,
A horse or a chair I will provide,
  And a servant to attend.
But if my dear shall hain the charge,
  As I expect she will,
And if she says, I 'll walk on foot,
  By my word she 'll hae her will.

If my dear wife shall bring me a son,
  As I expect she will,
Cake and wine I will provide,
  And a nurse to nurse the child.
But if my dear wife shall hain the charge,
  As I expect she will,
And if she says, She 'll nurs 't hersel,
  By my word she 'll hae her will.

This sly piece of Scotch humour was first published in a volume of old ditties, printed in 1824 under the title of the *North-Country Garland*, being one of the many services to the traditionary and historical literature of Scotland which have been rendered by Mr James Maidment, advocate.

[1] Save.

WHEN SHE CAM BEN SHE BOBBIT.

O when she cam ben she bob-bit fu' law, O
when she cam ben she bob-bit fu' law, And
when she cam ben, she kissed Cock - pen, And
syne she de-nied that she did it at a'.

O when she cam ben she bobbit fu' law,
O when she cam ben she bobbit fu' law,
And when she cam ben, she kissed Cockpen,
And syne she denied that she did it at a'.

And wasna Cockpen richt saucy witha',
And wasna Cockpen richt saucy witha',
In leaving the dochter of a lord,
And kissing a collier lassie an a'?

O never look doun, my lassie, at a',
O never look doun, my lassie, at a';
Thy lips are as sweet, and thy figure complete,
As the finest dame in castle or ha'.

Though thou hae nae silk and holland sae sma',
Though thou hae nae silk and holland sae sma',
Thy coat and thy sark are thy ain handywark,
And Lady Jean was never sae braw.

This is an old song brushed up by Burns. The air appears in Mrs Crockat's Manuscript, 1709, and it was published in Oswald's *Pocket Companion*. Cockpen is an estate now belonging to the Earl of Dalhousie, in the parish of the same name, Edinburghshire.

An admirable song, under the title of *The Laird of Cockpen*, was written to the same tune by Lady Nairn, and has very much assisted in throwing these old verses out of notice.

MY AULD MAN.

In the land of Fife there lived a wicked wife,
    And in the town of Cupar then,
Who sorely did lament, and made her complaint,
    Oh when will ye die, my auld man?

In cam her cousin Kate, when it was growing late,
    She said, What's guid for an auld man?
O wheit-breid and wine, and a kinnen new slain;
    That's guid for an auld man.

Cam ye in to jeer, or cam ye in to scorn,
    And what for cam ye in ?
For bear-bread and water, I 'm sure, is much better—
    It 's ower guid for an auld man.

Now the auld man 's deid, and, without remeid,
    Into his cauld grave he 's gane :
Lie still wi' my blessing ! of thee I hae nae missing ;
    I 'll ne'er mourn for an auld man.

Within a little mair than three-quarters of a year,
    She was married to a young man then,
Who drank at the wine, and tippled at the beer,
    And spent mair gear than he wan.

O black grew her brows, and howe grew her een,
    And cauld grew her pat and her pan :
And now she sighs, and aye she says,
    I wish I had my silly auld man ![1]

ROBIN REDBREAST'S TESTAMENT.

Guid day, now, bon-nie Ro-bin, How lang hae ye been here? I've been a bird a-bout this bush This mair than twenty year. But now I am the sick-est bird That ever sat on

[1] From Ritson's *Scottish Songs*, 1793.

brier; And I wad mak my tes - ta - ment, Guid-

man, if ye wad hear.

Guid day, now, bonnie Robin,
    How lang hae ye been here?
I've been a bird about this bush
    This mair than twenty year.

But now I am the sickest bird
    That ever sat on brier;
And I wad mak my testament,
    Guidman, if ye wad hear.

Gar tak this bonnie neb o' mine,
    That picks upon the corn;
And gie't to the Duke o' Hamilton,
    To be a hunting-horn.

Gar tak thae bonnie feathers o' mine,
    The feathers o' my neb;
And gie to the Lady Hamilton,
    To fill a feather-bed.

Gar tak this guid richt leg o' mine,
    And mend the brig o' Tay;
It will be a post and pillar guid,
    It will neither bow nor [gae].

And tak this other leg o' mine,
    And mend the brig o' Weir;
It will be a post and pillar guid,
    It will neither bow nor steer.

P

Gar tak thae bonnie feathers o' mine,
  The feathers o' my tail ;
And gie to the lads o' Hamilton
  To be a barn-flail.

And tak thae bonnie feathers o' mine,
  The feathers o' my breast ;
And gie them to the bonnie lad,
  Will bring to me a priest.

Now in there cam my Lady Wren,
  Wi' mony a sigh and groan,
O what care I for a' the lads,
  If my ain lad be gone !

Then Robin turn'd him round about,
  E'en like a little king ;
Gae pack ye out at my chamber-door,
  Ye little cutty-quean.[1]

THE WREN.

The wren scho lyes in care's bed, In
care's bed, in care's bed; The wren scho lyes in care's bed, In
meikle dule and pyne, O. When in cam Robin Red-breist,

[1] From Herd's Collection, 1776.

Redbreist Redbreist; When in cam Rob-in Redbreist, Wi'
suc-car saps and wine, O.

The wren scho lyes in care's bed,
    In care's bed, in care's bed ;
The wren scho lyes in care's bed,
    In meikle dule and pyne, O.
When in cam Robin Redbreist,
    Redbreist, Redbreist ;
When in cam Robin Redbreist,
    Wi' succar-saps and wine, O.

Now, maiden, will ye taste o' this,
    Taste o' this, taste o' this ;
Now, maiden, will ye taste o' this ?
    It 's succar-saps and wine, O.
Na, ne'er a drap, Robin,
    Robin, Robin ;
Na, ne'er a drap, Robin,
    Though it were ne'er sae fine, O.

     *   *   *   *

And where 's the ring that I gied ye,
    That I gied ye, that I gied ye ;
And where 's the ring that I gied ye,
    Ye little cutty-quean, O ?
I gied it till a soger,
    A soger, a soger ;
I gied it till a soger,
    A true sweetheart o' mine, O.[1]

        [1] From Herd's Collection.

BABITY BOWSTER.

Wha learned you to dance, Bab - i - ty Bowster, Bab - i - ty Bowster,

Wha learned you to dance, Bab - i - ty Bowster, braw - ly?

Wha learned you to dance,
    Babity Bowster, Babity Bowster,
Wha learned you to dance,
    Babity Bowster, brawly ?

My minny learned me to dance,
    Babity Bowster, Babity Bowster,
My minny learned me to dance,
    Babity Bowster, brawly.

Wha ga'e you the keys to keep,
    Babity Bowster, Babity Bowster,
Wha ga'e you the keys to keep,
    Babity Bowster, brawly ?

My minny ga'e me the keys to keep,
    Babity Bowster, Babity Bowster,
My minny ga'e me the keys to keep,
    Babity Bowster, brawly.

As sung by girls playing on the streets, in Glasgow.

JENNY'S BABEE.

And a' that e'er my Jen-ny had, My Jen-ny had, my Jen-ny had, And a' that e'er my Jen-ny had, Was ae ba-bee. There's your plack and my plack, And your plack and my plack, And my plack and your plack, And

Chorus.

Jen-ny's ba-bee. And a' that e'er my, &c.

And a' that e'er my Jenny had,
My Jenny had, my Jenny had,
And a' that e'er my Jenny had,
Was ae babee.

There's your plack and my plack,
And your plack and my plack,
And my plack and your plack,
And Jenny's babee.

We 'll put it in the pint stoup,
The pint stoup, the pint stoup,
We 'll put it in the pint stoup,
And birl 't a' three.[1]

Jenny's Babee is one of the simple rants which once had such popularity in Scotland—greatly exceeding in that respect strains by noted authors, charged with finest poetry and solidest sense. It is not even apparent what Jenny's babee means, whether an actual halfpenny, appreciated by a child; or metaphorically a young lady's fortune. The air was one often used as a dance. Within the present century two improved songs on the theme of Jenny's Babee have been offered for popular favour ; one of considerable effect, in a comic vein, by Sir Alexander Boswell ; another of a sentimental cast, for which the melody is given in slow time with surprisingly good effect.

[1] From Herd's Collection.

Sentimental Songs.

FIENT A CRUM OF THEE SHE FAWS.

OUR sentimental series opens with an elegy of unreturned affection by Alexander Scott, a poet who flourished in the time of Queen Mary, and wrote so elegantly and so copiously on amatory subjects that he has been called the SCOTTISH ANACREON. Of the personal life of Scott we know literally nothing. We find, however, that he addressed a New-year's congratulation to his fair young sovereign, on the first occurrence of the festival after her return to Scotland, wherein it appears that he did not sympathise strongly with the puritanic spirit which was then recently introduced into Scotland.

This specimen of Alexander Scott's poetry was recovered by Allan Ramsay, and printed by him, with some inexcusable corruptions, in the *Tea-table Miscellany*, 1724; likewise in the collection which he called the *Evergreen*. The verses here given are those which Lord Hailes extracted from the Bannatyne Manuscript. The air is one assigned to the song in Johnson's *Scots Musical Museum*.

Re - turn thee hameward, heart, a - gain, And
bide where thou was wont to be; Thou art ane fule, to
suf - fer pain, For luve of her that luves not thee: My
heart, let be sic fan - ta - sie, Luve nane but as they
mak thee cause; And let her seek ane heart for thee; For
fient a crum of thee she faws.

Return thee hameward, heart, again,
    And bide where thou was wont to be ;
Thou art ane fule, to suffer pain,
    For luve of her that luves not thee :
My heart, let be sic fantasie,
    Luve nane but as they mak thee cause ;
And let her seek ane heart for thee ;
    For fient a crum of thee she faws.

To what effect should thou be thrall
    But thank, sin' thou has thy free will ?
My heart, be not sae bestial,
    But knaw wha does thee guid or ill.

Remain with me and tarry still,
    And see wha playis best their paws,
And let fillock gae fling her fill,
    For fient a crum of thee she faws.

Though she be fair, I will not fenzie,
    She is the kind of others mae ;
For why ? there is a fellow menzie,
    That seemis guid and are not sae.
My heart, tak nowther pain nor wae,
    For Meg, for Marjory, or yet Mause,
But be thou glad and let her gae ;
    For fient a crum of thee she faws.

Because I find she took in ill,
    At her departing thou mak nae care ;
But all beguiled, go where she will,
    Ashrew the heart that mane maks mair !
My heart, be merry late and air,
    This is the final end and clause ;
And let her fallow ane filly fair,
    For fient a crum of thee she faws.

— ————

HEY, NOW THE DAY DAWS!

Dunbar, in one of his poems, ridicules the common minstrels of Edinburgh for having but two tunes :

    Your commone menstralis has no tone,
    But *Now the Day Daws*, and *Into June.*

This, of course, establishes that there was a popular air, called *Now the Day Daws*, as early as the beginning of the sixteenth century. We have, however, no copy of any tune so named before one which appears in Gordon's manuscript Lute-book, 1627 ; and the earliest song so entitled is one which appears in the works of Alexander Montgomery (died between 1607 and

1611). In the present collection, it has been thought proper to
present two of the seven verses of Montgomery's song, as giving
some idea of what was thought presentable song-minstrelsy in
the reign of James VI.—the refined lays of the lady's bower, in
contrast to the rude rants which sprang up among the common
people.

> Hey, now the day dawis,
> The jolly cock crawis,
> Now shrouds the shawis,
> 　　Through nature anon !
> The thrissle-cock cryis
> On lovers wha lyis ;
> Now skales the skyis ;
> 　　The night is near gone !
>
> The season excellis,
> Through sweetness that smellis ;
> Now Cupid compellis
> 　　Our heartis each one.
> On Venus, wha wakis
> To muse on our maikis,
> Syne sing, for their sakis,
> 　　The night is near gone !

Mr David Laing, in his notes on Johnson's *Museum* (p. 534),
has presented the notes of *The Day Dawis* from the Lute-book ;
but has failed to observe that it differs from the rhythm of
Montgomery's song, so that it is impossible to sing the one to
the other. This tune, indeed, is of a tinkling artificial character,
full of oddly abrupt transitions, perhaps well adapted for the
lute, but utterly unlike the flowing character of those melodies
to which the Scottish songs in general are sung. We are,
therefore, forced to conjecture that either the air has been incor-
rectly transcribed from the antiquated notation of the original,
or there were two songs of different metrical structure, called
The Day Dawis.

Mr Stenhouse, seeing the suitableness of Montgomery's song for the tune called *Hey Tuttie Taittie!* did not hesitate to assume that the latter was the true ancient tune of *The Day Dawis*, alluded to by the poet Dunbar. For this, however, there is no authority, any more than there is for the 'tradition' reported by Burns, that *Hey Tuttie Taittie* was Bruce's march at Bannockburn. All that we know of this notable melody is, that we find it in connection with a Jacobite song, beginning 'Here's to the king, sir,' and which has been included in our Historical Series.

THE BANKS OF HELICON.

In what is called the Maitland Manuscript (Pepys's Collection, Cambridge)—that is, a transcribed assemblage of poems of the sixteenth century, which we owe to Sir Richard Maitland and perhaps some other members of his family—appears a song called *The Banks of Helicon*, in the complicated measure which Montgomery in that age exemplified in *The Cherry and the Slae*, and which Burns was the last to employ (*Epistle to Davy*, &c.). It is the composition of a learned pen, and celebrates the charms of a mistress, with classic references, in a style approaching idolatry, but is not without a certain poetical *verve* far from displeasing. Modern literary antiquaries seem to think it possibly a composition of Alexander Montgomery, seeing it is in metre and some other respects so like his undoubted composition *The Cherry and the Slae*. Montgomery is believed to have died between 1607 and 1611.

Several musical manuscripts of the early part of the seventeenth century [1] present a tune called *The Banks of Helicon*, indicated in one as a work of Mr Andrew Blackhall, minister of Inveresk, who died in 1609, at the age of 73, and appears to have been

---

[1] See Sibbald's *Chronicle of Scottish Poetry*, iii. 191. Stenhouse's *Notes to Johnson's Museum*, p. 406. Laing's *Additional Notes to Stenhouse*, p. *453, and Introduction, p. lxxxiii.

a skilful musician, as there is extant a piece of five-part music
for the 101st psalm, stated to have been composed 'by Maister
Andro Blakehall in Halyrudehouse, 1569, and giffen in propyne
to the kyng.'   As this air perfectly suits the song in the Maitland
Manuscript, there can be little doubt that the one was composed
for the other.   It seems, therefore, allowable to give in this place
a selection from the somewhat tedious verses of the song, in
connection with the air; a fair specimen of the formal, well-bred,
but not very engaging chamber minstrelsy of the reign of the
Sixth James.

De - clare, ye banks of Hel - i - con, Par - nass - us hill, and

dales ilk one, And foun - tain Ca - bel - lein, Gif

o - ny of your Mus - es all Or nymph - is may be

per - e - gal Un - to my la - dy sheen. Or

if the la - dies that did lave Their bo - dies by your

brim, So seem - ly were or yet so suave, So

beau - ti - ful or trim. Con - tem - ple, ex-

am - ple Tak by her pro - per port, Gif

on - y so bon - nie Among you did re - sort.

Declare, ye banks of Helicon,
Parnassus hill, and dales ilk one,
    And fountain Cabellein,
Gif ony of your Muses all
Or nymphis may be peregal
    Unto my lady sheen.
Or if the ladies that did lave
    Their bodies by your brim,
So seemly were or yet so suave,
    So beautiful or trim.
       Contemple, example
         Tak by her proper port,
       Gif ony so bonnie
         Among you did resort.

No, no : forsooth was never none
That with this perfect paragon,
    In beauty might compare.
The Muses wad have given the grie
To her, as to the *A-per-se*
    And peerless pearl preclair.
Thinking with admiration
    Her person so perfyte,
Nature in her creation
    To form her took delight.

Confess then, express then,
    Your nymphs and all their race,
For beauty, of duty,
    Sould yield and give her place.

FAIR HELEN OF KIRKCONNELL.

In the burial ground of Kirkconnell, near the Border, is the grave of Helen Irving, recognised by tradition as *Fair Helen of Kirkconnell,* and who is supposed to have lived in the sixteenth century. It is also the grave of her lover, Adam Fleming—a name that once predominated in the district. Helen, according to the narration of Pennant, 'was beloved by two gentlemen at the same time. The one vowed to sacrifice the successful rival to his resentment, and watched an opportunity while the happy pair were sitting on the banks of the Kirtle, that washes these grounds. Helen perceived the desperate lover on the opposite side, and fondly thinking to save her favourite, interposed ; and,

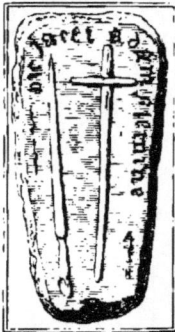
receiving the wound intended for her beloved, fell and expired in his arms. He instantly revenged her death ; then fled into Spain, and served for some time against the Infidels : on his return, he visited the grave of his unfortunate mistress, stretched himself on it, and expiring on the spot, was interred by her side. A cross and a sword are engraven on the tombstone, with "HIC JACET ADAMUS FLEMING ;" the only memorial of this unhappy gentleman, except an ancient ballad of no great merit, which records the tragical event.'[1]

---

[1] Pennant's *Tour in Scotland,* 1772, vol. ii. 101. According to a note in Graham's *Songs of Scotland* (iii. 172), the tombstone presents only the engraving of a sword, along with some letters now unintelligible, while the remains of an upright cross stand by. The above transcript from the stone would seem to shew that Pennant's description was correct.

I wish I were where Helen lies, For night and day on me she cries, I wish I were where Hel-en lies, On fair Kirk-con-nell lee.

I wish I were where Helen lies,
For night and day on me she cries,
I wish I were where Helen lies,
   On fair Kirkconnell lee.

Curst be the hand that shot the shot,
Likewise the gun that ga'e the crack,
Into my arms Burd Helen lap,
   And died for love of me.

Oh, think na ye my heart was sair,
To see her lie and speak nae mair!
There did she swoon wi' mickle care,
   On fair Kirkconnell lee.

I loutit down, my sword did draw,
I cuttit him in pieces sma',
I cuttit him in pieces sma',
   On fair Kirkconnell lee.

Oh, Helen fair, without compare,
I'll mak a garland o' thy hair,
And wear the same for evermair,
   Until the day I dee.

Q

I wish my grave were growing green,
A winding-sheet put ower my een,
And I in Helen's arms lying,
   On fair Kirkconnell lee.

Oh Helen chaste, thou were modest ;
Were I with thee I wad be blest,
Where thou lies low and takes thy rest,
   On fair Kirkconnell lee.

I wish I were where Helen lies,
For night and day on me she cries ;
I wish I were where Helen lies,
   On fair Kirkconnell lee.

The above is chiefly from the traditionary copy preserved by Mr Charles K. Sharpe, as he had been accustomed to hear it sung in Annandale in his childhood.[1] It is nearly the same with one presented in the Statistical Account of the parish, 1794. A version in the *Border Minstrelsy* gives the second verse thus :

Curst be the heart that thought the thought,
And curst the hand that fired the shot,
When in my arms Burd Helen dropt,
   And died to succour me—

being manifestly an editorial improvement.

The copy in the Statistical Account is prefaced with a number of verses, apparently of genuine antiquity, but referring to an earlier period of the story, and in an inferior strain of poetry. They are repeated in the *Border Minstrelsy* as a *first part* of the ballad :

My sweetest sweet, and fairest fair,
Of birth and worth beyond compare,
Thou art the causer of my care,
   Since first I loved thee.

---

[1] *Additions to Stenhouse: Johnson's Museum*, ii. 210*.

Yet God hath given to me a mind,
The which to thee shall prove as kind
As any one that thou shalt find
   Of high or low degree.

Yet, nevertheless, I am content,
And ne'er a whit my love repent,
But think my time it was weel spent,
   Though I disdained be.

The shall'est water makes maist din,
The deepest pool the deadest lin,
The richest man least truth within,
   Though he disdained be.

O Helen fair, without compare,
I'll wear a garland of thy hair,
Shall cover me for evermair,
   Until the day I die.

O Helen sweet and maist complete,
My captive spirit's at thy feet,
Thinks thou still fit thus for to treat
   Thy prisoner with cruelty?

O Helen brave! this still I crave,
On thy poor slave some pity have,
And do him save, that's near his grave,
   And dies for love of thee![1]

Odd as the idea is, one could almost suppose that these verses
were intended to express the feelings of the unsuccessful lover
while pressing his suit.

[1] [Sinclair's] *Stat. Acc. Scot.*, xiii. 275.

CROMLET'S LILT.

The traditionary story connected with this song has been confusedly handed down to us; but the facts probably were to the following general purport. Chisholm of Cromlecks, in Perthshire, was ardently attached to a daughter of Stirling of Ardoch, commonly called from her beauty *Fair Helen of Ardoch.* The pair lived during the reign of James VI. Obliged to go abroad for some years as a soldier of fortune, Cromlecks left a commission with a friend, for the conducting of a correspondence between himself and his mistress, who could not write; and the natural result was, that the friend became himself the lover of Helen, and, when other means failed, possessed her with a belief that Cromlecks had forgot, or become indifferent to her; so that she was induced to give an unwilling assent to the suit of the new lover.

After suffering much in spirit, Helen submitted to a marriage with the traitor, but had scarcely gone to bed that evening, when she started frantically from it, screaming out that, after three gentle taps on the wainscot at the bed-head, she had heard Cromlecks's voice crying, 'Helen, Helen, mind me!' Cromlecks soon after coming home, the treachery was discovered; the marriage annulled; and Helen became Lady Cromlecks.[1]

Since all thy vows, false maid, Are blown to air, And my poor heart betrayed To sad des-

[1] *Select Scottish Songs, with Critical Observations by Burns,* i. 80.

pair, In - to some wil - der - ness, My grief I

will ex - press, And thy hard heart - ed - ness,

O cru - el fair!

Since all thy vows, false maid,
    Are blown to air,
And my poor heart betrayed
    To sad despair,
Into some wilderness,
My grief I will express,
And thy hard heartedness,
    O cruel fair!

Have I not graven our loves
    On every tree,
In yonder spreading groves,
    Though false thou be?
Was not a solemn oath
Plighted betwixt us both,
Thou thy faith, I my troth,
    Constant to be?

Some gloomy place I 'll find,
    Some doleful shade,
Where neither sun nor wind
    E'er entrance had:

Into that hollow cave,
There will I sigh and rave,
Because thou dost behave
       So faithlessly.

Wild-fruit shall be my meat,
       I'll drink the spring;
Cold earth shall be my seat:
       For covering
I'll have the starry sky,
My head to canopy,
Until my soul on high
       Shall spread its wing.

I'll have no funeral fire,
       Nor tears for me:
No grave do I desire,
       Nor obsequies:
The courteous redbreast, he
With leaves will cover me,
And sing my elegy,
       With doleful voice.

And when a ghost I am,
       I'll visit thee,
O thou obdured dame,
       Whose cruelty
Hath killed the kindest heart
E'er pierced by Cupid's dart;
No grief my soul shall part
       From loving thee.

HER REPLY.

He whom I most affect
       Doth me disdain;
His causeless disrespect
       Makes me complain:

Wherefore I 'll me address
Into some wilderness,
Where unheard I 'll express
    My anxious pain.

Did we not both conjure
    By Stygian lake,
That sacred oath most pure
    The gods did take,
That we should both prove true:
You to me, I to you,
By that most solemn vow
    We both did make?

But thou perfidiously
    Didst violate
Thy promise made to me,
    To my regret;
For all the great respect,
Wherewith I thee affect,
Is paid with such neglect,
    Love 's turned to hate.

What tyrant e'er could hatch,
    Though inhumane,
A torturing rack and match
    To this my pain?
O barbarous cruelty,
That I, for loving thee,
Should basely murdered be
    By thy disdain!

I 'll go find out a cell,
    Where light ne'er shined:
There I 'll resolve to dwell,
    And be confined,

Until it pleaseth thee
With love to pity me,
Forsake thy cruelty,
   And prove more kind.

In that dark vault I'll call
   For bats and owls ;
The starth-owl, worst of all
   Prodigious fowls,
Shall be my mate by day ;
By night with her I'll stay,
In dark and uncouth way,
   'Mongst wandering souls.

And in that strange exile
   I'll thee arrest,
Amongst those monsters vile,
   To be my guest,
Until that thou relent,
And thy hard heart repent,
Freely to give consent
   To my request.

No cloth shall deck my skin,
   No raiment soft,
But haircloth rough and thin,
   That's comely wrought :
No bed will I lie on,
My pillow shall be a stone,
Each accent prove a groan
   Repeated oft.

No dainty dish I'll eat,
   Composed by art,
No sauces for my meat,
   Sweet, sour, or tart :

My food shall be wild-fruits,
Green herbs, and unboiled roots,
Such as poor hermits eat
      In wild deserts.

All solace, mirth, and game
      I will despise ;
A doleful mourning, then,
      With watery eyes,
Shall be my music sound,
Till all the hills resound,
And fill the valleys round
      With piteous cries.

Yet for all this I 'll not
      Abandon thee,
Nor alter in a jot
      My first decree,
But, in despite of fate,
Thy griefs to aggravate,
I 'll love thee, though thou hate,
      Until I die.

The first part of this song appeared in the *Orpheus Caledonius,*
1733, and has often been reprinted in our collections : the second
part was given from an old broadside, by Mr James Maidment,
in his *Scottish Songs and Ballads,* 1859.

ANNE BOTHWELL'S LAMENT.

Ba-loo, my boy, lie still and sleep, It grieves me
sair to hear thee weep: If thou 'lt be sil-ent, I 'll be

glad, Thy mourning makes my heart full sad. Ba - loo, my

boy, thy moth - er's joy, Thy fath - er bred me great an-

noy. Ba - loo, my dear, lie still and sleep, It grieves me

sair to hear thee weep.

Baloo, my boy, lie still and sleep,
It grieves me sair to hear thee weep:
If thou 'lt be silent, I 'll be glad,
Thy mourning makes my heart full sad.
Baloo, my boy, thy mother's joy,
Thy father bred me great annoy.
    Baloo, my dear, lie still and sleep,
    It grieves me sair to hear thee weep.

Baloo, my darling, sleep a while,
And when thou wakest, sweetly smile ;
But smile not as thy father did,
To cozen maids, may God forbid ;
For in thine eye his look I see,
The tempting look that ruined me.

When he began to court my love,
And with his sugared words to move,
His tempting face and flattering cheer,
In time to me did not appear ;

But now I see that cruel he
Cares neither for his babe nor me.

Farewell, farewell, thou falsest youth
That ever kissed a woman's mouth,
Let never any after me,
Submit unto thy courtesie :
For if they do, O cruel thou
Wilt her abuse and care not how.

I was too credulous at the first,
To yield thee all a maiden durst,
Thou swore for ever true to prove,
Thy faith unchanged, unchanged thy love ;
But quick as thought, the change is wrought,
Thy love's no more, thy promise nought.

I wish I were a maid again,
From young men's flattery I'd refrain ;
For now unto my grief I find,
They are all perjured and unkind ;
Bewitching charms bred all my harms,
Witness my babe lies in my arms.

* * * *

Baloo, my boy, weep not for me,
Whose greatest grief's for wronging thee,
Nor pity her deserved smart,
Who can blame none but her fond heart :
For too soon trusting latest finds
With fairest tongues are falsest minds.

Baloo, my boy, thy father's fled,
When he the thriftless son has played ;
Of vows and oaths forgetful he
Preferred the wars to thee and me ;
But now perhaps thy curse and mine
Makes him eat acorns with the swine.

But curse him not, perhaps now he,
Stung with remorse, is blessing thee :
Perhaps at death—for who can tell
Whether the Judge of heaven and hell,
By some proud foe, has struck the blow,
And laid the dear deceiver low.

I wish I were within the bounds,
Where he lies smothered in his wounds,
Repeating, as he pants for air,
My name, whom once he called his fair ;
No woman's yet so fiercely set,
But she 'll forgive, though not forget.

   *   *   *   *

Baloo, my boy, I 'll weep for thee ;
Too soon, alas ! thou 'lt weep for me :
Thy griefs are growing to a sum,
God grant thee patience when they come ;
Born to sustain thy mother's shame,
A hapless fate, a bastard's name.
  Baloo, my boy, lie still and sleep,
  It grieves me sair to hear thee weep.

It was the belief of Mr Charles Kirkpatrick Sharpe, founded on family traditions, supported by a passage in Father Hay's Manuscripts,[1] that this pathetic ballad was designed to embody the woes of a real sufferer by unfaithful love, a Mistress Anne Bothwell, daughter of the bishop of Orkney, who performed the Protestant nuptial ceremony over Mary in her union with the Earl of Bothwell, and afterwards made himself contemptible by appearing as evidence against her at York.[2] The lover was the lady's cousin, the Hon. Alexander Erskine, a younger son

---

[1] Advocates' Library.

[2] No Anne Bothwell appears in the meagre article on the family in Wood's *Peerage*. The lady is more likely to have been a granddaughter of the bishop.

of the seventh Earl of Marr by his second marriage. Mr Sharpe described a family portrait of this gentleman, as shewing him 'extremely handsome, with much vivacity of countenance, dark-blue eyes, a peaked beard, and moustaches.'[1] The time of the incident was early in the seventeenth century: Erskine would be a youth arrived at majority about 1620. In Broome's comedy of *The Northern Lass*, printed in 1632, there occurs a fragment of the ballad, probably as first composed:

> Peace, wayward bairn, O cease thy moan,
> Thy far more wayward daddy's gone;
> And never will recalled be
> By cries of either thee or me.
>   For should we cry
>   Until we die,
> We could not scant his cruelty.
>   Baloo, Baloo, &c.

The injured lady was thought to be avenged in the course of Providence, for Alexander Erskine, having joined the Covenanters, was one of the Earl of Haddington's party at Dunglass House, August 1640, when, by the vengeful treachery of a page, the place was blown up, and nearly all within perished.

Mr Dauney (*Ancient Melodies*, p. 286) transfers from a manuscript in the Advocates' Library, a song which bears a marked resemblance in style of thought and composition to *Anne Bothwell's Lament*:

THOU WILT NOT GO AND LEAVE ME HERE.

> Thou wilt not go and leave me here,
> O do not so, my dearest dear;
> The sun's departing clouds the sky,
> But thy departing makes me die.

---

[1] Additions to Stenhouse's *Notes on Johnson's Musical Museum*, ii. *204.

Thou canst not go, my dearest heart,
But I must quit my choicest part,
For with two hearts thou must be gone,
And I shall stay at home with none.

Meanwhile, my part shall be to mourn,
Telling the hours while thou return ;
My eyes shall be but eyes to weep,
And neither eyes to see nor sleep.

Prevent the hazard of this ill,
Go not at all, stay with me still ;
I 'll bathe thy lips with kisses then,
And look for more ease back again.

Since thou wilt needs go, well, away !
Leave, leave one heart with me to stay ;
Take mine, let thine in pain remain,
That quickly thou may come again.

Farewell, dear heart, since it must be,
That thou wilt not remain with me ;
My greatest grief it still shall be,
I love a love that loves not me.

I DO CONFESS THOU 'RT SMOOTH AND FAIR.

I do con-fess thou 'rt smooth and fair, And
I might have gone near to love thee; Had I not found the

slight - est prayer That   lips   could   speak, had power to move thee:

But   I   can   let   thee   now   a-lone, As   wor - thy   to   be

loved   by none. But   I   can   let   thee   now   a - lone, As

wor - thy   to   be   loved by none.

I do confess thou'rt smooth and fair,
    And I might have gone near to love thee ;
Had I not found the slightest prayer
    That lips could speak, had power to move thee :
But I can let thee now alone,
As worthy to be loved by none.

I do confess thou'rt sweet, yet find
    Thee such an unthrift of thy sweets,
Thy favours are but like the wind,
    That kisses everything it meets.
And since thou can with more than one,
Thou'rt worthy to be kiss'd by none.

The morning rose, that untouch'd stands,
 Arm'd with her briers, how sweetly smells !
But pluck'd and strain'd through ruder hands,
 Her sweets no longer with her dwells ;
But scent and beauty both are gone,
And leaves fall from her, one by one.

Such fate, ere long, will thee betide,
 When thou hast handled been a while ;
Like sere flowers to be thrown aside,
 And I will sigh, while some will smile,
To see thy love for more than one
Hath brought thee to be loved by none.

This song appears in Playford's *Select Ayres*, 1659, under the title of a '*Song to his Forsaken Mistress*, set to music by Henry Lawes.' Although in no respect a Scotch song, it is usually printed in Scottish collections, and represented as a composition of Sir Robert Ayton, secretary to Queen Anne, the consort of James I. The resemblance of the style of sentiment and diction to *Anne Bothwell's Lament* can scarcely be overlooked. It is also remarkable that the preceding song, *Thou wilt not go*, &c., is included in a collection of Sir Robert's poems, edited by Charles Rogers (Edin. 1844). If Ayton was the author of the two latter songs, he might also have written *Anne Bothwell's Lament*. Sir Robert Ayton, who was a Scotsman by birth, died in London in 1638, aged sixty-eight.

GUID NIGHT, AND JOY BE WI' YOU A'.

The two touching stanzas which follow, are given by Sir Walter Scott in his *Border Minstrelsy*, as those which tradition has preserved of the Good-night or Farewell of one of the Armstrongs, about to be executed for his concern in the murder of Sir John Carmichael of Edrom, warden of the Middle Marches of the Border of Scotland, an incident which happened in June

1600. The tune has long been a favourite in Scotland,[1] being usually played at the breaking up of convivial parties. It was in especial favour with Burns, who says in one of his letters: 'Ballad-making is now as completely my hobby-horse as ever fortification was Uncle Toby's; so I'll e'en canter it away till I come to the limit of my race (God grant that I may take the right side of the winning-post!), and then, cheerfully looking back on the honest folks with whom I have been happy, I shall say or sing, "Sae merry as we a' hae been!" and raising my looks to the whole of the human race, the last words of the voice of Coila shall be, "Good-night, and joy be wi' you a'!"' To this tune the bard wrote his well-known *Farewell to the Brethren of the Mason Lodge, Torbolton.*

O, this is my departing time, For here nae lang-er maun I stay; There's not a friend or foe o' mine But wish-es that I were a-way. What I hae done for lack o' wit, I nev-er, nev-er can re-ca'! I hope your're a' my friends as yet; Good-night, and joy be wi' you a'.

[1] It appears amongst Playford's Scotch Tunes, 1700.

R

O, this is my departing time,
　For here nae langer maun I stay;
There's not a friend or foe o' mine
　But wishes that I were away.

What I hae done for lack o' wit,
　I never, never can reca'!
I hope you're a' my friends as yet;
　Good-night, and joy be wi' you a'.

OLD LONG SYNE.

Burns thought the phrase, *Auld Lang Syne*, 'exceedingly expressive.' Its expressiveness in connection with the social feelings of the Scotsman—hallowing, as it were, all ordinary relations, and especially that of love—had struck the mind of a poet long before the days of the Ayrshire Ploughman. Probably as early as the reign of Charles I., its associations were conveyed in a song of many stanzas, which has been traced in broadsides prior to the close of the seventeenth century, and was gathered into James Watson's Collection, 1711. This song was as follows:

Should old ac - quaint - ance be for - got, And

nev - er thought up - on, The flames of love ex-

tin - guish - ed, And free - ly past and gone? Is

thy kind heart now grown so cold In that lov-ing breast of thine, That thou canst nev-er once re-flect On old long syne?

FIRST PART.

Should old acquaintance be forgot,
 And never thought upon,
The flames of love extinguished,
 And freely past and gone?
Is thy kind heart now grown so cold
 In that loving breast of thine,
That thou canst never once reflect
 On old long syne?

Where are thy protestations,
 Thy vows, and oaths, my dear,
Thou mad'st to me and I to thee,
 In register yet clear?
Is faith and truth so violate
 To th' immortal gods divine,
That thou canst never once reflect
 On old long syne?

Is 't Cupid's fears, or frosty cares,
 That makes thy spirits decay?
Or is 't some object of more worth
 That 's stolen thy heart away?

Or some desert makes thee neglect
   Him, so much once was thine,
That thou canst never once reflect
   On old long syne ?

Is 't worldly cares, so desperate,
   That makes thee to despair ?
Is 't that makes thee exasperate,
   And makes thee to forbear ?
If thou of that were free as I,
   Thou surely should be mine ;
If this were true, we should renew
   Kind old long syne.

But since that nothing can prevail,
   And all hope is in vain,
From these dejected eyes of mine
   Still showers of tears shall rain :
And though thou hast me now forgot,
   Yet I 'll continue thine,
And ne'er forget for to reflect
   On old long syne.

If e'er I have a house, my dear,
   That truly is call'd mine,
And can afford but country cheer,
   Or ought that 's good therein ;
Though thou were rebel to the king,
   And beat with wind and rain,
Assure thyself of welcome, love,
   For old long syne.

SECOND PART.

My soul is ravish'd with delight
   When you I think upon ;
All griefs and sorrows take the flight.
   And hastily are gone ;

The fair resemblance of your face
  So fills this breast of mine,
No fate nor force can it displace,
  For old long syne.

Since thoughts of you do banish grief,
  When I 'm from you removed ;
And if in them I find relief,
  When with sad cares I 'm moved,
How doth your presence me affect
  With ecstasies divine,
Especially when I reflect
  On old long syne.

Since thou hast robb'd me of my heart,
  By those resistless powers
Which Madam Nature doth impart
  To those fair eyes of yours,
With honour it doth not consist
  To hold a slave in pyne ;
Pray let your rigour, then, desist,
  For old long syne.

'Tis not my freedom I do crave,
  By deprecating pains ;
Sure, liberty he would not have
  Who glories in his chains :
But this I wish—the gods would move
  That noble soul of thine
To pity, if thou canst not love,
  For old long syne.

Allan Ramsay fructified upon the hint afforded by the
touching refrain of *Auld Lang Syne*, and produced a song of
more moderate length, which William Thomson gave with
music in his *Orpheus Caledonius*, and which may be found so

accompanied in Johnson's *Museum*. We cannot say much for Ramsay's verses ; but one may be selected as a favourable specimen :

> Methinks, around us, on each bough,
>   A thousand Cupids play;
> Whilst through the groves I walk with you,
>   Each object makes me gay.
> Since your return the sun and moon
>   With brighter beams do shine,
> Streams murmur soft notes while they run,
>   As they did lang syne.

Burns afterwards produced a brief and most expressive song involving the idea, most part being his own composition ; and this song, to the tune of *I Feed a Lass at Martinmas*, has found a lodgment in the hearts of Scotsmen in all parts of the earth, and must there remain while the words continue to be understood. It is appended here for the sake of the contrast with the elder song.

AULD LANG SYNE.

Should auld acquaintance be for - got, And nev - er brought to mind? Should auld ac - quaint - ance be for - got, And days o' lang syne? For auld lang syne, my dear, For

auld   lang   syne; We 'll tak'   a   cup   o'   kind - ness yet, For

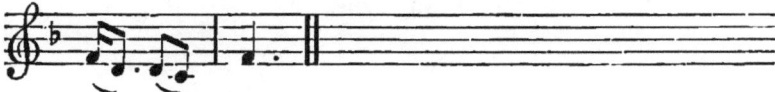

auld   lang   syne.

Should auld acquaintance be forgot,
  And never brought to mind ?
Should auld acquaintance be forgot,
  And days o' lang syne ?
    For auld lang syne, my dear,
    For auld lang syne ;
    We 'll tak' a cup o' kindness yet,
    For auld lang syne.

We twa ha'e run about the braes,
  And pu'd the gowans fine,
But we 've wandered mony a weary foot,
  Sin' auld lang syne.
    For auld lang syne, &c.

We twa ha'e paidelt in the burn,
  Frae morning sun till dine ;
But seas between us braid ha'e roar'd,
  Sin' auld lang syne.
    For auld lang syne, &c.

And here 's a hand, my trusty fere,
  And gi'e 's a hand o' thine ;
And we 'll tak' a richt-gude-willie waught,
  For auld lang syne.
    For auld lang syne, &c.

And surely ye'll be your pint-stoup,
    And surely I'll be mine ;
And we'll tak' a cup o' kindness yet,
    For auld lang syne.
        For auld lang syne, &c.

O WALY, WALY.

The song now to be introduced is one of the most beautiful and affecting in the whole range of the national minstrelsy. There appears no room to doubt that it forms part of a ballad composed upon an unhappy incident in the history of the great family of Douglas. James the second marquis, of the time of Charles II., was no very competent supporter of the credit and dignity of the line. There seems to have been an inclination on his part at one time to wed the daughter of 'Widow Jack, a taverner at Perth ;' but he subsequently (September 1670) took to wife the Lady Barbara Erskine, daughter of the ninth Earl of Marr. Owing, there can be little doubt, to his lordship's unworthy conduct, the alliance was productive of misery to the lady. She had even to bewail that her own honour was brought into question, chiefly, it would appear, through the influence of a chamberlain over her husband's mind. At length a separation with a suitable provision left her in the worst kind of widowhood, after she had brought the marquis one son (subsequently first commander of the Cameronian regiment, and who fell at the battle of Steenkirk). The verses are the lament of the unfortunate marchioness after the separation, and seems to have formed part of a ballad reciting her unfortunate case, and which has latterly been recovered.

O waly, waly up the bank,[1]
  And waly, waly down the brae,
And waly, waly yon burn-side,
  Where I and my love wont to gae !
I lean'd my back unto an aik,
  I thoucht it was a trusty tree ;
But first it bow'd, and syne it brak :
  Sae my true love did lichtly me.

[1] Waly, a Scottish exclamation of distress.

O waly, waly, but love be bonnie
    A little time while it is new ;
But when it 's auld it waxes cauld,
    And fades away like the morning dew.
O wherefore should I busk[1] my heid,
    Or wherefore should I kame my hair ?
For my true love has me forsook,
    And says he 'll never love me mair.

Now Arthur's Seat shall be my bed,
    The sheets shall ne'er be press'd by me,
St Anton's Well[2] shall be my drink,
    Since my true love has forsaken me.
Martinmas wind, when wilt thou blaw,
    And shake the green leaves aff the tree ?
O, gentle death, when wilt thou come ?
    For of my life I am wearie ?

'Tis not the frost that freezes fell,
    Nor blawing snaw's inclemencie ;
'Tis not sic cauld that makes me cry :
    But my love's heart 's grown cauld to me.
When we came in by Glasgow toun,
    We were a comely sicht to see ;
My love was clad in the black velvet,
    And I mysel in cramasie.

But had I wist, before I kissed,
    That love had been sae ill to win,
I 'd lock'd my heart in a case of gold,
    And pinn'd it wi' a siller pin.

[1] Dress, arrange.

[2] Arthur's Seat is a hill near Edinburgh, forming part of the chase which surrounds the royal palace of Holyrood. St Anton's, or St Anthony's Well, is a small crystal spring proceeding from the side of Arthur's Seat, and taking its name from a hermitage half-way up the hill, which it formerly supplied with water.

Oh, oh ! if my young babe were born,
    And set upon the nurse's knee,
And I mysel were dead and gane,
    And the green grass growing over me ![1]

BLINK OVER THE BURN, SWEET BETTY.

Blink ov - er the burn, sweet Bet - ty, It
is a cauld win - ter night; It
rains, it hails, and it thunders, The
moon she gi'es nae light: It's a' for the
sake o' sweet Betty, That ev - er I tint my

[1] This last line is substituted from an old nurse's copy, for one less delicate and pathetic, which has always hitherto been printed. The song appeared first in the *Tea-table Miscellany*, marked with the signature Z, indicating that the editor did not know its age.

way; O las - sie [gie me some shel - ter] Un-

til it be break o' day.

> Blink over the burn, sweet Betty,
>   It is a cauld winter night ;
> It rains, it hails, and it thunders,
>   The moon she gi'es nae light :
> It 's a' for the sake o' sweet Betty,
>   That ever I tint my way ;
> O lassie [gie me some shelter]
>   Until it be break o' day.

> O Betty shall bake my bread,
>   And Betty shall brew my ale,
> And Betty shall be my love,
>   When I come over the dale ;
> Blink over the burn, sweet Betty,
>   Blink over the burn to me ;
> And while I ha'e life, my dear lassie,
>   My ain sweet Betty thou's be.

There have been songs with some such phrase as ' Blink over the burn, sweet Betty,' for their groundwork, from comparatively an early period. Dr Rimbault traces the expression as far back as the reign of Henry VIII., soon after which it was moralised into a religious parody, beginning :

> Come over the burn, Bessy, thou pretty little Bessy,
>   Come over the burn, Bessy, to me ;
> The burn is this world blind, and Bessy is mankind, &c.

There was also a political parody, in which England hailed the advent of Elizabeth to the throne :

I am thy lover fair, hath chose thee to mine heir,
    And my name is merry England ;
Therefore come away, and make no more delay,
    Sweet Bessy, give me thy hand.

At what time the idea made its way into Scotland we cannot tell ; but the *Orpheus Caledonius* gives the air, with more than one set of verses. On this occasion, we pass over these refined but dull compositions, and give an old rustic Scotch song in connection with the melody.[1]

In Ritson's *Scottish Songs* (1794) appears the following stanza for *Blink over the Burn, sweet Betty :*

In simmer I mawed my meadow,
    In harvest I shure my corn,
In winter I married a widow,
    I wish I was free the morn.
    Blink over the burn, sweet Betty,
    Blink over the burn to me ;
    O it is a thousand pities
    But I was a widow for thee !

SAW YE MY FATHER.

The following romantic song occurs in Herd's Collection, 1776; but an English version of it is traced by Mr William Chapell[2] to a work called the *Songster's Companion*, of a few years' earlier date, and the air appears in Thompson's *Collection of Country Dances*, 1775. Mr Chapell evidently considers it as an English song, which has been transplanted in a Scotch form to the north of the Tweed. It is remarkable for relating an adventure of nocturnal courtship in a manner free of vulgarity ; which is not a circumstance very characteristic of Scottish song literature. Still the nativity of the song may fairly be held as matter of doubt.

[1] This old song has been preserved by Mr Stenhouse in his *Notes on Johnson's Museum,* p. 54.

[2] See Chapell's *Music of the Olden Time,* where a copy of the English version is printed.

'O saw ye my fath-er, or saw ye my moth-er, Or saw ye my true love John?' 'I saw not your fath-er, I saw not your mother, But I saw your true love John.'

'O saw ye my father, or saw ye my mother,
    Or saw ye my true love John?'
'I saw not your father, I saw not your mother,
    But I saw your true love John.'

'It's now ten at night, and the stars gi'e nae light,
    And the bells they ring ding dong;
He's met with some delay, that causeth him to stay;
    But he will be here ere long.'

The surly auld carle did naething but snarl,
    And Johnie's face it grew red;
Yet, though he often sighed, he ne'er a word replied,
    Till all were asleep in bed.

Up Johnie rose, and to the door he goes,
    And gently tirled at the pin.
The lassie, taking tent, unto the door she went,
    And she opened and let him in.

'And are ye come at last, and do I hold ye fast ?
   And is my Johnie true ?'
'I have nae time to tell, but sae lang's I like mysel,
   Sae lang sall I love you.'

'Flee up, flee up, my bonnie gray cock,
   And craw whan it is day :
Your neck shall be like the bonnie beaten gowd,
   And your wings of the silver gray.'

The cock proved fause, and untrue he was ;
   For he crew an hour ower sune.
The lassie thought it day, when she sent her love away,
   And it was but a blink o' the mune.

LEADER HAUGHS AND YARROW.

This is a song which may be safely set down to the end of
the seventeenth century, as a broadside copy of it, which from
some appearances is of that date, occurs in the Roxburghe Collection in the British Museum. It seems to have been designed
to embody a rustic bard's view of the chief places along the
valley of the Leader, in Berwickshire, with complimentary
references to some of them, particularly to Thirlstain Castle,
the seat of the Earls of Lauderdale, which, he says,

> —— stands as sweet on Leader side
> As Newark does on Yarrow.

There is some fancy in introducing the lapwing, the lark, and
the hare, as vehicles for the panegyrics of the poet. Notwithstanding, too, a certain grammatical roughness, most Scotsmen
will be sensible of a charm in the flow of the verses, which, in
their structure and euphony, and even in some of the local
names, as Burnmill, and the constant refrain of Yarrow, have
evidently acted as an inspiration and a model to the bard of
Rydal Mount, in his exquisite series of poems beginning with
Yarrow Unvisited. Regarding the authorship, the song itself

leaves us not in doubt, as it introduces him under the name of Minstrel Burne—a curious coincidence with the name of the greatest of our national bards. The Burne of Leader Haughs may be presumed from the term 'Minstrel,' and the feeling he expresses for the gentry of the district, to have been one who made his bread by wandering from house to house with a fiddle—

Companion of his lonely way—

wherewith to cheer the firesides at which he was entertained. This, indeed, is made more clear to us by the Roxburghe copy of the song, at the end of which is appended:

' The words of Burne the Violer,'

followed by three verses not heretofore printed. I was informed by an aged person at Earlstoun in 1826, that there used to be a portrait of Minstrel Burne in Thirlstain Castle, representing him as ' a douce auld man, leading a cow by a straw-rope.'

Pepys, in his Diary, under July 1666, has the following : 'To my Lord Lauderdale's house to speak with him, and find him and his lady, and some Scotch people, at supper. But at supper there played one of their servants upon the violin some Scotch tunes only ; several, and the best of their country, as they seem to esteem them, by their praising and admiring them ; but, Lord ! the strangest ayre that ever I heard in my life, and all of one cast.' Could this performer be Minstrel Burne ?

When Phœbus bright the azure skies With golden rays en-

light'neth, He makes all na - ture's beau - ties rise, Herbs,

trees, and flowers he quick'neth: A - mongst all those he

makes his choice, And with de - light goes thor - ow, With

ra - diant beams, the sil - ver streams Of

Lead - er Haughs and Yar - row.

When Phœbus bright the azure skies
    With golden rays enlight'neth,
He makes all nature's beauties rise,
    Herbs, trees, and flowers he quick'neth:
Amongst all those he makes his choice,
    And with delight goes thorow,
With radiant beams, the silver streams
    Of Leader Haughs and Yarrow.

When Aries the day and night
    In equal length divideth,
And frosty Saturn takes his flight,
    Nae langer he abideth;
Then Flora queen, with mantle green,
    Casts aff her former sorrow,
And vows to dwell with Ceres' sel,
    In Leader Haughs and Yarrow.

Pan, playing on his aiten-reed,
    And shepherds, him attending,
Do here resort, their flocks to feed,
    The hills and haughs commending;

s

With cur and kent, upon the bent,
   Sing to the sun, Good-morrow,
And swear nae fields mair pleasures yield,
   Than Leader Haughs and Yarrow.

A house there stands on Leader-side,
   Surmounting my descriving,
With rooms sae rare, and windows fair,[1]
   Like Daedalus' contriving :
Men passing by do aften cry,
   In sooth it hath no marrow ;
It stands as fair on Leader-side
   As Newark does on Yarrow.

A mile below, who lists to ride,
   Will hear the mavis singing ;
Into St Leonard's banks she bides,
   Sweet birks her head owerhinging.
The lint-white loud, and Progne proud,
   With tuneful throats and narrow,
Into St Leonard's banks they sing,
   As sweetly as in Yarrow.

The lapwing lilteth ower the lea,
   With nimble wing she sporteth ;
But vows she 'll flee far from the tree
   Where Philomel resorteth :
By break of day the lark can say,
   I 'll bid you a good-morrow ;
I 'll stretch my wing, and, mounting, sing
   O'er Leader Haughs and Yarrow.

[1] Variation in Roxburghe Collection :
     With case rooms rair and windows fair.

Park, Wanton-wa's, and Wooden-cleuch,
    The East and Wester Mainses,
The wood of Lauder's fair eneuch,
    The corns are good in the Blainslies : [1]
There aits are fine, and sald by kind,
    That if ye search all thorough
Mearns, Buchan, Marr, nane better are
    Than Leader Haughs and Yarrow.

In Burn-mill-bog and Whitslaid Shaws,
    The fearful hare she haunteth ;
Brig-haugh and Braidwoodshiel she knaws,
    And Chapel-wood frequenteth :
Yet, when she irks, to Kaidslie Birks,
    She rins, and sighs for sorrow,
That she should leave sweet Leader Haughs,
    And cannot win to Yarrow

What sweeter music wad ye hear,
    Than hounds and beagles crying ?
The started hare rins hard with fear,
    Upon her speed relying :
But yet her strength it fails at length ;
    Nae bielding can she borrow,
In Sorrowless-fields, Clackmae, or Hags ;
    And sighs to be in Yarrow.

[1] There used to be two sorts of oats in Scotland—the *dour*, or late seed, and the early seed. 'The early were of two sorts : one from *Blainslie*, in Lauderdale, and the other from the *Fans*, in the adjacent district of the Merse. Once in every four or five years, most of the Lothian farmers got a boll or two of them from one or other of these two places, from which they raised on their best lands as much seed as in two or three years at furthest supplied their whole farm.'—Robertson's *Rural Recollections*. 'Three villages called Blainslies, remarkable for their fine oats, which are carried to the most parts of the kingdom, and some of them to the south of London : they are regarded not so much for their whiteness, as for their earliness and increase ; they are commonly sold three or four shillings above the ordinary rate of the market.'— Rev. A. Milne's *Account of Melrose Parish*, 1743.

For Rockwood, Ringwood, Spotty, Shag,
 With sight and scent pursue her ;
Till, ah, her pith begins to flag ;
 Nae cunning can rescue her :
Ower dub and dyke, ower sheuch and syke,
 She 'll rin the fields all thorough,
Till, fail'd, she fa's in Leader Haughs,
 And bids fareweel to Yarrow.

Sing Erslington [1] and Cowdenknowes,
 Where Humes had ance commanding ;
And Drygrange, with the milk-white yowes,
 'Twixt Tweed and Leader standing :
The bird that flees through Redpath trees
 And Gladswood banks ilk morrow,
May chant and sing sweet Leader Haughs
 And bonnie howms of Yarrow.

But Minstrel Burne can not assuage
 His grief, while life endureth,
To see the changes of this age,
 Which fleeting time procureth :
For mony a place stands in hard case,
 Where blithe folk ken'd nae sorrow,
With Humes that dwelt on Leader-side,
 And Scotts that dwelt on Yarrow.

The following are the three additional verses as given in the Roxburghe Collection :

THE WORDS OF BURNE THE VIOLER.

What, shall my viol silent be,
 Or leave her wonted scriding ?
But choise some sadder elegie,
 Not sports and mirds deriding.

---

[1] Earlstoun, formerly spelled Ercildoun.

It must be fain with lower strain,
  Than it was wont before, O,
To sound the praise of Leader Haughs
  And the bonnie banks of Yarrow.

But floods has overflown the banks,
  The greenish haughs disgracing,
And trees in woods grows thin in ranks,
  About the fields defacing.
For waters waxes, woods do waind ;
  More, if I could for sorrow,
In rural verse I could rehearse
  Of Leader Haughs and Yarrow.

But sighs and sobs o'ersets my breath,
  Sore saltish tears forth sending,
All things sublunar here on earth
  Are subject to an ending.
So must my song, though somewhat long,
  Yet late at even and morrow
I'll sigh and sing sweet Leader Haughs
  And the bonnie banks of Yarrow.
                    Hic terminus haeret.

It may be remarked that a line in these verses serves to
localise the poet as connected with Lauderdale, Thomas the
Rhymer of Earlstoun having long before said :

  The waters shall wax, and the woods shall wane,
  But the bannock'll be ne'er the braider.

OMNIA VINCIT AMOR.

As I went forth to view the spring, Which Flora had a-
dorn-èd In gorgeous rai-ment, eve-ry-thing A
win-ter's rage out-scorn-èd; I cast mine eye, and
did es-py A youth that made great clamour, And,
draw-ing nigh, I heard him cry, Ah, Om-ni-a vin-cit
a - mor!

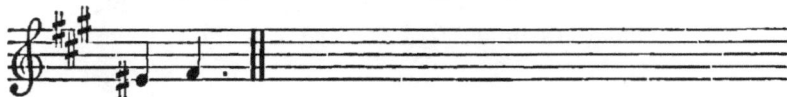

As I went forth to view the spring,
  Which Flora had adornèd
In gorgeous raiment, everything
  A winter's rage outscornèd ;

I cast mine eye, and did espy
  A youth that made great clamour,
And, drawing nigh, I heard him cry,
  Ah, *Omnia vincit amor !*

Upon his breast he lay along,
  Hard by a murmuring river,
And mournfully his doleful song
  With sighs he did deliver :
' On Jeanie's face lies comely grace,
  Her locks that shine like lammer,
With burning rays have cut my days—
  For *Omnia vincit amor !*

' Her glancy een, like comet's sheen,
  The morning sun outshining,
Have caught my heart in Cupid's net,
  And made me die with pining.
Durst I complain, Nature's to blame
  So curiously to frame her,
Whose beauties rare make me, with care,
  Cry, *Omnia vincit amor !*

' Ye crystal streams that swiftly glide,
  Be partners of my mourning ;
Ye fragrant fields and meadows wide,
  Condemn her for her scorning.
Let every tree a witness be
  How justly I may blame her ;
Ye chanting birds, note these my words,
  Ah ! *Omnia vincit amor !*

' Had she been kind as she was fair,
  She long had been admired,
And been adored for virtues rare,
  Who 'f life now makes me tired.'

This said, his breath began to fail,
　　He could not speak, but stammer ;
He sighed full sore, and said no more
　　But, *Omnia vincit amor !*

When I observed him near to death,
　　I ran in haste to save him,
But quickly he resigned his breath,
　　So deep the wound love gave him ;
Now, for her sake, this vow I'll make,
　　My tongue shall aye defame her ;
While on his hearse I'll write this verse,
　　Ah, *Omnia vincit amor !*

Straight I considered in my mind,
　　Upon the matter rightly,
And found, though Cupid he be blind,
　　He proves in pith most mighty.
For warlike Mars and thundering Jove,
　　And Vulcan with his hammer,
Did ever prove the slaves of love,
　　For *Omnia vincit amor !*

Hence we may see th' effects of love,
　　Which gods and men keep under,
That nothing can his bonds remove,
　　Or torments break asunder ;
Nor wise nor fool need go to school,
　　To learn this from his grammar ;
His heart's the book where he's to look
　　For *Omnia vincit amor !*

The idea of a song with *Omnia vincit amor* for its burden is as
old at least as the reign of Charles I., for such is the title of one
of the tunes in the Skene Manuscript. The present composition
cannot be traced further back than to a broadside apparently of
King William's time, which is inserted in the Roxburghe

Collection (British Museum). Ramsay gave it a place in his *Tea-table Miscellany*, with the signature Q., to denote that it was an old song with alterations. It was presented, with its tune, in Johnson's *Museum*—not, however, the tune called *Omnia Vincit Amor* in the Skene Manuscript.

The style of the verse, and even of the grammar and syntax, as well as the introduction of heathen deities, bring us strongly in remembrance of the preceding song, *Leader Haughs and Yarrow*. Most probably, therefore, *Omnia Vincit Amor* is another of Minstrel Burne's productions.

THE BIRKS OF ABERGELDY.

Bon - nie las - sie, will ye go,

Will ye go, will ye go,

Bon - nie las - sie, will ye go To the

Birks of A - ber - gel - dy? O

ye shall get a gown o' silk, A

gown   o'   silk,   a   gown   o'   silk;   O

ye   shall   get   a   gown   o'   silk,   And   a

coat   o'   cal - i - man - co.

Bon - nie   las - sie,   will   ye   go,

Will   ye   go,   will   ye   go,

Bon - nie   las - sie,   will   ye   go   To   the

Birks   of   A - ber - gel - dy?

Bonnie lassie, will ye go,
Will ye go, will ye go,
Bonnie lassie, will ye go
    To the Birks of Abergeldy?

O ye shall get a gown o' silk,
A gown o' silk, a gown o' silk ;
O ye shall get a gown o' silk,
    And a coat o' calimanco.

Na, kind sir, I darena gang,
I darena gang, I darena gang ;
Na, kind sir, I darena gang,
    For my minnie she 'll be angry.

Sair, sair wad she flyte,
Wad she flyte, wad she flyte,
Sair, sair wad she flyte,
    And sair wad she bang me.

This is one of the simple old songs of Scotland, conveying little meaning, but yet, with the aid of a good melody, more facile to sing than many superior compositions. It is localised to Aberdeenshire, for Abergeldy is a beautiful district on Deeside, once the property of a gentleman named Gordon, but now that of her Majesty Queen Victoria, being adjacent to the royal residence of Balmoral. The birch was long ago the natural and abundant wood of the district, and must have formed an attractive scene for the imagination of the poetical lover ; but it has for many years been superseded by oak and other more profitable timber. An air styled *The Birks of Abergeldie* appears in Playford's Collection, 1700.

The rustic simplicity of the Birks, the gown o' silk, and coat o' calimanco, proved unsatisfactory to the more refined lovers of Scottish song in the last century, and accordingly we find in Herd, under the title of the air *Birks of Abergeldy*, a long and rather common-place ditty, in which a gentleman bewails the disappointments incidental to the married state—as follows, for example :

Alack a day, what will I do,
What will I do, what will I do ?
Alack a day, what will I do,
   The honey month is done, jo !
My glittering gold is all turned dross,
And siller scarcely will be brass,
I 've nothing but a bonnie lass,
   And she 's quite out of tune, jo !

Finally, came Burns, with his beautiful song in compliment
to a place of nearly the same name in a different part of the
Highlands :

THE BIRKS OF ABERFELDY.

Bonnie lassie, will ye go,
Will ye go, will ye go,
Bonnie lassie, will ye go,
   To the Birks of Aberfeldy ?

Now simmer blinks on flowery braes,
And o'er the crystal streamlet plays ;
Come, let us spend the lichtsome days
   In the Birks of Aberfeldy.
     Bonnie lassie, &c.

While o'er their head the hazels hing,
The little birdies blithely sing,
Or lichtly flit on wanton wing,
   In the Birks of Aberfeldy.

The braes ascend like lofty wa's,
The foamin' stream deep-roaring fa's,
O'erhung wi' fragrant spreadin' shaws,
   The Birks of Aberfeldy.

The hoary cliffs are crown'd wi' flow'rs,
White ower the lin the burnie pours,
And, risin', weets wi' misty show'rs
    The Birks of Aberfeldy.

Let fortune's gifts at random flee,
They ne'er shall draw a wish frae me,
Supremely bless'd wi' love and thee,
    In the Birks of Aberfeldy.

JOHN HAY'S BONNIE LASSIE.

The song which follows appeared in Ramsay's *Tea-table
Miscellany* and in the *Orpheus Caledonius*, and has usually been
included in subsequent collections.   Burns learned somewhere,
from the voice of tradition, that the John Hay in question was
no less a person than the first Marquis of Tweeddale, and the
bonnie lassie his lordship's daughter Margaret, who became
Countess of Roxburghe, and died at Broomlands, near Kelso,
January 23, 1753, after a widowhood of seventy-two years.[1]   The
present editor, in the course of his wanderings in Scotland many
years ago, heard the same story, with the addition that the song
was the composition of a working-joiner, who had vainly lifted
his poetical fancy to the level of a marquis's daughter.   Both
statements, however, must be taken with reservation.   The
locality assumed 'by smooth-winding Tay' does not suit a
connection with the family of Tweeddale.

[1] Her ladyship's husband, Robert, Earl of Roxburghe was lost in the
Gloucester frigate, on Yarmouth Sands, in coming down to Scotland with
the Duke of York, May 7, 1682.

By smooth winding Tay a swain was re-

clin - ing, Aft cried he, Oh, hey! maun I still live

pin - ing My - sel thus a - way, And daur - na dis-

cov - er To my bon - nie Hay, that I am her

lov - er! Nae mair it will hide; the flame waxes

stranger; If she's not my bride, my days are nae

lang - er: Then I'll take a heart, and try at a

ven - ture; May · be, ere we part, my

vows may con - tent her.

By smooth-winding Tay a swain was reclining,
Aft cried he, Oh, hey ! maun I still live pining
Mysel thus away, and daurna discover
To my bonnie Hay, that I am her lover !

Nae mair it will hide ; the flame waxes stranger ;
If she's not my bride, my days are nae langer :
Then I 'll take a heart, and try at a venture ;
May be, ere we part, my vows may content her.

She's fresh as the spring, and sweet as Aurora,
When birds mount and sing, bidding day a good-morrow :
The sward of the mead, enamell'd with daisies,
Looks wither'd and dead, when twined of her graces.

But if she appear where verdure invite her,
The fountains run clear, and the flowers smell the sweeter.
'Tis heaven to be by, when her wit is a-flowing :
Her smiles and bright eyes set my spirits a-glowing.

The mair that I gaze, the deeper I'm wounded ;
Struck dumb with amaze, my mind is confounded :
I'm all in a fire, dear maid, to caress ye ;
For a' my desire is John Hay's bonnie lassie.

WITHIN A MILE OF EDINBURGH.

The following song is a noted example of those composed by English wits in imitation of *the Scots Manner*, and which were, with little discrimination, accepted as Scots songs in Scotland itself. It is wholly of English origin; the verses by Thomas D'Urfey, and the air by Mr James Hook, elder brother of the celebrated wit Theodore Hook. The verses (of which the present is a slightly altered copy) first appeared in the collection of songs called *Wit and Mirth,* 1698.

'Twas with - in a mile of Ed - in - bu-rgh town, In the

ro - sy time of the year; Sweet flowers bloom'd, and the

grass was down, And each shep - herd woo'd his dear.

Bonnie Jockey, blithe and gay, Kiss'd sweet Jen-ny, making hay, The

lassie blush'd, and frowning cried, 'No, no, it will not do; I

can - not, can - not, won - not, won - not, man - not   buckle   to.'

'Twas within a mile of Edinburgh town,
   In the rosy time of the year ;
Sweet flowers bloom'd, and the grass was down,
   And each shepherd woo'd his dear.
      Bonnie Jockey, blithe and gay,
      Kiss'd sweet Jenny, making hay,
The lassie blush'd, and frowning cried, 'No, no, it will not do ;
I cannot, cannot, wonnot, wonnot, mannot buckle to.'

Jockey was a wag that never would wed,
   Though long he had followed the lass ;
Contented she earned and ate her brown bread,
   And merrily turn'd up the grass.
      Bonnie Jockey, blithe and free,
      Won her heart right merrily :
Yet still she blush'd, and frowning cried, 'No, no, it will not do ;
I cannot, cannot, wonnot, wonnot, mannot buckle to.'

But when he vow'd he would make her his bride,
   Though his flocks and herds were not few,
She gave him her hand, and a kiss beside,
   And vow'd she 'd for ever be true.
      Bonnie Jockey, blithe and free,
      Won her heart right merrily :
At church she no more frowning cried, 'No, no, it will not do ;
I cannot, cannot, wonnot, wonnot, mannot buckle to.'

T

KATHERINE OGIE.

As an Anglo-Scottish production, this may be considered as a twin-piece with *Within a Mile of Edinburgh*, although we only have a rude sketch of it in D'Urfey's Collection.[1] The present version, in which the English origin is apparently obscured by its having passed through a Scottish alembic, is from the *Tea-table Miscellany*. The air, a very beautiful one, has been brought conspicuously forward, in consequence of Burns having composed to it his exquisite elegiac song of *Highland Mary*.

As walk - ing forth to view the plain, Up-

on a morn - ing ear - ly, While May's sweet scent did

cheer my brain, From flowers which grow so rare - ly,

[1] Of the original there presented, the opening verse, in all its peculiarities of spelling, may be given as a curiosity :

As I cam down by Hay Land town,
　　There was lasses many
Sat in a rank, on either bank,
　　And ane more gay than any ;
Ise leekt about for ane kind face,
　　And Ise spy'd *Willy Scroggy* ;
Ise speir'd of him what was her name,
　　And he caw'd her *Kathern Loggy*.

I chanced to meet a pretty maid; She

shined tho' it was fog-gy; I ask'd her name: Sweet

sir, she said, My name is Kath'-rine Og-ie.

As walking forth to view the plain,
   Upon a morning early,
While May's sweet scent did cheer my brain,
   From flowers which grow so rarely,
I chanced to meet a pretty maid ;
   She shined, though it was foggy ;
I ask'd her name : sweet sir, she said,
   My name is Katherine Ogie.

I stood awhile, and did admire,
   To see a nymph so stately ;
So brisk an air there did appear,
   In a country maid so neatly:
Such natural sweetness she display'd,
   Like a lilie in a bogie ;
Diana's self was ne'er array'd
   Like this same Katherine Ogie.

Thou flower of females, beauty's queen,
   Who sees thee, sure must prize thee ;
Though thou art drest in robes but mean,
   Yet these cannot disguise thee :

Thy handsome air, and graceful look,
　　Far excels any clownish rogie ;
Thou art a match for lord or duke,
　　My charming Katherine Ogie.

O were I but some shepherd swain !
　　To feed my flock beside thee,
At boughting-time to leave the plain,
　　In milking to abide thee ;
I'd think myself a happier man,
　　With Kate, my club, and dogie,
Than he that hugs his thousands ten,
　　Had I but Katherine Ogie.

Then I'd despise the imperial throne,
　　And statesmen's dangerous stations :
I'd be no king, I'd wear no crown,
　　I'd smile at conquering nations :
Might I caress, and still possess
　　This lass, of whom I'm vogie ;
For these are toys, and still look less.
　　Compared with Katherine Ogie.

But I fear the gods have not decreed
　　For me so fine a creature,
Whose beauty rare makes her exceed
　　All other works in nature.
Clouds of despair surround my love,
　　That are both dark and fogie ;
Pity my case, ye powers above,
　　Else I die for Katherine Ogie.

ANNIE LAURIE.

There is a song long popular in the south of Scotland, though only recently introduced into print, of which the following is an authentic copy :

Max - wel - ton banks are bon - nie, Where ear - ly fa's the dew; Where me and An - nie Lau - rie Made up the pro - mise true; Made up the pro - mise true, And ne'er for - get will I; And for bon - nie An - nie Lau - rie I 'll lay me doun and die.

Maxwelton banks are bonnie,
Where early fa's the dew ;
Where me and Annie Laurie
Made up the promise true ;
Made up the promise true,
And ne'er forget will I ;
And for bonnie Annie Laurie
I 'll lay me doun and die.

> She's backit like the peacock ;
> She's breistit like the swan ;
> She's jimp about the middle ;
> Her waist ye weel micht span :
> Her waist ye weel micht span,
> And she has a rolling eye ;
> And for bonnie Annie Laurie
> I'll lay me doun and die.

Maxwelton is the mansion of a family of rank, beautifully situated on the side of the valley of the Cairn, in Dumfriesshire. It is believed that these verses were composed by a Mr Douglas of Fingland upon Anne, one of the four daughters of Sir Robert Laurie, first baronet of Maxwelton—so created in 1685. The lady, it appears, was not destined to be won by her poetical lover, but became the wife of Mr Fergusson of Craigdarroch.[1]

A living lady of rank has produced a song on the basis of this original one, and which has attained a wide popularity.[2]

WERE NA MY HEART LICHT I WAD DEE.

Towards the end of the seventeenth century, the upper and more educated classes seem to have become sensible of the beauty of the national melodies, and probably saw that in many instances the substitution of pure for licentious verses was desirable. Now, accordingly, we find the beginning of a series of song-writers of aristocratic grade, the first being Lady Grizel Baillie, a lady who may almost be said to have a place in our national history on other accounts. She was the daughter of the celebrated Patrick Hume, whose destiny it was to attain the

----

[1] See a *Ballad Book*, Edinburgh, 1824 (being a small collection by Mr Charles Kirkpatrick Sharpe), where the song was first printed.

[2] This, with the music, will be found in Wood's *Songs of Scotland*, iii. 24.

rank of an earldom (Marchmont) and the highest state employments under the regime of King William, but who, in the
preceding reign, had been a proscribed fugitive and an exile.
At a dark crisis, when compelled to seek concealment for weeks
in the charnel-house of his family under Polwarth Church, his
heroic daughter Grizel braved all dangers and supplied him with
food. The narration of the affair, given by her daughter Lady
Murray of Stanhope, is one of the most interesting in the
language.

Lady Grizel, who, in the happier days of her family, became
the wife of Mr Baillie of Jerviswood (son of another sufferer
under the House of Stuart), addicted herself to verse-making
from an early age. Her daughter possessed a manuscript volume,
which she had used in Holland, while residing there with her
father, for jotting down snatches of song which she had composed.
But of all her productions only two have as yet seen the light.
The most important is a pathetic pastoral strain, which was
published in her ladyship's lifetime in the *Orpheus Caledonius.*
Lady Grizel died in 1746, aged eighty-one.

There was anes a may, and she loo'd na men: She
bigg - it her bon - nie bouir doun i' yon glen; But
now she cries, Dule and a well - a - day! Come
doun the green gate, and come here a - way.

There was anes a may, and she loo'd na men :
She biggit her bonnie bouir doun i' yon glen ;
But now she cries, Dule and a well-a-day !
Come doun the green gate, and come here away.

When bonnie young Johnie cam over the sea,
He said he saw naething sae bonnie as me ;
He hecht me baith rings and monie braw things ;
And were na my heart licht I wad dee.

He had a wee titty that loo'd na me,
Because I was twice as bonnie as she ;
She raised such a pother 'twixt him and his mother,
That were na my heart licht I wad dee.

The day it was set, and the bridal to be :
The wife took a dwam, and lay down to dee.
She main'd, and she graned, out o' dolour and pain,
Till he vow'd that he ne'er wad see me again.

His kin was for ane of a higher degree,
Said, what had he to do wi' the like of me ?
Albeit I was bonnie, I was na for Johnie :
And were na my heart licht I wad dee.

They said I had neither cow nor calf,
Nor dribbles o' drink rins through the draff,
Nor pickles o' meal rins through the mill-e'e ;
And were na my heart licht I wad dee.

His titty she was baith wylie and slee,
She spied me as I cam ower the lea ;
And then she ran in, and made a loud din ;
Believe your ain een an ye trow na me.

His bonnet stood aye fou round on his brow ;
His auld ane look'd aye as well as some's new ;
But now he lets 't wear ony gate it will hing,
And casts himself dowie upon the corn-bing.

And now he gaes drooping about the dykes,
And a' he dow do is to hund the tykes :
The live-lang nicht he ne'er steeks his e'e ;
And were na my heart licht I wad dee.

Were I young for thee as I hae been,
We should ha' been gallopin' down on yon green,
And linkin' it on the lilie-white lea ;
And wow gin I were but young for thee ![1]

THE EWE-BUCHTIN'S BONNIE.

The only other song of Lady Grizel Baillie which has been
brought before the world is a fragment, but one breathing
strongly of the soft and tender style of the author. The late
Mr Charles Kirkpatrick Sharpe published it in a sheet, along
with an air which his father had composed for it, at a
surprisingly early period of life.[2]

O, the ewe-buchtin's bonnie, baith e'ening and morn,
When our blithe shepherds play on the bog-reed and horn ;
While we 're milking, they 're lilting, baith pleasant and clear—
But my heart's like to break when I think on my dear.

O the shepherds take pleasure to blow on the horn,
To raise up their flocks o' sheep soon i' the morn ;
On the bonnie green banks they feed pleasant and free,
But, alas, my dear heart, all my sighing 's for thee !

[1] From the *Tea-table Miscellany*, 1724.   [2] For the air, see p. 455.

THE YELLOW-HAIRED LADDIE.

The yel - low haired lad - die sat on yon burn brae, Cries, Milk the ewes, lass - ie, let nane o' them gae; And aye she milk - ed and aye she sang, The yel - low haired lad - die shall be my guid - man.

The yellow-haired laddie sat on yon burn brae,
Cries, Milk the ewes, lassie, let nane o' them gae ;
And aye she milked and aye she sang,
The yellow-haired laddie shall be my guidman.
     And aye she milked, &c.

The weather is cauld, and my claithing is thin,
The ewes are new clipped, they winna bught in ;
They winna bught in, although I should die,
O yellow-haired laddie, be kind unto me.
     They winna bught in, &c.

The guidwife cries but the house, ' Jenny, come ben,
The cheese is to mak, and the butter's to kirn.'
Though butter and cheese and a' should sour,
I 'll crack wi' my love for another half-hour—
   Ae half-hour, and we 'll e'en mak it three,
   For the yellow-haired laddie my husband shall be.

This appears in the *Tea-table Miscellany* (1724), as the original
simple rustic song to the beautiful melody of *The Yellow-Haired
Laddie*. The air by itself had been published in Mrs Crockat's
Music Book, in 1709. Ramsay composed a song to the air,
beginning—

   ' In April when primroses paint the sweet plain,'

which is far from being devoid of merit : he also composed for it
a song in *The Gentle Shepherd*—

   ' When first my dear laddie gaed to the green hill '—

a not less pleasing song. Yet it may be said that the old country
ditty, which milkmaids used to sing, and which perhaps a
milkmaid composed, has a superior charm to all that has been
attempted to the same strain.

THE YELLOW-HAIRED LADDIE.

(RAMSAY'S VERSION).

In April, when primroses paint the sweet plain,
And summer approaching rejoiceth the swain,
The yellow-haired laddie would oftentimes go
To woods and deep glens where the hawthorn-trees grow.

There, under the shade of an old sacred thorn,
With freedom he sung his loves, evening and morn :
He sung with so soft and enchanting a sound,
That sylvans and fairies, unseen, danced around.

The shepherd thus sung : 'Though young Maddie be fair,
Her beauty is dash'd with a scornful proud air ;
But Susie was handsome, and sweetly could sing ;
Her breath 's like the breezes perfumed in the spring ;

'That Maddie, in all the gay bloom of her youth,
Like the moon, was inconstant, and never spoke truth ;
But Susie was faithful, good-humoured, and free,
And fair as the goddess that sprung from the sea.

'That mamma's fine daughter, with all her great dower,
Was awkwardly airy, and frequently sour.'
Then sighing, he wish'd, would but parents agree,
The witty sweet Susie his mistress might be.[1]

THE WAUKIN' O' THE FAULD.

In the old rural economy of Scotland, it was necessary for a
shepherd and one of the female servants of the farm to keep up
a night-watch upon the ewe-bughts or fold, in order to prevent
the weaned lambs from getting back to their dams. In the
mild twilight nights of July, it was no great hardship to stay
from eve till dewy morn in the open air, and when the pair
were of congenial minds, still more if they were declared lovers,
it was of course considered as a luxury. The occasion is com-
memorated in a charming song by Ramsay, which forms the
opening of his *Gentle Shepherd*.

[1] From the *Tea-table Miscellany*, 1724.

My Peg-gie is a young thing, Just enter'd in her teens; Fair

as the day, and sweet as May, Fair as the day, and always gay: My

Peg-gie is a young thing, And I'm nae ve-ry auld, And

weel I like to meet her at The waukin' o' the fauld. My

Peg-gie speaks sae sweetly When-e'er we meet a-lane, I

wish nae mair to lay my care, I wish nae mair o' a' that's rare: My

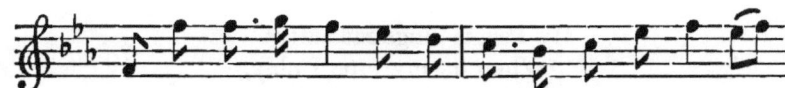

Peg-gie speaks sae sweetly, To a' the lave I'm cauld, But

she gars a' my spir-its glow At waukin' o' the fauld.

My Peggie is a young thing,
    Just enter'd in her teens ;
Fair as the day, and sweet as May,
Fair as the day, and always gay :
    My Peggie is a young thing,
        And I 'm nae very auld,
    And weel I like to meet her at
        The waukin' o' the fauld.

My Peggie speaks sae sweetly
    Whene'er we meet alane,
I wish nae mair to lay my care,
I wish nae mair o' a' that 's rare :
    My Peggie speaks sae sweetly,
        To a' the lave I 'm cauld,
    But she gars a' my spirits glow
        At waukin' o' the fauld.

My Peggie smiles sae kindly
    Whene'er I whisper love,
That I look doun on a' the toun,
That I look doun upon a croun :
    My Peggie smiles sae kindly,
        It maks me blithe and bauld,
    And naething gi'es me sic delight
        As waukin' o' the fauld.

My Peggie sings sae saftly
    When on my pipe I play,
By a' the rest it is confest,
By a' the rest, that she sings best :
    My Peggie sings sae saftly,
        And in her sangs are tauld,
    With innocence, the wale o' sense,
        At waukin' o' the fauld.

BESSY BELL AND MARY GRAY.

O Bessy Bell and Mary Gray,
    They are twa bonnie lasses ;
They bigg'd a bower on yon burn brae,
    And theek'd it o'er with rashes.
Fair Bessy Bell I loo'd yestreen,
    And thought I ne'er could alter ;
But Mary Gray's twa pawky een,
    Gard a' my fancy falter.

Now Bessy's hair's like a lint tap,
    She smiles like a May morning,
When Phœbus starts frae Thetis' lap,
    The hills with rays adorning.
White is her neck, soft is her hand,
    Her waist and feet fu' genty ;
With ilka grace she can command
    Her lips ; O wow ! they're dainty.

And Mary's locks are like a craw,
    Her een like diamonds glances ;
She's aye sae clean, redd up, and braw,
    She kills whene'er she dances ;
Blithe as a kid, with wit at will,
    She blooming, tight, and tall is ;
And guides her airs sae gracefu' still,
    O Jove ! she's like thy Pallas.

Dear Bessy Bell and Mary Gray,
    Ye unco sair oppress us,
Our fancies jee between ye twa,
    Ye are sic bonnie lasses.
Wae's me ! for baith I canna get,
    To ane by law we're stented,
Then I'll draw cuts, and tak my fate
    And be with ane contented.

This song was composed by Allan Ramsay on the basis of a preceding one, of which he retained only the first four lines. The air, a lively one, is inserted in Playford's Collection, 1700. There is a tradition that the two heroines were the daughters of respectable citizens of Perth, and that on the plague breaking out there, they retired to a rush-thatched cot or bower on the braes of Lednoch, where a lover of one or both visited them occasionally, bringing provisions. Unfortunately he brought also the disease, which cut off both the damsels, and their bodies were buried together near their cot, on a spot which has been enclosed by a rail.

A fragment of an original ballad on this painful tragedy has been preserved :

> They wadna lie in Methven kirkyard,
> Amang their gentle kin ;
> But they wad lie on Dronach haugh,
> To beak fornent the sun.

The discrepancy between the original story of Bessy Bell and Mary Gray, and Ramsay's lively song upon their distracting charms, is not easily to be accounted for.

THE LAST TIME I CAM O'ER THE MUIR.

The Skene Manuscript, written about 1630, contains an air entitled *Alas, that I Cam o'er the Muir, and left my Love behind me*, which, with some modifications, had survived to the time of Ramsay. He, probably finding it fitted with words unpresentable to delicate ears, composed a new song to the air, altering the idea expressed in its title. This is not one of Allan's best productions ; but even Burns failed to supersede it with new verses.

The   last   time   I   cam   o'er   the   muir,   I

left my   love   be - hind   me ;   Ye   powers! what pains do

U

I en - dure When soft i - de - as mind me!

Soon as the rud - dy morn dis - played The

beam - ing day en - su - ing, I met be - times my

love - ly maid In fit re - treats for woo - ing.

The last time I cam o'er the muir,
   I left my love behind me ;
Ye powers ! what pains do I endure
   When soft ideas mind me !
Soon as the ruddy morn displayed
   The beaming day ensuing,
I met betimes my lovely maid
   In fit retreats for wooing.

Beneath the cooling shades we lay,
   Gazing and chastely sporting,
Until the sun's last setting beam
   Was in the ocean glowing.
I pitied all beneath the skies,
   Even kings, when she was nigh me ;
In raptures I beheld her eyes,
   Which could but ill deny me.

Should I be called where cannons roar,
    Where mortal steel may wound me,
Or cast upon some foreign shore,
    Where dangers may surround me ;
Yet hopes again to see my love,
    To feast on glowing kisses,
Shall make my cares at distance move,
    In prospect of such blisses.

In all my soul there's not one place
    To let a rival enter :
Since she excels in ev'ry grace,
    In her my love shall centre.
Sooner the seas shall cease to flow,
    Their waves the Alps shall cover,
On Greenland ice shall roses grow,
    Before I cease to love her.

The neist time I gang o'er the muir,
    She shall a lover find me ;
And that my faith is firm and pure,
    Though I left her behind me ;
Then Hymen's sacred bonds shall chain
    My heart to her fair bosom ;
There, while my being does remain,
    My love more fresh shall blossom.

THE YOUNG LAIRD AND EDINBURGH KATIE.

This song of Ramsay's introduces us to the social life of Edinburgh, at a time when it was confined to the Old Town, and when the Hill—that is, the Castle Hill—was the only place available for a lover's promenade ; when, moreover, young ladies were accustomed, out of doors, to screen their faces with a plaid, the equivalent of the Spanish mantilla.

Now wat ye wha I met yes - treen,

Com - ing down the street, my joe? My

mis - tress, in her tar - tan screen, Fu'

bon - nie, braw, and sweet, my joe! My

dear, quoth I, thanks to the nicht, That

nev - er wiss'd a lov - er ill, Sin'

ye 're out o' your mith - er's sicht, Let's

tak' a walk up to the Hill.

Now wat ye wha I met yestreen,
   Coming down the street, my joe ?
My mistress, in her tartan screen,
   Fu' bonnie, braw, and sweet, my joe !
My dear, quoth I, thanks to the nicht,
   That never wiss'd a lover ill,
Sin' ye 're out o' your mither's sicht,
   Let 's tak' a walk up to the Hill.

Oh, Katie, wilt thou gang wi' me,
   And leave the dinsome toun a while ?
The blossom 's sprouting frae the tree,
   And a' creation 's gaun to smile.
The mavis, nichtingale, and lark,
   The bleating lambs and whistling hynd,
In ilka dale, green shaw, and park,
   Will nourish health, and glad your mind.

Sune as the clear guidman o' day
   Does bend his mornin' draught o' dew,
We 'll gae to some burn-side and play,
   And gather flouirs to busk your brow.
We 'll pou the daisies on the green,
   The lucken-gowans frae the bog ;
Between hands, now and then, we 'll lean
   And sport upon the velvet fog.

There 's, up into a pleasant glen,
   A wee piece frae my father's tower,
A canny, saft, and flowery den,
   Which circling birks have formed a bower.
Whene'er the sun grows high and warm,
   We 'll to the caller shade remove ;
There will I lock thee in my arm,
   And love and kiss, and kiss and love.

KATIE'S ANSWER.

My moth-er's aye glow-rin' ower me, Though
she did the same be-fore me; I can-na get leave To
look at my love, Or else she'd be like to devour me. Right fain wad I tak' your of-fer, Sweet
sir, but I'll tyne my tocher; Then, San-dy, ye'll fret, And
wyte your puir Kate, Whene'er ye keek in your toom cof-fer.

My mother's aye glowrin' ower me,
Though she did the same before me ;
    I canna get leave
    To look at my love,
Or else she'd be like to devour me.

Right fain wad I tak' your offer,
Sweet sir, but I'll tyne my tocher;
    Then, Sandy, ye'll fret,
    And wyte your puir Kate,
Whene'er ye keek in your toom coffer.

For though my father has plenty
Of silver, and plenishing dainty,
    Yet he's unco sweir
    To twine wi' his gear;
And sae we had need to be tenty.

Tutor my parents wi' caution,
Be wylie in ilka motion;
    Brag weel o' your land,
    And, there's my leal hand,
Win them, I'll be at your devotion.[1]

THE LASS O' PATIE'S MILL.

Allan Ramsay, paying a visit to the Earl of Loudon at Loudon Castle, and riding out one day with his lordship, observed a rustic girl of uncommon beauty *tedding hay* in a field at a place called Pate's Mill. The consequence of the encounter was this song, adapted to a beautiful old air; both of which were published in the *Orpheus Caledonius*.

[1] The tune for *Katie's Answer* is identical with an English country dance-tune, called *A Health to Betty.*—W. CHAPELL.

The lass o' Patie's Mill, Sae bon-nie, blithe, and gay, In spite o' a' my skill, Has stown my heart a-way. When ted-ding of the hay, Bare-head-ed on the green, Love midst her locks did play, And wan-toned in her een.

The lass o' Patie's Mill,
　Sae bonnie, blithe, and gay,
In spite o' a' my skill,
　Has stown my heart away.
When tedding of the hay,
　Bareheaded on the green,
Love midst her locks did play,
　And wantoned in her een.

Without the help of art,
　　Like flowers that grace the wild,
She did her sweets impart,
　　Whene'er she spoke or smiled ;
Her looks they were so mild,
　　Free from affected pride,
She me to love beguiled,
　　I wished her for my bride.

O, had I all that wealth,
　　Hopetoun's high mountains fill,
Insured lang life and health,
　　And pleasure at my will ;
I'd promise and fulfil,
　　That none but bonnie she,
The lass o' Patie's Mill,
　　Should share the same wi' me.

WOE'S MY HEART THAT WE SHOULD SUNDER.

With brok - en words and down - cast eyes, Poor

Col - in spoke his pas - sion ten - der, And

part - ing with his Griz - zy cries, Ah woe's my heart that

we should sun - der; To oth - ers I am

cold   as snow, But   kin - dle with   thine

eyes like tin - der, From thee with pain I 'm forced to go, It

breaks my   heart   that we should sun - der.

With broken words and downcast eyes,
    Poor Colin spoke his passion tender,
And parting with his Grizzy cries,
    Ah woe 's my heart that we should sunder ;
To others I am cold as snow,
    But kindle with thine eyes like tinder,
From thee with pain I 'm forced to go,
    It breaks my heart that we should sunder.

Chained to thy charms, I cannot range,
    No beauty now my love shall hinder,
Nor time, nor place, shall ever change
    My vows, though we 're obliged to sunder.
The image of thy graceful air,
    And beauties which invite our wonder,
Thy lively wit, and prudence rare,
    Shall still be present though we sunder.

Dear nymph, believe thy swain in this,
    You 'll ne'er engage a heart that 's kinder,
Then seal a promise with a kiss,
    Always to love me, though we sunder.

Ye powers, take care of my dear lass,
    That as I leave her I may find her.
When that blessed time shall come to pass,
    We'll meet again, and never sunder.

This song was composed by Ramsay, to supersede a homely one which had long possessed popular favour. An air under the title of *Alace my Heart that we should Sunder* appears in Playford's Collection, 1700. There is also one, essentially different from the above, in the Skene Manuscript, under the title of *Alace this Night that we suld Sinder.*

THE HIGHLAND LADDIE.

The old tune of the *Highland Laddie,* consisting of but one part, was fitted by Ramsay with the following words, and published in the *Orpheus Caledonius.* A second part was afterwards added. The song, however, has long been adapted by the irresistible will of the people to the air here subjoined.

The Low-land lads they think they're fine, But O they're vain and id-ly gaw-dy! How much un-like the graceful mien And man-ly looks of my Highland lad-die. O my bon-nie Highland lad-die, My handsome, charming, Highland lad-die! May

heaven still guard, and love re - ward, The Low-land lass and her

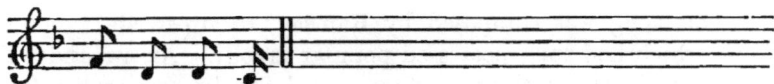

Highland lad - die!

The Lowland lads they think they're fine,
But O they're vain and idly gawdy!
How much unlike the graceful mien
And manly looks of my Highland laddie.
O my bonnie Highland laddie,
My handsome, charming, Highland laddie!
May heaven still guard, and love reward,
The Lowland lass and her Highland laddie!

If I were free at will to choose
To be the wealthiest Lawland lady,
I'd take young Donald without trews,
With bonnet blue and belted plaidy.

The brawest beau in borrows-toun,
In a' his airs, with art made ready,
Compared to him, he's but a clown;
He's finer far in's tartan plaidy.

O'er benty hill with him I'll run,
And leave my Lawland kin and daddy;
Frae winter's cauld, and summer's sun,
He'll screen me with his Highland plaidy.

Few compliments between us pass;
I ca' him my dear Highland laddie;
And he ca's me his Lawland lass,
Syne rows me in beneath his plaidy.

Nae greater joy I 'll e'er pretend,
   Than that his love prove true and steady,
Like mine to him, which ne'er shall end,
   While Heaven preserves my Highland laddie.

LOCHABER NO MORE.

Fare-well to Loch-a-ber, and fare-well, my

Jean, Where heart-some wi' her I ha'e mon-y a day

been; For Loch-a-ber no more, Loch-a-ber no

more, We'll may-be re-turn to Loch-a-ber no

more. These tears that I shed they are a' for my

dear, And no for the dan-gers at-tend-ing on

weir; Tho' borne on rough   seas to   a   far dis - tant

shore, May - be   to   re - turn to Loch - a - ber   no more.

Farewell to Lochaber, and farewell, my Jean,
Where heartsome wi' her I ha'e mony a day been ;
For Lochaber no more, Lochaber no more,
We 'll may-be return to Lochaber no more.
These tears that I shed they are a' for my dear,
And no for the dangers attending on weir ;
Though borne on rough seas to a far-distant shore,
May-be to return to Lochaber no more.

Though hurricanes rise, though rise every wind,
No tempest can equal the storm in my mind ;
Though loudest of thunders on louder waves roar,
There 's naething like leavin' my love on the shore.
To leave thee behind me my heart is sair pained,
But by ease that 's inglorious no fame can be gained,
And beauty and love 's the command of the brave,
And I maun deserve it before I can crave.

Then glory, my Jeanie, maun plead my excuse ;
Since honour commands me, how can I refuse ?
Without it I ne'er could have merit for thee,
And losing thy favour I 'd better not be.
I gae, then, my lass, to win honour and fame,
And if I should chance to come glorious hame,
I 'll bring a heart to thee, with love running o'er,
And then I 'll leave thee and Lochaber no more.

This song is by Ramsay. The air is based upon a simple

ballad air of one strain, called *Lord Ronald my Son.* There is
another air called *King James's March to Ireland,* which has
evidently been founded on the same ballad air.

The pathos of *Lochaber no More,* when the song is well sung,
usually has a powerful effect on Scotchmen, especially if they be
at a distance from Scotland. There is a story constantly told
and believed, to the effect that it was necessary for the officers
of a Highland regiment in the West Indies to order the playing
of this air by the band to be discontinued, on account of its
fatal effect in creating home-sickness among the men.

ETTRICK BANKS.

All that is known of this delightful pastoral, and its air, is
that they were inserted in the *Orpheus Caledonius,* 1725.

On Et - trick banks, in a sum - mer's night, At

gloam - ing, when the sheep drave hame, I met my lass - ie

braw and tight, Came wad - ing, bare - foot, a' her lane;

My heart grew light, I ran, I flang My

arms about her lil - y neck, And kissed and clapped her

there fu' lang; My words they were na mon - y feck.

On Ettrick banks, in a summer's night,
   At gloaming, when the sheep drave hame,
I met my lassie braw and tight,
   Came wading, barefoot, a' her lane ;
My heart grew light, I ran, I flang
   My arms about her lily neck,
And kissed and clapped her there fu' lang ;
   My words they were na mony feck.

I said, My lassie, will ye go
   To the Highland hills, the Erse to learn ;
I 'll baith gi'e thee a cow and ewe,
   When ye come to the brig o' Earn.
At Leith auld meal comes in, ne'er fash,
   And herrings at the Broomielaw,
Cheer up your heart, my bonnie lass,
   There 's gear to win ye never saw.

All day when we have wrought enough,
   When winter frosts and snaw begin
Soon as the sun gaes west the loch,
   At night when ye sit down to spin,
I 'll screw my pipes and play a spring,
   And thus the weary night will end,
Till the tender kid and lamb-time bring
   Our pleasant summer back again.

Syne when the trees are in their bloom,
  And gowans glint o'er ilka field,
I'll meet my lass amang the broom,
  And lead you to my summer shiel.
Then far frae a' their scornfu' din,
  That make the kindly hearts their sport,
We'll laugh and kiss, and dance and sing,
  And gar the langest day seem short.   *

TWEEDSIDE.

It would have been surprising if the beautiful stream which pervades the pastoral region of southern Scotland had not been taken up as a subject both by the musician and the poet. It was in reality so at a comparatively early period, if tradition is right in assigning the following canzonet to Lord Yester—born 1645, died 1713—eventually the second Marquis of Tweeddale—a distinguished statesman of the reigns of William and Anne, and noted for his concern in promoting that union of the kingdoms which lost for the Tweed its only unenviable characteristic as the division between two portions of an island designed by nature to be one. It cannot be said that the four simple verses ascribed to Lord Yester are of signal merit; yet it is possible that, with the aid of the beautiful melody, they might be tolerably effective. I have heard that when Lady Grizel Baillie sang this song, she generally drew tears from her auditory.

When Maggie and I were acquaint,
  I carried my noddle fu' hie;
Nae lintwhite in a' the gay plain,
  Nae gowdspink sae bonnie as she!
I whistled, I piped, and I sang;
  I wooed, but I cam nae great speed;
Therefore I maun wander abroad,
  And lay my banes far frae the Tweed.

v

To Maggie my love I did tell,
  My tears did my passion express ;
Alas ! for I lo'ed her ower weel,
  And the women lo'e sic a man less.
Her heart it was frozen and cauld ;
  Her pride had my ruin decreed ;
Therefore I maun wander abroad,
  And lay my banes far frae the Tweed.

In the reign of George I., when our national melodies and songs were beginning to make their way into good company, there was a young gentleman named Robert Crawford, who manifested a decided gift in pastoral poesy. There has been some doubt as to his family, and even his Christian name ; but it may now be regarded as settled that he was not William Crawford of the Auchinames family, in Renfrewshire, as was at one time commonly set forth, but Robert Crawford, second son of Patrick Crawford of Drumsoy, in that county. Having an elder brother named Thomas, who was successively secretary to the embassy of the Earl of Stair, and envoy extraordinary to the court of Versailles, Robert came, by a natural train of circumstances, to spend some years in France, and it is believed that he died in returning from that country in the year 1732. There is so much obscurity about him, that we are glad to lay hold of any tolerably well-authenticated fact which brings him as a reality before us ; and therefore I here recall that Mr Ramsay of Auchtertyre, writing to Robert Burns in 1787, speaks of a conversation he had just had with a Colonel Edmondstone, who remembered being at his cousin Robert Crawford's funeral fifty-five years before. Colonel Edmondstone added the interesting particular, that he was 'a pretty young man.'

Robert Crawford's poetical genius was entirely for the Scottish pastoral, an idealisation of the life of the hard-working peasantry of his native country into shepherds with pipes and crooks and coy damosels, seated among purling brooks and shady groves. His strains had at the same time a mellowness and flow—even

a tenderness—that suited well the rising taste of the people and
the age. Crawford was pleased to sing of Tweed, the Bush aboon
Traquair, and the Broom of the Cowdenknowes, instead of any of
the less romantic scenes of his own west-country, as the following series of his pieces will evince. His song entitled *Tweedside*
appeared with the music in his own lifetime, being presented
in Thomson's *Orpheus Caledonius*, 1725.

What beau-ties does Flo-ra dis - close! How

sweet are her smiles up-on Tweed! Yet Ma-ry's, still

sweet-er than those, Both na-ture and fan-cy ex-

ceed. No dai-sy, nor sweet blushing rose, Not

all the gay flowers of the field, Not

Tweed, glid-ing gent-ly through those, Such beau-ty and

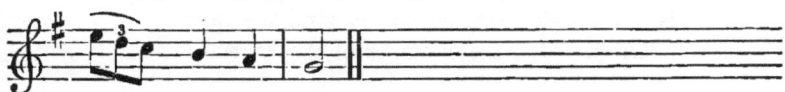

plea-sure does yield.

What beauties does Flora disclose !
How sweet are her smiles upon Tweed !
Yet Mary's, still sweeter than those,
Both nature and fancy exceed.
No daisy, nor sweet blushing rose,
Not all the gay flowers of the field,
Not Tweed, gliding gently through those,
Such beauty and pleasure does yield.

The warblers are heard in the grove,
The linnet, the lark, and the thrush ;
The blackbird, and sweet cooing dove,
With music enchant ev'ry bush.
Come, let us go forth to the mead ;
Let us see how the primroses spring ;
We'll lodge in some village on Tweed,
And love while the feather'd folk sing.

How does my love pass the long day ?
Does Mary not tend a few sheep ?
Do they never carelessly stray
While happily she lies asleep ?
Should Tweed's murmurs lull her to rest,
Kind nature indulgin' my bliss,
To ease the soft pains of my breast,
I'd steal an ambrosial kiss.

'Tis she does the virgins excel ;
No beauty with her may compare ;
Love's graces around her do dwell ;
She's fairest where thousands are fair.
Say, charmer, where do thy flocks stray ?
Oh, tell me at morn where they feed ?
Shall I seek them on sweet-winding Tay
Or the pleasanter banks of the Tweed ?

The tradition of Scottish society has preserved for us the

object of Crawford's poetic affections in the person of Mary Scott, second daughter of John Scott of Harden. She was a woman of uncommon personal attractions, as is amply proved by a portrait of her by Allan Ramsay, junior, in Hamilton Palace— the subject of an almost raving admiration to Pennant, in his *Tour of Scotland.* It was about 1725 that Mary Scott was in the zenith of her charms, and Crawford was not the only bard who celebrated them. There was an old and now lost ditty, with a simple air of one strain, commemorating Mary Scott, 'the Flower of Yarrow,' as she was called—namely, a daughter of Scott of Dryhope in Yarrow, who married the famous Walter Scott of Harden in the time of Queen Mary, and who consequently was an ancestress of the now reigning beauty. On this strain, which was probably unfit for ears polite, Allan Ramsay built up a short song in his usual manner, designed as a compliment to the contemporary beauty, and repeating in her favour the title of 'the Flower of Yarrow,' in spite of its inappropriateness as regarded her nativity and residence. It begins thus :

> Happy the love which meets return,
> But mine meets only slight and scorn ;
> Oh, that I ne'er had seen yon tower,
> That shelters Yarrow's fairest flower !
> 'Mang circling hills that guard her hame,
> The bonnie loch's clear waters gleam,
> And there lives she whom nane can marrow,
> Mary Scott, the Flower of Yarrow.[1]

I had the advantage, many years ago, of hearing Sir Walter Scott speak of this poetic heroine, whom he called the *Second* Flower of Yarrow, as one whom he had himself known, although

---

[1] 'L. M. M. R.,' in *Notes and Queries,* March 18, 1854, gives a verse of the old song of *Mary Scott, the Flower of Yarrow,* as the only one he remembers :

> Mary 's black, and Mary 's white,
> Mary is the king's delight,
> The king's delight, the prince's marrow,
> Mary Scott, the Flower of Yarrow !

at rather an early period of his life. She was commonly recognised in fashionable circles by the name of *Cadie Scott*, from
having once, by way of a girlish frolic, gone to a fancy-ball in the
dress of a *cadie*, or street-porter. 'I remember her,' he said, 'as
an old lady, distinguished for elegant manners and high spirit,
though struggling with the disadvantages of a narrow income,
as her father's estate, being entailed on heirs-male, went to
another branch of the Harden family. I have heard a hundred
times from those who lived at the time, that *Tweedside* and *Mary
Scott the Flower of Yarrow*, were both written upon this much
admired lady.' Sir Walter added : 'The facts could not but be
well known to me, as living in the utmost intimacy with the
Harden family, and being descended from their eldest cadet,
Scott of Raeburn.' [1]

THE BUSH ABOON TRAQUAIR.

At Traquair, in Peeblesshire, on a piece of sloping ground on
the west side of the valley, a mile above the old mansion-
house, was a grove of birches, such as might well form an assig-
nation-ground for lovers. In what way it came to attract the
attention of Robert Crawford—for the place is remote, and
Robert, as connected with the Whig Earl of Stair, could, one
would think, be little likely to visit the Stuart-devoted Traquair
family—cannot be imagined. There, however, long after it has
decayed away to a few melancholy stumps, it remains imperishable
in his sweet pastoral strains.

---

[1] The words here quoted, being quite consistent with my recollection
of Sir Walter's conversation, are transcribed from a manuscript note
by him upon a copy of Cromek's *Reliques of Burns*, formerly in the
possession of Mr Samuel Aitken, bookseller, Edinburgh.

Hear me, ye nymphs, and ev'-ry swain, I'll
tell how Peg-gy grieves me; Though thus I lan-guish
and com-plain, A-las! she ne'er be-lieves me.
My vows and sighs, like sil-ent air, Un-
heed-ed, nev-er move her; At the
bon-nie Bush a-bune Tra-quair, 'Twas
there I first did love her.

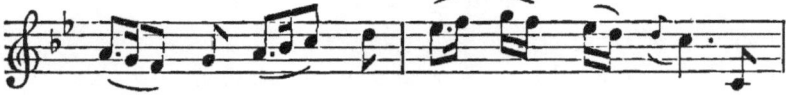

Hear me, ye nymphs, and every swain,
I'll tell how Peggy grieves me;
Though thus I languish and complain,
Alas! she ne'er believes me.

My vows and sighs, like silent air,
  Unheeded, never move her ;
At the bonnie Bush abune Traquair,
  'Twas there I first did love her.

That day she smiled and made me glad,
  No maid seem'd ever kinder ;
I thought myself the luckiest lad,
  So sweetly there to find her ;
I tried to soothe my amorous flame,
  In words that I thought tender ;
If more there pass'd, I 'm not to blame—
  I meant not to offend her.

Yet now she scornful flees the plain,
  The fields we then frequented ;
If e'er we meet she shews disdain,
  She looks as ne'er acquainted.
The bonnie bush bloom'd fair in May,
  Its sweets I 'll aye remember ;
But now her frowns make it decay—
  It fades as in December.

Ye rural powers, who hear my strains,
  Why thus should Peggy grieve me !
O make her partner in my pains,
  Then let her smiles relieve me :
If not, my love will turn despair,
  My passion no more tender ;
I 'll leave the Bush abune Traquair—
  To lonely wilds I 'll wander.

MY DEARIE, IF THOU DEE.

There was an old and simple song, of which the verses ended with 'My dearie, an thou die.' It was superseded by an elegant song of Robert Crawford, which appeared in both the *Tea-table Miscellany* and the *Orpheus Caledonius;* in the latter case, with an air evidently the representative of one inserted in the Skene Manuscript, under the title of *O Sillie Soul alace!* In repeating the song, however, in this place, a copy given as the genuine old one by Mr Stenhouse, and which may certainly be accepted as such, is preferred. Amongst modern lovers of our national melodies, it will be recognised as the tune adopted for a song of recent date, beginning, 'What ails this heart o' mine?'

Love never more shall give me pain, My fan-cy's fix'd on thee; Nor ev-er maid my heart shall gain, My Peggie, if thou dee. Thy beau-ties did such pleasure give, Thy love's so true to me; With-out thee I shall nev-er live, My dearie, if thou dee.

Love never more shall give me pain,
   My fancy's fix'd on thee ;
Nor ever maid my heart shall gain,
   My Peggie, if thou dee.
Thy beauties did such pleasure give,
   Thy love's so true to me ;
Without thee I shall never live,
   My dearie, if thou dee.

If fate shall tear thee from my breast,
   How shall I lonely stray !
In dreary dreams the night I 'll waste,
   In sighs the silent day.
I ne'er can so much virtue find,
   Nor such perfection see :
Then I 'll renounce all womankind,
   My Peggie, after thee.

No new-blown beauty fires my heart,
   With Cupid's raving rage ;
But thine, which can such sweets impart,
   Must all the world engage.
'Twas this that, like the morning sun,
   Gave joy and life to me ;
And, when its destined day is done,
   With Peggie let me dee.

Ye powers that smile on virtuous love,
   And in such pleasures share,
Ye who its faithful flames approve,
   With pity view the fair :
Restore my Peggie's wonted charms,
   Those charms so dear to me ;
Oh, never rob them from those arms—
   I 'm lost if Peggie dee !

ONE DAY I HEARD MARY SAY.

This song by Crawford—unfortunate in the name assigned to the lover, but yet a pleasant specimen of the genius of its author —was composed to an old air, called from the original song *I'll Never Leave Thee*, which commenced as follows:

> Leave thee, lad, leave thee, lad,
> I'll never leave thee.
> Gang the world as it will,
> I'll never leave thee.

One Day I heard Mary say was printed in the *Tea-table Miscellany* and the *Orpheus Caledonius*, and has been included in all subsequent collections. About 1770, the Italian singer Tenducci made a great success in introducing it to his Edinburgh audiences; and so lately as 1848, the editor had the pleasure of hearing a representation of that great vocalist's manner of singing this song, from a gentleman who not only remembered it well, but could imitate it with tolerable effect. As might be expected, a strong rise in passionate energy at 'Alas, my fond heart will break!' was the *tour de force* of the performance.

One day I heard Ma - ry say, How shall I leave thee? Stay, dearest A - don - is, stay; Why wilt thou grieve me? A - las! my fond heart will break,

If thou should leave me: I'll live and die

for thy sake, Yet nev - er leave thee.

One day I heard Mary say,
   How shall I leave thee?
Stay, dearest Adonis, stay;
   Why wilt thou grieve me?
Alas! my fond heart will break,
   If thou should leave me:
I'll live and die for thy sake,
   Yet never leave thee.

Say, lovely Adonis, say,
   Has Mary deceived thee?
Did e'er her young heart betray
   New love, that has grieved thee?
My constant mind ne'er shall stray;
   Thou may believe me.
I'll love thee, lad, night and day,
   And never leave thee.

Adonis, my charming youth,
   What can relieve thee?
Can Mary thy anguish soothe?
   This breast shall receive thee.
My passion can ne'er decay,
   Never deceive thee;
Delight shall drive pain away,
   Pleasure revive thee.

But leave thee, leave thee, lad,
   How shall I leave thee ?
Oh ! that thought makes me sad ;
   I 'll never leave thee !
Where would my Adonis fly ?
   Why does he grieve me ?
Alas ! my poor heart will die,
   If I should leave thee.

DOWN THE BURN, DAVIE.

This song by Crawford appeared with its air in the *Orpheus Caledonius*. In the present and other modern reprints, an improved version of the last verse, from the pen of Burns, is adopted.

When trees did bud, and fields were green, And broom bloom'd fair to see; When Ma - ry was com-plete fif - teen, And love laugh'd in her e'e; Blithe Davie's blinks her heart did move To speak her mind thus

free: Gang   down   the   burn,   Da - vie, love, And

I   will   fol - low   thee.

When trees did bud, and fields were green,
    And broom bloom'd fair to see ;
When Mary was complete fifteen,
    And love laugh'd in her e'e ;
Blithe Davie's blinks her heart did move
    To speak her mind thus free :
Gang down the burn, Davie, love,
    And I will follow thee.

Now Davie did each lad surpass
    That dwelt on this burnside ;
And Mary was the bonniest lass,
    Just meet to be a bride :
Her cheeks were rosie, red and white ;
    Her een were bonnie blue ;
Her looks were like the morning bright,
    Her lips like dropping dew.

As down the burn they took their way,
    And through the flow'ry dale ;
His cheek to hers he aft did lay,
    And love was aye the tale.
With, Mary, when shall we return,
    Sic pleasure to renew ?
Quoth Mary, Love, I like the burn,
    And aye will follow you.[1]

[1] Burns was informed that the air of this song was composed by David Maigh, who, in his time, had been keeper of the blood-hounds to the Laird of Riddel, in Roxburghshire.

TO MRS A. H.,

ON SEEING HER AT A CONCERT.

This little occasional canzonet of Crawford's is a fair specimen of his amatory verses, and a characteristic production. A general admirer of the fair, he sees a young lady at a concert, deems her the prettiest creature extant, and immediately throws off two stanzas in her praise, to the appropriate tune of *The Bonniest Lass in a' the World.* It appears that the lady in question was *Miss* Anne Hamilton (as we should now entitle her), a relative of William Hamilton of Bangour, and subsequently married to 'Professor M——, in the university of Edinburgh.'

The modern reader, who only *reads* the verses, will perhaps set little store by them; but if he be so fortunate as hear them well sung to their proper melody, he will probably own that they possess a certain charm.

Look where my dear Ha - mil - la smiles, Ha-
mil - la, love - ly charm - er! See how with all their
arts and wiles The Loves and Gra - ces arm her!
A blush dwells glow - ing on her cheeks, Fair

seats   of youth - ful pleasures; There   Love   in   smil - ing

lan - guage speaks, There spreads his   ros - y   trea - sures.

Look where my dear Hamilla smiles,
     Hamilla, lovely charmer !
See how with all their arts and wiles
     The Loves and Graces arm her !
A blush dwells glowing on her cheeks,
     Fair seats of youthful pleasures ;
There Love in smiling language speaks,
     There spreads his rosy treasures.

O fairest maid, I own thy power,
     I gaze, I sigh, I languish ;
Yet ever, ever will adore,
     And triumph in my anguish.
But ease, dear charmer, ease my care,
     And let my torments move thee :
As thou art fairest of the fair,
     So I the dearest love thee.

BUSK YE, BUSK YE.

The refined society of Edinburgh, in the reign of George I., boasted of another poetical ornament besides Robert Crawford, in the person of William Hamilton of Bangour. An amiable enthusiast in love and Jacobitism, he passed through a bachelor life of fifty years, which might have been prolonged if he had not subjected himself to severe personal hardships and exile, by his adherence to the Stuart cause in 1745. Hamilton wrote moralising and descriptive epics in the manner then prevalent, and these pieces have twice been admitted into the canon of the British poets; but Johnson's insensibility to their merits, as recorded by Boswell, would probably be sanctioned by modern criticism. More may be said for him as the author of a few of our favourite Scottish songs, and particularly of the one here immediately following, which, in addition to its own inherent merits, has the incidental one of having stimulated Wordsworth to the production of his *Yarrow Unvisited,* and its sequels.

The air is that of a previously existing ballad, the incidents of which suggested the song to Hamilton.

Busk ye, busk ye, my bon-nie, bon-nie bride!

Busk ye, busk ye, my win-some mar-row!

Busk ye, busk ye, my bon-nie, bon-nie bride, And

think nae mair of the braes of Yar-row.' 'Where gat ye that

bon-nie, bon-nie bride? Where gat ye that

w

win - some mar - row?' 'I gat her where I

daur - na weel be seen, I'u' - ing the birks on the

braes of Yar - row.'

A. 'Busk ye, busk ye, my bonnie, bonnie bride!
    Busk ye, busk ye, my winsome marrow!
  Busk ye, busk ye, my bonnie, bonnie bride,
    And think nae mair of the braes of Yarrow.'

B. 'Where gat ye that bonnie, bonnie bride?
    Where gat ye that winsome marrow?'
A. 'I gat her where I daurna weel be seen,
    Puing the birks on the braes of Yarrow.

  'Weip not, weip not, my bonnie, bonnie bride,
    Weip not, weip not, my winsome marrow!
  Nor let thy heart lament to leive
    Puing the birks on the braes of Yarrow.'

B. 'Why does she weip, thy bonnie, bonnie bride?
    Why does she weip, thy winsome marrow?
  And why daur ye nae mair weel be seen,
    Puing the birks on the braes of Yarrow?'

A. 'Lang maun she weip, lang, lang maun she weip,
    Lang maun she weip wi' dule and sorrow;
  And lang maun I nae mair weel be seen
    Puing the birks on the braes of Yarrow.

' For she has tint her luver deir,
  Her luver deir, the cause of sorrow ;
And I ha'e slain the comeliest swain
  That e'er pu'd birks on the braes of Yarrow.

' Why runs thy stream, O Yarrow, red ?
  Why on thy braes heard the voice of sorrow ?
And why yon melancholious weids,
  Hung on the bonnie birks of Yarrow ?

' What's youder floats on the rueful flude ?
  What's yonder floats ?—Oh, dule and sorrow !
'Tis he, the comely swain I slew
  Upon the dulefu' braes of Yarrow !

' Wash, oh, wash his wounds in tears,
  His wounds in tears o' dule and sorrow ;
And wrap his limbs in mourning weids,
  And lay him on the banks of Yarrow.

' Then build, then build, ye sisters sad,
  Ye sisters sad, his tomb wi' sorrow ;
And weip around, in waefu' wise,
  His hapless fate on the braes of Yarrow !

' Curse ye, curse ye, his useless shield,
  The arm that wrocht the deed of sorrow,
The fatal spear that pierced his breist,
  His comely breist, on the braes of Yarrow !

' Did I not warn thee not to love,
  And warn from fight ?   But, to my sorrow,
Too rashly bold, a stronger arm thou met'st,
  Thou met'st, and fell on the braes of Yarrow.

' Sweit smells the birk ; green grows the grass ;
  Yellow on Yarrow's braes the gowan ;
Fair hangs the apple frae the rock ;
  Sweit the wave of Yarrow flowin' !

'Flows Yarrow sweit? as sweit flows Tweed ;
   As green its grass ; its gowan as yellow ;
As sweit smells on its braes the birk ;
   The apple from its rocks as mellow !

' Fair was thy love ! fair, fair, indeed, thy love !
   In flowery bands thou didst him fetter ;
Though he was fair, and well-beloved again,
   Than me he never loved thee better.

' Busk ye, then, busk, my bonnie, bonnie bride !
   Busk ye, busk ye, my winsome marrow !
Busk ye, and lo'e me on the banks of Tweed,
   And think nae mair on the braes of Yarrow.'

C. ' How can I busk a bonnie, bonnie bride ?
   How can I busk a winsome marrow ?
How can I lo'e him on the banks of Tweed
   That slew my love on the braes of Yarrow ?

' Oh, Yarrow fields, may never rain
   Nor dew thy tender blossoms cover !
For there was basely slain my love,
   My love, as he had not been a lover.

' The boy put on his robes of green,
   His purple vest—'twas my ain sewin' ;
Ah, wretched me ! I little, little kenn'd
   He was in these to meet his ruin.

' The boy took out his milk-white steed,
   Unmindful of my dule and sorrow :
But, ere the too-fa' of the nicht,[1]
   He lay a corpse on the banks of Yarrow !

---

[1] Ere the fall of the evening.

'Much I rejoiced, that waefu' day ;
    I sang, my voice the woods returning ;
But, lang ere nicht, the spear was flown
    That slew my love, and left me mourning.

' What can my barbarous father do,
    But with his cruel rage pursue me ?
My lover's blude is on thy spear—
    How canst thou, barbarous man, then, woo me ?

' My happy sisters may be proud,
    With cruel and ungentle scoffing,
May bid me seek, on Yarrow braes,
    My lover nailed in his coffin.

' My brother Douglas may upbraid,
    And strive, with threat'ning words, to move me ;
My lover's blude is on thy spear—
    How canst thou ever bid me love thee ?

' Yes, yes, prepare the bed of love !
    With bridal-sheets my body cover !
Unbar, ye bridal-maids, the door !
    Let in th' expected husband-lover !

' But who the expected husband is ?
    His hands, methinks, are bathed in slaughter !
Ah, me ! what ghastly spectre 's yon,
    Comes, in his pale shroud, bleeding after ?

' Pale as he is, here lay him down ;
    O lay his cold head on my pillow !
Take off, take off these bridal-weids,
    And crown my careful head with willow.

' Pale though thou art, yet best beloved,
    Oh, could my warmth to life restore thee !
Yet lie all night between my breasts—
    No youth lay ever there before thee !

'Pale, pale, indeed, oh lovely youth,
　　Forgive, forgive so foul a slaughter,
And lie all night between my breasts,
　　No youth shall ever lie there after!'

A. 'Return, return, O mournful bride!
　　Return, and dry thy useless sorrow!
Thy lover heids nocht of thy sighs;
　　He lies a corpse on the braes of Yarrow.'

AH, THE POOR SHEPHERD'S MOURNFUL FATE.

This is a piece by Hamilton of Bangour, scarcely to be distinguished in style from those of Crawford. It is to a tune entitled *Sour Plums o' Galashiels*, or briefly *Galashiels*, which is stated by Mr Stenhouse to have been composed by the Laird of Galashiels's piper, about the beginning of the eighteenth century.

Ah, the poor shep - herd's mourn - ful fate, When
doom'd to love and doom'd to lan - guish, To
bear the scorn - ful fair one's hate, Nor
dare dis - close his an - guish! Yet

eag - er looks and dy - ing sighs My

se - cret soul dis - cov - er, While

rap - ture, trem - bling through mine eyes, Re-

veals how much I love her. The

tend - er glance, the red - den - ing cheek, O'er-

spread with ris - ing blush - es, A

thou - sand var - i - ous ways they speak A

thou - sand var - i - ous wish - es.

Ah, the poor shepherd's mournful fate,
  When doom'd to love and doom'd to languish,
To bear the scornful fair one's hate,
  Nor dare disclose his anguish!
Yet eager looks and dying sighs
  My secret soul discover,
While rapture, trembling through mine eyes,
  Reveals how much I love her.
The tender glance, the reddening cheek,
  O'erspread with rising blushes,
A thousand various ways they speak
  A thousand various wishes.

For, oh! that form so heavenly fair,
  Those languid eyes so sweetly smiling,
That artless blush and modest air
  So fatally beguiling;
Thy every look, and every grace,
  So charm, whene'er I view thee,
Till death o'ertake me in the chase
  Still will my hopes pursue thee.
Then, when my tedious hours are past,
  Be this last blessing given,
Low at thy feet to breathe my last,
  And die in sight of heaven.

THE BRUME O' THE COWDENKNOWES.

How blithe, ilk morn, was I to see My
swain come o'er the hill! He skipt the burn and

flew to me: I met him with good - will. Oh, the brume, the

bon - nie, bon - nie brume! The brume o' the Cow - den-

knowes! I wish I were with my dear swain, With

his pipe and my yowes.

How blithe, ilk morn, was I to see
My swain come o'er the hill!
He skipt the burn and flew to me:
I met him with good-will.
Oh, the brume, the bonnie, bonnie brume!
The brume o' the Cowdenknowes!
I wish I were with my dear swain,
With his pipe and my yowes.

I wanted neither yowe nor lamb,
While his flock near me lay;
He gathered in my sheep at night,
And cheered me a' the day.

He tuned his pipe, and played sae sweet,
The birds sat listening bye;
E'en the dull cattle stood and gazed,
Charmed with the melodye.

While thus we spent our time, by turns,
    Betwixt our flocks and play,
I envied not the fairest dame,
    Though e'er so rich or gay.

Hard fate, that I should banished be,
    Gang heavily, and mourn,
Because I loved the kindest swain
    That ever yet was born.

He did oblige me every hour;
    Could I but faithful be?
He stawe my heart; could I refuse
    Whate'er he ask'd of me?

My doggie, and my little kit
    That held my wee soup whey,
My plaidie, brooch, and crookit stick,
    May now lie useless by.

Adieu, ye Cowdenknowes, adieu!
    Fareweel, a' pleasures there!
Ye gods, restore me to my swain—
    Is a' I crave or care.
      Oh, the brume, the bonnie, bonnie brume!
      The brume o' the Cowdenknowes!
    I wish I were with my dear swain,
      With his pipe and my yowes!

COWDENKNOWES.

When summer comes, the swains on Tweed
    Sing their successful loves;
Around the ewes the lambkins feed,
    And music fills the groves.

But my loved song is then the broom,
  So fair on Cowdenknowes ;
For sure so sweet, so soft a bloom
  Elsewhere there never grows !

There Colin tuned his aiten reed,
  And won my yielding heart ;
No shepherd e'er that dwelt on Tweed
  Could play with half such art.

He sung of Tay, of Forth, of Clyde,
  The hills and dales around,
Of Leader-haughs and Leader-side ;
  Oh, how I blessed the sound !

Yet more delightful is the broom
  So fair on Cowdenknowes ;
For sure so fresh, so fair a bloom,
  Elsewhere there never grows.

Not Teviot braes, so green and gay,
  May with this broom compare ;
Not Yarrow's banks, in flow'ry May,
  Nor the Bush aboon Traquair.

More pleasing far are Cowdenknowes,
  My peaceful happy home,
Where I was wont to milk my yowes
  At even, among the broom.

Ye powers, that haunt the woods and plains,
  Where Tweed with Teviot flows,
Convey me to the best of swains,
  And my loved Cowdenknowes ? [1]

These two favourite specimens of the Scottish pastoral muse
date from the early years of the eighteenth century, both of them

[1] From the *Tea-table Miscellany*, 1724.

appearing in the *Tea-table Miscellany*, 1724. The second is by Crawford, and a fair example of his manner. Regarding the authorship of the first, we only know that it is signed in the *Tea-table Miscellany* with the initials S. R. The tune, which is a ballad one in one part, was recommended to Dr Pepusch by its sweetness and simplicity, and adopted by him as the parting strain of Macheath and Polly in the *Beggar's Opera*.

These pastoral songs, however, are a comparatively modern creation, probably on the basis of some lost original, of which we see another and English offshoot in a vulgar ballad of the preceding century, of which a broadside copy, mostly in black-letter, is preserved in the Roxburghe Collection, British Museum.[1] What is here transcribed of this composition will be sufficient to give the reader some idea of it.

THE LOVELY NORTHERN LASS.

Who in this ditty here complaining shews
What harm she got milking her daddy's ewes.
    To a pleasant Scotch tune, called *The Broome of Cowdenknowes.*

> Through Liddersdale as lately I went,
>   I musing on did passe,
> I heard a maid was discontent,
>   She sighed and said, Alas !
> All maids that ever deceived was,
>   Bear a part of these my woes,
> For once I was a bonny lass,
>   When I milked my daddy's ewes.
> With O the broome, the bonny, bonny broome,
>   The broome of Cowdenknowes ;
> Fain would I be in the North Countrie,
>   To milk my daddy's ewes.
>
> My love into the fields did come,
>   When my daddy was at home ;
> Sugared words he gave me there,
>   Praised me for such a one ;

---

[1] *Roxburghe Ballads*, Vol. i., No. 190.

His honey breath, and lips so soft,
  And his alluring eye,
And tempting tongue, [that] wooed me oft,
  Now forces me to cry :
All maids, &c.
      *   *   *   *

In Danby forest I was born,
  My beauty did excel.
      *   *   *   *

I might have been a prince's peer,
  When I came over the knowes,
Till the shepherd-boy beguiled me,
  Milking my daddy's ewes.
      *   *   *   *

A young man, hearing her complaint,
  Did pity this her case,
Saying to her, Sweet beauteous saint,
  I grieve so fair a face
Should sorrow so—then, sweeting, know,
  To ease thee of thy woes,
I'll go with thee to the North Countrie,
  To milk thy daddy's ewes.

Leander-like, I will remain
  Still constant to thee ever,
As Pyramus or Troilus,
  Till death our lives shall sever ;
Let me be hated evermore,
  Of all men that me knows,
If false to thee, sweet heart, I be,
  Milking thy daddy's ewes.

Then modestly she did reply,
  Might I so happy be,
Of you to find a husband kind,
  And for to marry me.
Then to you I would, during life,
  Continue constant still,
And be a true obedient wife,
  Observing of your will.

With O the broome, the bonny, bonny broome,
The broome of Cowdenknowes;
Fain would I be in the North Countrie,
Milking my daddy's ewes.[1]

* * * *

Cowles, it may be remarked, was a publisher of broadside ballads in the reign of Charles II., if not also somewhat earlier. A considerable number of those published by him and preserved in the Roxburghe Collection, including this of *The Northern Lass*, are in a certain style marking one authorship—a style distinguished by its involving a great deal of mythological allusion, thus somewhat recalling the manner of Burn the Violer. One of these pieces bears the initials 'L. P.,' which we may consequently regard as a shadow of the name of the author of *The Northern Lass*.

In Playford's *Dancing Master*, as early as 1650, occurs a tune called *Broom, the Bonny Bonny Broom*, which perfectly suits this song, and is believed by Mr William Chappell to have been its proper melody : it is probably that alluded to in the well-known book of that period, Burton's *Anatomy of Melancholy*, under the name of *O the Broom, the Bonny Bonny Broom*. Thus we pretty clearly take back the date of this famous air to the middle of the seventeenth century.

It is the opinion, however, of Mr Chappell [2]—and no opinion on such a subject can be entitled to greater weight—that the tune was of still earlier origin. There is in the Pepys Collection another black-letter emanation of the press of Francis Cowles, entitled *The New Broome*, and opening thus :

Poor Coridon did sometimes sit
Hard by the broome alone,
And secretly complained to it,
Against his only one.

[1] Printed at London for F. Cowles.
[2] *Popular Music of the Olden Time*, ii. 458.

He bids the broome that blooms him by,
    Beare witness to his wrong,
And, thinking that none else was nigh,
    He thus began his song :
        The broome, the broome, the well-favoured broome,
            The broome blooms fair on hill ;
        What ailed my love to lightly me,
            And I working her will.

Mr Chappell remarks that this song recalls ' the bunch of
ballads and songs all ancient, as *Broom, Broom on Hill,*' &c.,
which are mentioned in Laneham's *Letter from Kenilworth,* 1575,
and also, we may add, the tune *Brume, Brume on Hil,* introduced
in the list of melodies in the *Complaynt of Scotland,* 1548. We
thus seem to obtain a hint that our *Broom of the Cowdenknowes*
is the representative of an air of uncommon antiquity, and
which, in all its mutations, has constantly been connected with
the idea of broom—broom growing on elevated ground—though
not from the first on Cowdenknowes in the valley of the Leader,
in Berwickshire.   It is, for this and other reasons, the opinion of
Mr Chappell, that the tune is of English origin, and only came to
be called a Scotch tune on the front of *The Northern Lass,* from
the song being on a Scotch subject, and in imitation of the
Scotch dialect.   The case, however, is—to say the very least—
' not proven.'

SAW YE JOHNIE COMING ?

This is one of the old rustic productions of the Scottish muse,
for which there is no trace of authorship. Burns considered the
song unrivalled in humour, and the air in ' lively originality,'
and yet to most minds the pathetic earnestness of the girl will be
as striking as any drollery involved in the dialogue ; while no
one has more heartily admitted the capability of the air, when
played slow, for conveying mournful ideas than Burns himself.
He had the advantage of hearing it played with the most

touching effect by Mr Thomas Fraser, an oboist connected with the Dumfries theatre, and was thus induced to compose to it his pathetic song, *Thou hast Left me ever, Jamie.*

Saw ye Johnie comin'? quo' she, Saw ye Johnie comin'?

Saw ye Johnie comin'? quo' she, Saw ye Johnie comin'?   Wi'

his blue bon-net on his head, And his dog-gie rinnin'? quo' she,

And his dog-gie rin-nin'?

Saw ye Johnie comin'? quo' she,
    Saw ye Johnie comin'?
Saw ye Johnie comin'? quo' she,
    Saw ye Johnie comin'?
Saw ye Johnie comin'? quo' she,
    Saw ye Johnie comin',
Wi' his blue bonnet on his head,
    And his doggie rinnin'? quo' she,
    And his doggie rinnin'.

Fee him, father, fee him, quo' she,
    Fee him, father, fee him;
Fee him, father, fee him, quo' she,
    Fee him, father, fee him;

For he is a gallant lad,
   And a weel-doin';
And a' the wark about the toun
   Gangs wi' me when I see him, quo' she,
   Gangs wi' me when I see him.

O what will I do wi' him ? quo' he,
   What will I do wi' him ?
He has ne'er a coat upon his back,
   And I hae nane to gie him.
I hae twa coats into my kist,
   And ane o' them I'll gie him ;
And for a merk o' mair fee
   Dinna stand [1] wi' him, quo' she,
   Dinna stand wi' him :

For weel do I lo'e him, quo' she,
   Weel do I lo'e him ;
For weel do I lo'e him, quo' she,
   Weel do I lo'e him.
O, fee him, father, fee him, quo' she,
   Fee him, father, fee him ;
He'll haud the pleuch, thrash in the barn,
   And crack wi' me at e'en, quo' she,
   And crack wi' me at e'en.[2]

DUMBARTON'S DRUMS.

The following song, from the *Tea-table Miscellany,* is not of
the first order of merit, but could not well be omitted from the
present collection. Burns was under an impression that the
song was localised to Dumbarton Castle ; but the drums, more
probably, were those of Dumbarton's regiment, a corps named
from its first commander, Douglas, Earl of Dumbarton, who died
in exile in 1692.

[1] As much as to say, Don't stickle with him.
[2] From Herd's Collection, 1776.

x

Dum - bar - ton's drums beat bon - nie, O, When they

mind me of my dear John - ie, O ; How

hap - pie am I When my sol - dier is by, While he

kiss - es and bless - es his An - nie, O ! 'Tis a

sol - dier a - lone can de - light me, O, For his

grace - ful looks do in - vite me, O; While

guard-ed in his arms, I 'll fear no war's alarms, Neither

dan - ger nor death shall e'er fright me, O.

Dumbarton's drums beat bonnie, O,
When they mind me of my dear Johnie, O ;
  How happie am I
  When my soldier is by,
While he kisses and blesses his Annie, O !
'Tis a soldier alone can delight me, O,
For his graceful looks do invite me, O ;
  While guarded in his arms,
  I 'll fear no war's alarms,
Neither danger nor death shall e'er fright me, O.

My love is a handsome laddie, O,
Genteel, but ne'er foppish nor gaudy, O.
  Though commissions are dear,
  Yet I 'll buy him one this year,
For he 'll serve no longer a cadie, O.
A soldier has honour and bravery, O ;
Unacquainted with rogues and their knavery, O,
  He minds no other thing
  But the ladies or the king ;
For every other care is but slavery, O.

Then I 'll be the captain's lady, O,
Farewell all my friends and my daddy, O ;
  I 'll wait no more at home,
  But I 'll follow with the drum,
And whene'er that beats I 'll be ready, O.
Dumbarton's drums sound bonnie, O,
They are sprightly like my dear Johnie, O :
  How happy shall I be
  When on my soldier's knee,
And he kisses and blesses his Annie, O !

AN THOU WERT MY AIN THING.

An thou wert my ain thing, O, I would love thee,
I would love thee; An thou wert my ain thing, how
dear - ly would I love thee! Then
I would clasp thee in my arms, Then I'd se - cure thee
from all harms; For a - bove mor - tal
thou hast charms: How dear - ly do I
love thee!

An thou wert my ain thing, O,
    I would love thee, I would love thee;
An thou wert my ain thing,
    How dearly would I love thee!

Then I would clasp thee in my arms,
Then I'd secure thee from all harms;
For above mortal thou hast charms:
   How dearly do I love thee!

Of race divine thou needs must be,
Since nothing earthly equals thee,
So I must still presumptuous be,
   To shew how much I love thee.

The gods one thing peculiar have,
To ruin none whom they can save;
O, for their sake, support a slave,
   Who only lives to love thee!

To merit I no claim can make,
But that I love, and, for your sake,
What man can more, I'll undertake,
   So dearly do I love thee.

My passion, constant as the sun,
Flames stronger still, will ne'er have done,
Till fates my thread of life have spun,
   Which breathing out, I'll love thee.

This beautiful song, with its fine air, appeared in Ramsay's *Tea-table Miscellany*, excepting the second verse, which was added in a repetition of the song in Thomson's *Orpheus Caledonius*. It was regarded by these editors as a song of unknown authorship, and so it remains to this day.

An Thou wer Myn Own Thing is the name of a tune in the manuscript Lute-book, written by Gordon of Straloch in the year 1627.

THE EWE-BUCHTS.

The following song is another of the better productions of the rustic muse, probably dating from an early period of the eighteenth century, as it is published in Ramsay's *Tea-table Miscellany*, 1724, and, with its fine melody, in the *Orpheus Caledonius*, 1725. Bishop Percy paid it the compliment of inserting it in his *Reliques*.

Will ye go to the ewe - buchts, Ma - rion, And weir in the sheep wi' me? The sun shines sweet, my Ma - rion, But nae hauf sae sweet as thee. The sun shines sweet, my Ma - rion, But nae hauf sae sweet as thee.

Will ye go to the ewe-buchts, Marion,
And weir in the sheep wi' me?
The sun shines sweet, my Marion,
But nae hauf sae sweet as thee.

O, Marion's a bonnie lass,
    And the blithe blink's in her e'e ;
And fain wad I marry Marion,
    Gin Marion wad marry me.

There's gowd in your garters, Marion,
    And silk on your white hause-bane ;
Fou fain wad I kiss my Marion,
    At e'en, when I come hame.
There's braw lads in Earnslaw, Marion,
    Wha gape, and glower wi' their e'e,
At kirk when they see my Marion ;
    But nane o' them lo'es like me.

I've nine milk-ewes, my Marion,
    A cow and a brawny quey ;
I'll gie them a' to my Marion,
    Just on her bridal-day.
And ye'se get a green sey apron,
    And waistcoat o' London broun ;
And wow but we'se be vap'rin'
    Whene'er ye gang to the toun.

I'm young and stout, my Marion ;
    Nane dances like me on the green :
And, gin ye forsake me, Marion,
    I'll e'en gae draw up wi' Jean.
Sae put on your pearlins, Marion,
    And kirtle o' cramasie ;
And, as sune as my chin has nae hair on,
    I will come west, and see ye.[1]

---

[1] In a version of *The Ewe-buchts*, popular in the south of Scotland, the following chorus is added :

    Come round about the Merry-knowes, my Marion;
      Come round about the Merry-knowes wi' me;
    Come round about the Merry-knowes, my Marion;
      For Whitsled is lying lee.

As Whitsled is a farm in the parish of Ashkirk, and county of Selkirk,

THE BIRKS OF INVERMAY.

At the time when Crawford and Hamilton were celebrating the fair ladies of Edinburgh under the guise of shepherdesses, a young man from the skirts of the Perthshire Highlands, named David Malloch, occupied the humble position of janitor of the High School. He was afterwards able to push his way to a good education, and a position of some notability in the literary circles of London, under the slightly changed name of David Mallet ; and, finally, we find him acting as the editor of Bolingbroke's Works. While living in Edinburgh, he caught the *furore* for pastoral verse which was then and there raging, and produced the following song to a beautiful tune of contemporaneous origin :

The smil-ing morn, the breath-ing spring, In-vite the tune-fu' birds to sing; And,

while the Merry-knowes is the name of a particular spot on the farm, it is probable that the song is a native of that Arcadia of Scotland, the Vale of the Tweed.

To readers of fastidious taste, the following might be a more acceptable version of the last stanza :

I'm young and stout, my Marion ;
   Nane dances like me on the green ;
I could work a haill day, my Marion,
   For ae blink o' your een.
Sae put on your pearlins, Marion,
   And kirtle o' cramasie ;
And, as sune as it is the gloamin',
   I will come west, and see ye.

while they war - ble from the spray, Love

melts the un - i - vers - al lay. Let

us, A - man - da, time - ly wise, Like

them, im - prove the hour that flies; And

in soft rap - tures waste the day, A-

mong the birks of In - ver - may.

The smiling morn, the breathing spring,
Invite the tunefu' birds to sing ;
And, while they warble from the spray,
Love melts the universal lay.
Let us, Amanda, timely wise,
Like them, improve the hour that flies ;
And in soft raptures waste the day,
Among the birks of Invermay.

For soon the winter of the year,
And age, life's winter, will appear ;
At this thy living bloom will fade,
As that will strip the verdant shade.
Our taste of pleasure then is o'er,
The feathered songsters are no more ;
And when they drop, and we decay,
Adieu the birks of Invermay ![1]

ROSLIN CASTLE.

The beautiful air of this song was long thought to be a production of James Oswald ; but Mr Stenhouse states, that it appears in the prior collection of M'Gibbon, under the name of *The House of Glams.*   It is certainly of no great age.

The song, which may be considered as an imitation of the dulcet strains of Mallet and Thomson, was composed by Richard Hewitt, a young man, a native of Cumberland, who served Dr Blacklock, the blind poet, for some years as an amanuensis, and died in 1764, in the capacity of secretary to the Lord Justice-Clerk Milton, *sous-ministre* for Scotland, under Archibald, Duke of Argyle.

The song first appeared in Herd's Collection.

'Twas   in   that   sea - son   of   the year, When

all   things   gay   and   sweet   ap - pear,   That

[1] Invermay is a small woody glen, on the northern skirts of the Ochil range, rendered attractive by a cascade of its rivulet, the May.

Col - in, with the morn - ing ray, A-

rose and sung his ru - ral lay. Of

Nan - nie's charms the shep - herd sung: The

hills and dales with Nan - nie rung; While

Ros - lin Cas - tle heard the swain, And

ech - oed back his cheer - ful strain.

'Twas in that season of the year,
When all things gay and sweet appear,
That Colin, with the morning ray,
Arose and sung his rural lay.
Of Nannie's charms the shepherd sung:
The hills and dales with Nannie rung;
While Roslin Castle heard the swain,
And echoed back his cheerful strain.

Awake, sweet Muse ! The breathing spring
With rapture warms : awake, and sing !
Awake and join the vocal throng,
And hail the morning with a song :
To Nannie raise the cheerful lay ;
O, bid her haste and come away ;
In sweetest smiles herself adorn,
And add new graces to the morn !

O look, my love ! on every spray
A feather'd warbler tunes his lay ;
'Tis beauty fires the ravish'd throng,
And love inspires the melting song :
Then let the raptured notes arise :
For beauty darts from Nannie's eyes ;
And love my rising bosom warms,
And fills my soul with sweet alarms.

Oh, come, my love ! Thy Colin's lay
With rapture calls : O, come away !
Come, while the Muse this wreath shall twine
Around that modest brow of thine.
O ! hither haste, and with thee bring
That beauty blooming like the spring,
Those graces that divinely shine,
And charm this ravish'd heart of mine !

PINKIE HOUSE.

This song appears in Herd's Collection, 1776, being apparently designed as an improvement upon one of David Mallet's,
beginning 'As Sylvia in a forest lay,' which had been printed
in the *Tea-table Miscellany* and *Orpheus Caledonius*, as to the
tune of *Rothes's Lament or Pinkie House*. The present song is
believed to have been a composition of Joseph Mitchell, a bard
of medium merit, who flourished in Edinburgh in the reign of
George II.

By Pinkie House [1] oft let me walk,
    And muse o'er Nelly's charms !
Her placid air, her winning talk,
    Even envy's self disarms.
O let me, ever fond, behold
    Those graces void of art—
Those cheerful smiles that sweetly hold,
    In willing chains, my heart !

[1] Pinkie House, the seat of Sir Archibald Hope, Bart., is a Scottish manor-house, in the taste of the time of King James VI., situated in the midst of a fine old grove, close by the town of Musselburgh.

O come, my love ! and bring anew
   That gentle turn of mind ;
That gracefulness of air in you
   By nature's hand designed.
These, lovely as the blushing rose,
   First lighted up this flame,
Which, like the sun, for ever glows
   Within my breast the same.

Ye light coquettes ! ye airy things !
   How vain is all your art !
How seldom it a lover brings !
   How rarely keeps a heart !
O gather from my Nelly's charms
   That sweet, that graceful ease,
That blushing modesty that warms,
   That native art to please !

Come then, my love ! O, come along !
   And feed me with thy charms ;
Come, fair inspirer of my song !
   Oh, fill my longing arms !
A flame like mine can never die,
   While charms so bright as thine,
So heavenly fair, both please the eye,
   And fill the soul divine !

TARRY WOO.

There are very few sentimental songs of the north countrie
otherwise than upon love. One of that exceptive character, long
held in great favour in the pastoral regions of Tweed and Teviot,
is devoted to the exaltation of the pastoral craft, under the
general idea of the tarry wool in which it deals. This ditty was
published in the *Tea-table Miscellany,* and the air in M'Gibbon's
first collection.

Tar - ry woo, O, tar - ry woo, Tarry woo is

ill to spin; Card it weil, O card it weil,

Card it weil, ere ye be - gin, When it's card - it,

row'd, and spun, Then the wark is haf - lins done;

But, when wov - en, dress'd, and clean, It may be clead - in'

for a queen.

Tarry woo, O, tarry woo,
    Tarry woo is ill to spin ;
Card it weil, O card it weil,
    Card it weil, ere ye begin,
When it's cardit, row'd, and spun,
Then the wark is haflins done ;
But, when woven, dress'd, and clean,
It may be cleadin' for a queen.

Sing my bonnie harmless sheep,
That feed upon the mountains steep,
Bleating sweetly, as ye go
Through the winter's frost and snow.
Hart, and hynd, and fallow-deer,
No by half sae useful are :
Frae kings, to him that hauds the plou',
All are obliged to tarry woo.

Up, ye shepherds, dance and skip ;
Ower the hills and valleys trip ;
Sing up the praise of tarry woo ;
Sing the flocks that bear it too :
Harmless creatures, without blame,
That clead the back, and cram the wame ;
Keep us warm and hearty fou—
Leeze me on the tarry woo !

How happy is the shepherd's life,
Far frae courts and free of strife !
While the gimmers bleat and bae,
And the lambkins answer mae ;
No such music to his ear !
Of thief or fox he has no fear :
Sturdy kent, and collie true,
Weil defend the tarry woo.

He lives content, and envies none :
Not even a monarch on his throne,
Though he the royal sceptre sways,
Has such pleasant holidays.
Who'd be king, can ony tell,
When a shepherd sings sae well ?
Sings sae well, and pays his due
With honest heart and tarry woo.

Sir Walter Scott used annually to join in the festivities of
the woollen manufacturers of Galashiels, on the day of the

inauguration of their deacon-convener. On one or two of these occasions, notwithstanding disqualifications equal to those of the Nightingale Club, he was induced to regale the company (at an advanced period of the evening) with *Tarry Woo*.

MY SHEEP I NEGLECTED.

This is an effort in the pastoral style of Crawford by a man who occupied rather a broad space in the public eye in Scotland, in the middle of the eighteenth century. Sir Gilbert Elliot of Minto, the third baronet of the series, appears to have been a man of fine sagacity, very considerable accomplishments, and good talents for public business. The Rev. Dr Somerville of Jedburgh, who was intimately acquainted with him, speaks in the highest terms of Sir Gilbert's talents and of his amiable general character. As member for Roxburghshire, he rose to be Treasurer of the Navy, and was at one time in some likelihood of being appointed Speaker. He died in the vigour of life in January 1777.

Sir Gilbert displayed a gift of verse-making at the early age of fourteen, when he composed some lines in compliment to Mr Murray, on his defending the magistrates of Edinburgh in parliament against the charge brought against them on account of the Porteous Riot.[1] Like his sister, Miss Jeanie, he wrote one Scotch song, which has been ever held in esteem :

My sheep I ne-glect-ed— I lost my sheep-
hook, And all the gay haunts of my

[1] These verses are in the *Gentleman's Magazine*, 1737, p. 509.

youth   I   for - sook; No   more   for   A-

mynt - ta fresh gar - lands   I   wove; For am-

bi - tion,   I   said, would soon cure me of   love. Oh,

what had   my youth with am - bi - tion   to   do? Why

left I   A - myn - ta? Why broke I   my   vow? Oh,

give me   my sheep, and   my   sheep - hook   re-

store, And I'll   wan - der   from   love   and A-

myn - ta   no   more.

My sheep I neglected—I lost my sheep-hook,
And all the gay haunts of my youth I forsook ;
No more for Amynta fresh garlands I wove ;
For ambition, I said, would soon cure me of love.
   Oh, what had my youth with ambition to do ?
   Why left I Amynta ? Why broke I my vow ?
   Oh, give me my sheep, and my sheep-hook restore,
   And I 'll wander from love and Amynta no more.

Through regions remote in vain do I rove,
And bid the wide ocean secure me from love !
Oh, fool ! to imagine that aught could subdue
A love so well-founded, a passion so true !
Alas, 'tis too late at thy fate to repine !
Poor shepherd ! Amynta no more can be thine ;
Thy tears are all fruitless, thy wishes are vain,
The moments neglected return not again.

The air for which this song was written is one commonly
called in old collections *My Apron, Dearie*, from a rude song in
which these words were conspicuous, of which it was the original
music.

In connection with the poetical gifts of the brother and sister
Gilbert and Jean Elliot, it is interesting to know that their
father Sir Gilbert, a judge of the Court of Session under the
title of Lord Minto, and who died in 1763, was a lover of poetry,
and shewed in himself a gift for verse. The only composition of
his which has been brought to light, is an Italian canzonet which
he wrote for Signora Passini, to be sung to a Scotch air at some
of the concerts at which she appeared about the 'fifties.'

      Veduto in prato
       Il mio pastor,
     Il crin coronato,
       D'un serto di fior'.
     Il sole negli occhi
       La fide nel sen',
     Ah ! dove s' asconde ?
      Il caro mio ben' ?

Al bosco, al monte,
La cerco in van,
E, presso al fonte
Non trovo ch' il can ;
Ah ! cane fedele
Deh ! dimmi perche ;
Il mio crudele
S' asconde di me ?[1]

SAE MERRY AS WE TWA HA'E BEEN !

Sae Merry as We have been appears as a refrain of old date
in our poetical history. It occurs as the name of one of the
tunes in the Skene Manuscript, circa 1630—a tune, however,
which does not now exist in any such connection. It appears as
the title of an air also in Ramsay's *Tea-table Miscellany*, being
the melody assigned to a song probably of Ramsay's own,
addressed 'to Mrs E. C.,' and beginning, 'Now Phœbus advances
on high,' but containing no such phrase or refrain as this in the
body of the poem. The phrase is one of those expressions, like
' auld lang syne,' which can never fail to awaken kindly social
feelings, and it is not surprising that there should have at length
been a song fully developing the idea—one which Burns felt to
be ' beautiful '—whose chorus, in particular, he deemed 'truly
pathetic '—as follows :[2]

A lass that was lad - en'd with care, Sat
heav - i - ly un - der yon thorn; I list - en'd a

[1] *Scottish Ballads and Songs*, Edinburgh, 1859.
[2] This song appeared in Herd's Collection. There is another version,
containing a few attempts at improvement, in some later collections.

while for to hear, When thus she be - gan for to

mourn. When - e'er my dear shep - herd was there, The

birds did me - lo - dious - ly sing, And cold nip - ping

win - ter did wear A face that re - sem - bled the

spring. Sae mer - ry as we twa ha'e been, Sae

mer - ry as we twa ha'e been, My heart it is

like for to break When I think on the

days we ha'e seen.

A lass that was laden'd with care,
  Sat heavily under yon thorn ;
I listen'd a while for to hear,
  When thus she began for to mourn.
Whenc'er my dear shepherd was there,
  The birds did melodiously sing,
And cold nipping winter did wear
  A face that resembled the spring.
    Sae merry as we twa ha'e been,
      Sae merry as we twa ha'e been,
    My heart it is like for to break
      When I think on the days we ha'e seen.

Our flocks feeding close by his side,
  He gently pressing my hand,
I view'd the wide world in its pride,
  And laugh'd at the pomp of command !
My dear, he would oft to me say,
  What makes you hard-hearted to me !
Oh ! why do you thus turn away,
  From him who is dying for thee ?

But now he is far from my sight,
  Perhaps a deceiver may prove,
Which makes me lament day and night,
  That ever I granted my love.
At eve, when the rest of the folk
  Are merrily seated to spin,
I set myself under an oak,
  And heavily sighed for him.

An interesting anecdote connected with this song is given in the Abbé Morellet's *Memoirs:* 'Franklin was very fond of Scotch songs ; he recollected, he said, the strong and agreeable impression which they had made on him. He related to us that, while travelling in America, he found himself beyond the Alleghany Mountains, in the house of a Scotchman, living remote from society, after the loss of his fortune, with his wife, who had been handsome, and their daughter, fifteen or sixteen years of age ; and that, on a beautiful evening, sitting before their door, the wife had sung the Scotch air *So Merry as We have been,* in so sweet and touching a way that he burst into tears ; and that the recollection of this impression was still vivid, after more than thirty years.'

JOHNIE'S GRAY BREEKS.

A homely song, entitled *Johnie's Gray Breeks,* has been long a favourite in Scotland. Its air, one of the finest of the whole series of our sentimental melodies, Mr Stenhouse believed to be the composition of James Oswald. The best song extant to this air, out of many, is the following :

When I was in my se'n-teen year, I was baith blithe and bon-nie, O; The lads lo'ed me baith far and near, But I lo'ed nane but John-ie, O: He gain'd my heart in twa three weeks, He spake sae blithe and

kind - ly,   O; And   I made   him   new gray breeks, That

fit - ted   him   most   fine - ly,   O.

When I was in my se'nteen year,
    I was baith blithe and bonnie, O ;
The lads lo'ed me baith far and near,
    But I lo'ed nane but Johnie, O :
He gain'd my heart in twa three weeks,
    He spake sae blithe and kindly, O ;
And I made him new gray breeks,
    That fitted him most finely, O.

He was a handsome fellow ;
    His humour was baith frank and free ;
His bonnie locks sae yellow,
    Like gowd they glitter'd in my e'e :
His dimpled chin and rosy cheeks,
    And face sae fair and ruddy, O ;
And then-a-days his gray breeks
    Were neither auld nor duddy, O.

But now they 're threadbare worn,
    They 're wider than they wont to be ;
They 're tash'd-like and sair torn,
    And clouted upon ilka knee.
But gin I had a simmer's day,
    As I ha'e had right monie, O,
I 'd make a web o' new gray,
    To be breeks to my Johnie, O.

For he 's weel wordy o' them,
    And better, gin I had to gie,
And I 'll tak pains upo' them,
    Frae faults I 'll strive to keep them free.
To cleid him weel shall be my care,
    To please him a' my study, O !
But he maun wear the auld pair
    A wee, though they be duddy, O.

For when the lad was in his prime,
    Like him there warna monie, O.
He ca'd me aye his bonnie thing,
    Sae wha wadna lo'e Johnie, O ?
O, I lo'e Johnie's gray breeks,
    For a' the care they 've gi'en me yet,
And gin we live another year,
    We 'll mak them hale between us yet.

SHAME FA' THE GEAR.

When I think on this warld's pelf, And the
lit - tle wee share I ha'e o't to my - self, And
how the lass that wants it is by the lads for-got, May the
shame fa' the gear and the bleth - rie o't!

When I think on this warld's pelf,
And the little wee share I ha'e o't to myself,
And how the lass that wants it is by the lads forgot,
May the shame fa' the gear and the blethrie o't !

Jockie was the laddie that held the pleuch,
But now he's got gowd and gear eneuch,
He thinks nae mair o' me that wears the plaidin' coat ;
May the shame fa' the gear and the blethrie o't !

Jenny was the lassie that muckit the byre,
But now she is clad in her silken attire ;
And Jockie says he lo'es her, and me has forgot—
May the shame fa' the gear and the blethrie o't !

But all this shall never daunton me,
Sae lang as I keep my fancy free ;
For the lad that's sae inconstant is no worth a groat—
May the shame fa' the gear and the blethrie o't !

'Shame fa' the gear and the blethrie [that is, the senseless-
ness] o't' is an old Scottish proverb, adduced on any occasion
when conduct has been unduly affected by sordid considerations,
as when a young woman, for the sake of a good 'down-sitting,'
marries an old man. Kelly, in his *Scotch Proverbs*, published in
1721, alludes to a song embodying the idea. There are two
versions of such a song : one here given from Johnson's *Museum;*
another which appeared in Yair's *Charmer*, 1751, of which the
morale is strikingly inferior. It represents a man as reflecting
sarcastically on his own poverty, simply in contrast with old
companions now well-off, and adding finally a line which hints
an ample explanation of his low condition—

While I ha'e the tither penny to pay the tither pot,
May the shame fa' the gear and the blethrie o't !

LOGIE O' BUCHAN.

The song here presented has long been in great favour in Scotland. According to Mr Peter Buchan, it was the composition of Mr George Halket, and was written by him while schoolmaster of Rathen, in Aberdeenshire, about the year 1736. 'The poetry of this individual,' says Mr Buchan, 'was chiefly Jacobitical, and long remained familiar amongst the peasantry in that quarter of the country. One of the best known of these, at the present, is *Wherry, Whigs, awa', Man!* In 1746, Mr Halket wrote a dialogue betwixt George II. and the Devil, which falling into the hands of the Duke of Cumberland while on his march to Culloden, he offered one hundred pounds' reward for the person or the head of its author. Mr Halket died in 1756.

'The Logie here mentioned is in one of the adjoining parishes (Crimond), where Mr Halket then resided; and the hero of the piece was a James Robertson, gardener at the place of Logie.'

The song and air first appeared in Johnson's *Museum.*

O, Lo-gie o' Buch-an, O, Lo-gie, the laird, They ha'e ta'en a-wa' Jam-ie that delved in the yard; He play'd on the pipe and the vi-ol sae sma'; They ha'e ta'en a-wa' Jam-ie, the flower o' them

a'. He said, Think na lang, lass-ie, though I gang a-

wa'; He said, Think na lang, lass-ie, though I gang a-

wa'; For the sim-mer will come, when cauld win-ter's a-

wa', And I'll come and see thee in spite o' them a'.

O, Logie o' Buchan, O, Logie, the laird,
They ha'e ta'en awa' Jamie that delved in the yard;
He play'd on the pipe and the viol sae sma';
They ha'e ta'en awa' Jamie, the flower o' them a'.
  He said, Think na lang, lassie, though I gang awa';
  He said, Think na lang, lassie, though I gang awa';
  For the simmer will come, when cauld winter's awa',
  And I'll come and see thee in spite o' them a'.

Though Sandie has owsen, and siller, and kye,
A house and a haddin',[1] and a' things forbye,
Yet I wad ha'e Jamie, wi's bonnet in's hand,
Before I'd ha'e Sandie wi' houses and land.

My daddie looks sulky, my minnie looks sour,
They frown upon Jamie, because he is poor;
But daddie and minnie although that they be,
There's nane o' them a' like my Jamie to me.

[1] A holding.

I sit on my creepie,[1] and spin at my wheel,
And think on the laddie that lo'ed me sae weel ;
He had but ae sixpence—he brak it in twa,
And he gi'ed me the hauf o't when he gaed awa'.
   Then haste ye back, Jamie, and bide na awa',
   Then haste ye back, Jamie, and bide na awa';
   The simmer is comin', cauld winter 's awa',
   And ye 'll come and see me in spite o' them a'.

JENNY NETTLES.

Every child in rural Scotland has heard nurse-maids singing
a ranting and lively song, beginning with the following verses :

> Saw ye Jenny Nettles,
>   Jenny Nettles, Jenny Nettles?
> Saw ye Jenny Nettles,
>   Coming frae the market?
> Wi' bag and baggage on her back,
> Her fee and bountith in her lap,
> Wi' bag and baggage on her back,
>   And a baby in her oxter.
>
> I met ayont the cairnie,
>   Jenny Nettles, Jenny Nettles,
> Singing till her bairnie, &c.[2]

The obscurity of this poor girl has not prevented her tale of
hapless love from attaining that celebrity which even the home-
liest of rustic verse can sometimes give. Jenny, disowned by an
ungrateful lover, and unable to bear the scorn of society, put an
end to her life, and was buried between two lairds' lands near
the Lomond Hills, where a cairn of stones was afterwards formed
to mark the spot, according to ancient usage. It seems strange
that so tragic a tale should be connected with so merry a melody

---

[1] A low stool.
[2] The entire song is in Herd's Collection.

as that here presented. Upwards of thirty years ago, and probably much above a century after the composition of the song, a gentleman paying a visit in Fife, found himself in the neighbourhood of the spot where the cairn of Jenny Nettles had once stood. Causing a digging to be commenced, he found at the depth of eighteen inches a skull and some other bones, with two ear-rings and twenty-four beads—supposed to be relics of this unfortunate maiden.[1]

A song of greater elegance and more refined sentiment, but not of a high degree of merit, was composed at a later period in honour of the name of Jenny Nettles.

I met ayont the cairnie, Jenny Nettles trig and braw, A-mang the shaws o' Bar-nie, Skipping light-ly bare-foot: The spreading ros-es wet with dew Are no sae sweet as Jenny's mou', Her dimpled cheeks and een so blue, A-mang the heather barefoot.

> I met ayont the cairnie,
> Jenny Nettles trig and braw,
> Amang the shaws o' Barnie,
> Skipping lightly barefoot :

[1] Some of these relics were long in the possession of the late Mr Robert Frazer, honorary curator of the museum of the Society of the Antiquaries of Scotland. See Notes to Johnson's *Scots Musical Museum*. The skull is in possession of Mr Joseph Paton, Dunfermline.

The spreading roses wet with dew
Are no sae sweet as Jenny's mou',
Her dimpled cheeks and een so blue,
    Amang the heather barefoot.

I took her hand, I pressed it—
I asked if she could fancy me ;
My heart ye ha'e distressed it,
    Coming frae the market.
My bonnie lass both trig and neat,
Nae fairer trips on London street,
Your glancing een subdues my heart,
    Amang the heather barefoot.

My haddin' stands on yonder glen,
I ha'e a but, I ha'e a ben ;
Gin ye 'll be lady o' my ain,
    Ye 'll gang nae langer barefoot.
I met ayont the cairnie,
Jenny Nettles trig and braw,
Amang the shaws o' Barnie,
    Skipping lightly barefoot.

A silken gown then ye shall hae,
A cleaden new frae tap to tae,
A pair o' shoon and stockings tae,
    To keep you frae gaun barefoot.
I met ayont the cairnie,
Jenny Nettles trig and braw,
Amang the shaws o' Barnie,
    Skipping lightly barefoot.

LOW DOUN IN THE BRUME.

This rustic ditty is not of great age, but nevertheless enjoys a large measure of popular admiration. The origin and authorship of the words and music are involved in doubt.[1]

My dad-die is a cankert carle, He'll no twine wi' his gear; My

min-nie she's a scauldin' wife, Hauds a' the house a-steer; But

let them say, or let them do, It's a' ane to me, For he's

low doun, he's in the brume, That's wait-in' on me:

[1] 'This song is said to be the production of James Carnegie, Esq. of Balnamoon, a beautiful estate upon the slope of the Grampians, about five miles north-west of Brechin. A correspondent, who has kindly furnished the substance of this notice, says: " I have conversed with a worthy farmer of fourscore, who has lived on the Balnamoon estate from infancy. The garrulous old fellow observed, 'I kent the auld laird weel; he was a curious body, and there's nae doubt but he made up the sang.' He was firmly attached to the House of Stuart, and went out in the Forty-five. After the quelling of that unhappy rebellion, he lived for some time in the capacity of a shepherd to one of his hill-farmers; but the interest of the Arbuthnot family, with which he was connected by marriage, soon restored him to his home and to the world." '—*Harp of Caledonia*, vol. ii. p. 387.

Wait - in' on me, my love, He's wait - in' on me: For he's

low doun, he's in the brume, That's wait - in' on me.

My daddie is a cankert carle,
 He'll no twine wi' his gear ;
My minnie she's a scauldin' wife,
 Hands a' the house asteer.
  But let them say, or let them do,
  It's a' ane to me,
  For he's low doun, he's in the brume,
  That's waitin' on me :
  Waitin' on me, my love,
  He's waitin' on me :
  For he's low doun, he's in the brume,
  That's waitin' on me.

My auntie Kate sits at her wheel,
 And sair she lightlies me ;
But weel I ken it's a' envy,
 For ne'er a joe has she.
  And let them say, &c.

My cousin Kate was sair beguiled
 Wi' Johnie o' the Glen ;
And aye sinsyne she cries, Beware
 O' fause deluding men.

Gleed Sandy he cam west yestreen,
 And speir'd when I saw Pate ;
And aye sinsyne the neebors round
 They jeer me air and late.

z

THE SHEPHERD'S WIFE.

In Herd's Collection is a long rambling dialogue song, of not much merit, but sustained by a melody of uncommon beauty, and, for a Scotch sentimental air, animation. After the song had been in a great measure laid aside, the air retained popularity, and of late years it has been insured a sort of immortality by being adapted for the melody of Burns's charming song, *A Rose-bud by my early walk.* The present editor, unwilling to see the original rustic song entirely perish, has here condensed and purified it, so as to fit it for modern society.

The shep - herd's wife cries o'er the lee, Cries

o'er the lee, cries o'er the lee, The shepherd's wife cries

o'er the lee, Will ye come hame a - gain e'en, jo? What

shall I ha'e gin I come hame, Gin I come hame, gin

I come hame, What shall I ha'e gin I come hame, Gin

I come hame a - gain e'en, jo?

The shepherd's wife cries o'er the lee,
Cries o'er the lee, cries o'er the lee,
The shepherd's wife cries o'er the lee,
Will ye come hame again e'en, jo ?

What shall I ha'e gin I come hame,
Gin I come hame, gin I come hame,
What shall I ha'e gin I come hame,
Gin I come hame again e'en, jo ?

Ye 'll ha'e a panfu' o' plumping porridge,
And butter in them, and butter in them,
Ye 'll ha'e a panfu' o' plumping porridge,
Gin ye 'll come hame again e'en, jo.

Ha ha how, that 's naething that dow,
I winna come hame, I winna come hame ;
Ha ha how, that 's naething that dow,
I winna come hame again e'en, jo !

Ye 'll ha'e your wifie's welcome smile,
Her welcome smile, her welcome smile,
Ye 'll ha'e your loving wifie's smile,
Gin ye 'll come hame again e'en, jo.

Ha ha now, that 's something that dow,
I will come hame, I will come hame ;
Ha ha now, that 's something that dow,
I will come hame again e'en, jo.

THE PLOUGHMAN.

The Ploughman appears in Herd's Collection. Subsequently Johnson gave the air in his *Museum*, but with the song thrown into a new form by Burns. There is another version, very much corrupted, in Cunningham's *Songs of Scotland*. In the present case, the air and the old verses are given together.

The plough-man he's a bon-nie lad, And
a' his wark's at lei - sure; And,
when that he comes hame at e'en, He
kiss-es me wi' plea-sure. Up wi't now, my ploughman lad!
Up wi't now, my plough - man! Of
a' the lads that I do see, Commend me to the plough-man.

The ploughman he 's a bonnie lad,
 And a' his wark 's at leisure ;
And, when that he comes hame at e'en,
 He kisses me wi' pleasure.
  Up wi 't now,[1] my ploughman lad !
  Up wi 't now, my ploughman !
  Of a' the lads that I do see,
   Commend me to the ploughman.

Now the blooming spring comes on,
 He takes his yoking early,
And, 'whistling o'er the furrowed land,' [2]
 He goes to fallow clearly.

When my ploughman comes hame at e'en,
 He 's often wet and wearie ;
Cast aft the wet, put on the dry,
 And gae to bed, my dearie.

I will wash my ploughman's hose,
 And I will wash his owerlay,
And I will make my ploughman's bed,
 And cheer him late and early.

  Merry but, and merry ben,
  Merry is my ploughman ;
  Of a' the trades that I do ken,
   Commend me to the ploughman.

Plough yon hill, and plough yon dale,
 Plough yon faugh and fallow ;
Wha winna drink the ploughman's health,
 Is but a dirty fellow !

[1] A Scottish phrase of high exultation, which seems to be only used in
songs :
   Up wi 't, Ailie, Ailie,
   Up wi 't, Ailie, now !
      Old Song.

[2] MILTON.

AYE WAUKIN' O!

There are various versions of this simple old song, but none so good as the following, which was taken from recitation many years ago, and inserted in a collection edited by Mr Robert Chambers in 1829. Burns furnished an improved version to Johnson's *Museum*.

O spring's a pleasant time, Flowers o' ev'-ry col-our—The sweet bird builds her nest, And I lang for my lov-er. Aye wau-kin' O, Wau-kin' aye, and wear-y, Sleep I can get nane, For think-in' o' my dear-ie.

O spring's a pleasant time,
  Flowers o' every colour—
The sweet bird builds her nest,
  And I lang for my lover.
Aye waukin' O,
  Waukin' aye, and weary,
Sleep I can get nane,
  For thinkin' o' my dearie.

O I 'm wat, wat,
  O I 'm wat and weary ;
Yet fain I 'd rise and run
  If I thought to meet my dearie.

When I sleep I dream,
  When I wauk I 'm eerie ;
Sleep I can get nane,
  For thinkin' o' my dearie.

Lanely night comes on ;
  A' the lave are sleeping ;
I think on my love,
  And blear my een wi' greeting.

Feather-beds are soft,
  Painted rooms are bonnie ;
But a kiss o' my dear love
  Is better far than ony.

O for Friday's night,
  Friday at the gloaming !
O for Friday's night !
  Friday 's lang o' coming.

THE LEE-RIG.

There was an old rustic song, of which the first verse only has been preserved :

    I 'll rowe thee o'er the lee-rig,
      My ain kind dearie, O ;
    I 'll rowe thee o'er the lee-rig,
      My ain kind dearie, O.
    Although the night were ne'er sae wet,
      And I were ne'er sae weary, O,
    I 'll rowe thee o'er the lee-rig,
      My ain kind dearie, O.

While the verses were homely and unfit for the polite, the air had liveliness and character sufficient to recommend it for preservation in Oswald's Collection. Robert Fergusson afterwards composed to it the song here presented. At a subsequent period, Burns composed a song to the same air.

Will ye gang o'er the lee - rig, My
ain kind dear - ie, O, And
cud - dle there sae kind - ly Wi'
me, my kind dear - ie, O? At
thorn - y dike and birk - en tree, We'll
daff and ne'er be wear - y, O, They'll
scug ill een frae you and me, My
ain kind dear - ie, O.

Will ye gang o'er the lee-rig,
  My ain kind dearie, O,
And cuddle there sae kindly
  Wi' me, my kind dearie, O ?

At thorny dike and birken-tree,
  We'll daff and ne'er be weary, O,
They'll scug ill een frae you and me,
  My ain kind dearie, O.

Nae herds wi' kent and colly there
  Shall ever come to fear ye, O ;
But laverocks whistling in the air
  Shall woo, like me, their dearie, O.

While others herd their lambs and ewes,
  And toil for warld's gear, my jo,
Upon the lee my pleasure grows,
  Wi' you, my kind dearie, O.

KIND ROBIN LO'ES ME.

There was a very old song called *Kind Robin Lo'es Me*, but of a rude and homely character, and of which no more than two verses have been preserved :

Hech, hey, Robin, quo' she,
Hech, hey, Robin, quo' she,
Hech, hey, Robin, quo' she,
  Kind Robin lo'es me, &c.

In Herd's Collection appeared the song here presented, which has been much a favourite in Scotland.

Ro - bin is my on - ly jo, For Ro - bin has the
art to lo'e; Sae to his suit I mean to bow, Because I ken he lo'es me. Hap - py, hap - py
was the shower, That led me to his birk - en bower, Where
first of love I fand the power, And kenn'd that Ro - bin
lo'ed me.

Robin is my only jo,
For Robin has the art to lo'e ;
Sae to his suit I mean to bow,
   Because I ken he lo'es me.
Happy, happy was the shower,
That led me to his birken bower,
Where first of love I fand the power,
   And kenn'd that Robin lo'ed me.

They speak of napkins, speak of rings,
Speak of gluves and kissin' strings ;
And name a thousand bonnie things,
    And ca' them signs he lo'es me.
But I 'd prefer a smack o' Rob,
Seated on the velvet fog,
To gifts as lang's a plaiden wab ;
    Because I ken he lo'es me.

He 's tall and sonsie, frank and free,
Lo'ed by a', and dear to me ;
Wi' him I 'd live, wi' him I 'd dee,
    Because my Robin lo'es me.
My tittie Mary said to me,
Our courtship but a joke wad be,
And I or lang be made to see
    That Robin didna lo'e me.

But little kens she what has been,
Me and my honest Rob between ;
And in his wooing, O sae keen
    Kind Robin is that lo'es me.
Then fly, ye lazy hours, away,
And hasten on the happy day,
When, Join your hands, Mess John will say,
    And mak him mine that lo'es me.

Till then, let every chance unite
To fix our love and give delight,
And I 'll look down on such wi' spite,
    Wha doubt that Robin lo'es me.
        O hey, Robin ! quo' she,
        O hey, Robin ! quo' she,
        O hey, Robin ! quo' she ;
           Kind Robin lo'es me.

THE LOWLANDS OF HOLLAND.

This touching little rustic ballad appeared in Herd's Collection. It was reproduced in Johnson's *Museum*, with some changes, and with the air, which Mr Stenhouse considers as having afforded a basis for William Marshall's well-known tune, *Miss Admiral Gordon's Strathspey*, to which Burns composed *Of a' the Airts the Wind can Blaw*.

My love he's built a bonnie ship, and set her on the sea, With seven score guid mariners to bear her companie. There's three score is sunk, and three score dead at sea; And the lowlands of Holland ha'e twined my love and me.

My love he's built a bonnie ship, and set her on the sea,
With seven score guid mariners to bear her companie.
There's three score is sunk, and three score dead at sea ;
And the lowlands of Holland ha'e twined my love and me.

My love he built another ship, and set her on the main,
And nane but twenty mariners for to bring her hame ;
But the weary wind began to rise, and the sea began to rout ;
My love, then, and his bonnie ship, turn'd withershins [1] about.

There shall neither coif come on my head, nor kame come in
    my hair ;
There shall neither coal nor candle-licht come in my bouir mair ;
Nor will I love another man until the day I dee,
For I never loved a love but ane, and he's drown'd in the sea.

O, haud your tongue, my daughter dear, be still and be content ;
There are mair lads in Galloway, ye need na sair lament.
O ! there is nane in Galloway, there's nane at a' for me ;
For I never loved a love but ane, and he's drown'd in the sea.

WANDERING WILLIE.

Here a-wa', there a-wa', wan-der-ing Wil-lie,
Here a-wa', there a-wa', here a-wa' hame! Lang have I
sought thee, dear have I bought thee, Now I have
got-ten my Wil-lie a-gain!

[1] In a direction contrary to the course of the sun.

Here awa', there awa', wandering Willie,
  'Here awa', there awa', here awa' hame !
Lang have I sought thee, dear have I bought thee,
  Now I have gotten my Willie again !

Through the lang muir I have followed my Willie ;
  Through the lang muir I have followed him hame.
Whatever betide us, nought shall divide us ;
  Love now rewards all my sorrow and pain.

Here awa', there awa', wandering Willie,
  Here awa', there awa', here awa' hame !
Come, love, believe me, nothing can grieve me,
  Ilka thing pleases while Willie's at hame.

For this beautiful song—verses and air—we are indebted to
the collections of Herd and Oswald. Burns, who admired the
latter extremely, composed to it a ballad of his own, representative of the feelings of his friend Mrs M'Lehose (Clarinda)
regarding the husband who had deserted her.

I LO'E NE'ER A LADDIE BUT ANE.

I lo'e ne'er a lad - die but ane, He
lo'es ne'er a lass - ie but me: He's
pro - mised to mak me his ain, And his

ain I am will - ing to be. He

coft me a roke - lay o' blue, And a

pair o' mit - tens o' green ; The

price was a kiss o' my mou'; And I

paid him the debt yes - treen.

I lo'e ne'er a laddie but ane,
    He lo'es ne'er a lassie but me :
He 's promised to mak me his ain,
    And his ain I am willing to be.
He coft me a rokelay o' blue,
    And a pair o' mittens o' green ;
The price was a kiss o' my mou' ;
    And I paid him the debt yestreen.

Let ithers brag weel o' their gear,
    Their land, and their lordly degree ;
I carena for ought but my dear,
    For he 's ilka thing lordly to me :

His words are sae sugar'd, sae sweet!
His sense drives ilk fear far awa'!
I listen—poor fool! and I greet;
Yet how sweet are the tears as they fa'!

Dear lassie, he cries wi' a jeer,
Ne'er heed what the auld anes will say;
Though we've little to brag o'—ne'er fear;
What's gowd to a heart that is wae?
Our laird has baith honours and wealth,
Yet see how he's dwining wi' care;
Now we, though we've naething but health,
Are cantie and leal evermair.

O Marion! the heart that is true,
Has something mair costly than gear;
Ilk e'en it has naething to rue—
Ilk morn it has naething to fear.
Ye warldlings, gae hoard up your store,
And tremble for fear ought you tyne;
Guard your treasures wi' lock, bar, and door,
While here in my arms I lock mine!

He ends wi' a kiss and a smile—
Wae's me, can I tak it amiss?
My laddie's unpractised in guile,
He's free aye to daut and to kiss!
Ye lasses wha lo'e to torment
Your wooers wi' fause scorn and strife,
Play your pranks—I ha'e gi'en my consent,
And this night I am Jamie's for life.

The first verse of this song, and another verse not reproduced here, are stated by Ritson to have been composed by 'J. D.;' but Burns ascribes them to Mr John Clunie, minister of Borthwick, Edinburghshire. This reverend gentleman, who is remembered as a good singer of Scotch songs, died on the 13th April 1819, at the age of sixty-two. The remaining verses were the composition of Hector Macneill.

WEBSTER'S LINES.

Oh, how could I venture to love one like thee,
And you not despise a poor conquest like me,
On lords, thy admirers, could look wi' disdain,
And knew I was naething, yet pitied my pain ?
You said, while they teased you with nonsense and dress,
When real the passion, the vanity 's less ;
You saw through that silence which others despise,
And, while beaux were a-talking, read love in my eyes.

Oh, how shall I fauld thee, and kiss a' thy charms,
Till, fainting wi' pleasure, I die in your arms ;
Through all the wild transports of ecstasy tost,
Till, sinking together, together we 're lost !
Oh, where is the maid that like thee ne'er can cloy,
Whose wit can enliven each dull pause of joy ;
And when the short raptures are all at an end,
From beautiful mistress turn sensible friend ?

In vain do I praise thee, or strive to reveal
(Too nice for expression), what only we feel :
In a' that ye do, in each look and each mien,
The graces in waiting adorn you unseen.
When I see you I love you, when hearing adore ;
I wonder and think you a woman no more :
Till, mad wi' admiring, I canna contain,
And, kissing your lips, you turn woman again.

With thee in my bosom, how can I despair ?
I 'll gaze on thy beauties, and look awa' care ;
I 'll ask thy advice, when with troubles opprest,
Which never displeases, but always is best.

In all that I write I'll thy judgment require ;
Thy wit shall correct what thy charms did inspire.
I'll kiss thee and press thee till youth is all o'er,
And then live in friendship, when passion's no more.

What appears as the first draught of this amatory lyric was
printed in the *Scots Magazine* for November 1747, and subsequently in the *Charmer*, 1751, with the signature 'A. W——r.'
The person here hinted at was a notable evangelical divine and
leader in the church-courts through all the middle years of the
last century, the Rev. Alexander Webster.   Previous to his death
in 1784, he had been for the greater part of his life minister of
the Tolbooth Church, Edinburgh, where he gathered about
him a congregation of special zeal and faithfulness in Calvinistic
convictions, who came to be commonly recognised as the
Tolbooth Whigs.   The great fact of his life was his organ-
isation of the scheme of a Fund for the Widows of Ministers
of the Scotch Kirk—a most beneficial institution.   One of
inferior moment, but still remarkable, was his leading the persecution against those of his brethren who had been concerned
in bringing forward the tragedy of *Douglas.*   Powerful evangelical preaching, immense capacity for claret, strong head
for calculations, opposition to theatricals, good-fellowship over
corporation and presbyterial dinners, were the somewhat incon-
gruous characteristics of Alexander Webster.   It is but another
oddity in so strange a composition, that he should have written
so erotic an effusion as his *Lines.*   The legend on that subject
is that, acting as *black-foot* for a friend who was in love with a
lady of rank, he unexpectedly made a favourable impression on
the fair one himself, and was consequently inspired with this
song breathing gratitude as well as love.   The lady, who became
Dr Webster's wife, was Mary Erskine, daughter of Colonel
John Erskine (brother of Alva) by Eupheme, sister of Thomas,
eighth Earl of Dundonald.   She was born in 1715, and died
in 1766.

BIDE YE YET.

We are indebted to Herd for the preservation of this cheerful little song, and to Johnson for giving us its air.

Gin I had a wee house and a

can - tie wee fire, A bon - nie wee wif - ie to

praise and ad - mire, A bon - nie wee yard - ie be-

side a wee burn, Fare - weel to the bod - ies that

Chorus.

yammer and mourn. And bide ye yet, and bide ye yet, Ye

lit - tle ken what may be - tide ye yet; Some

bon - nie wee bod - ie may fa' to my lot, And I'll

aye be can - tie wi' think - in' o't.

Gin I had a wee house and a cantie wee fire,
A bonnie wee wifie to praise and admire,
A bonnie wee yardie beside a wee burn,
Fareweel to the bodies that yammer and mourn.
    And bide ye yet, and bide ye yet,
    Ye little ken what may betide ye yet ;
    Some bonnie wee bodie may fa' to my lot,
    And I 'll aye be cantie wi' thinkin' o't.

When I gang afield and come hame at e'en,
I 'll get my wee wifie fu' neat and fu' clean ;
And a bonnie wee bairnie upon her knee,
That 'll cry Papa, or Daddie, to me.

And if there ever should happen to be
A difference atween my wee wifie and me ;
In hearty good-humour, although she be teased,
I 'll kiss her and clap her until she be pleased.

FOR LACK OF GOLD.

Miss Jean Drummond, daughter of John Drummond of Megginch, in Perthshire, was on some terms of affection with Dr Austin, an accomplished physician in Edinburgh, when unluckily the Duke of Athole called one day at her father's house, was struck by her tall elegant figure, and sought and won her for his bride. The forsaken swain gave vent to his feelings in the following song, which attained a certain degree of popularity, and found its way into Herd's Collection. The marriage of the duke to Miss Drummond took place on the 7th May 1749. Surviving her husband without issue, she married, for a second, Lord Adam Gordon, fourth son of Alexander, second Duke of Gordon, and commander of the forces in Scotland. She died in 1795, and was buried at Inveresk, where a handsome monument to her memory may be seen. Notwithstanding the jilted lover's declaration of eternal celibacy, he married and had a large family.

The song was composed to an air previously in existence in connection with a song, beginning 'For the lack of gold I lost her, O.'

For lack of gold she has left me, O, And of all that's dear she's be-reft me, O; She me for-sook for A-thole's duke, And to endless woe she has left me, O. A star and gart-er have more art Than youth, a true and faith-ful heart; For emp-ty ti-tles we must part— For glitt'-ring show she has left me, O.

For lack of gold she has left me, O,
And of all that 's dear she 's bereft me, O ;
She me forsook for Athole's duke,
   And to endless woe she has left me, O.
A star and garter have more art
Than youth, a true and faithful heart ;
For empty titles we must part—
   For glitt'ring show she has left me, O.

No cruel fair shall ever move
My injured heart again to love ;
Through distant climates I must rove,
   Since Jeany she has left me, O.
Ye powers above, I to your care
Resign my faithless, lovely fair ;
Your choicest blessing be her share,
   Though she has ever left me, O.

THERE 'S NAE LUCK ABOUT THE HOUSE.

This most felicitous song first appeared on the streets about
1772, and it was soon after taken into Herd's Collection. The
authorship is a matter of doubt. A copy of it, like a first draught,
was found among the papers of William Julius Mickle, the
elegant translator of the *Lusiad*, and the song has hence been
believed to be his, notwithstanding that he did not include it
in his own works. On the other hand, there has been some
plausible argument to shew that it must have been the work of
a Mrs Jean Adams, who kept a school at Crawford's Dyke,
near Greenock. The solution of the question seems now
unattainable.

And are ye sure the news is true? And
are ye sure he's weil? Is this a time to
think o' wark? Ye jauds, fling by your wheel. Is
this a time to think o' wark, When Col-in's at the
door? Rax down my cloak—I'll to the quay, And
see him come a-shore. For there's nae luck a-
bout the house, There's nae luck at a', There's
nae luck a-bout the house, When our guidman's a-wa'.

And are ye sure the news is true?
And are ye sure he's weil?
Is this a time to think o' wark?
Ye jauds, fling by your wheel.

Is this a time to think o' wark,
   When Colin 's at the door ?
Rax down my cloak—I 'll to the quay,
   And see him come ashore.
      For there 's nae luck about the house,
        There 's nae luck at a',
      There 's nae luck about the house,
        When our guidman 's awa'.

Rise up and make a clean fireside,
   Put on the mickle pat ;
Gie little Kate her cotton goun,
   And Jock his Sunday's coat.
And mak their shoon as black as slaes,
   Their stockins white as snaw ;
It 's a' to pleasure our guidman—
   He likes to see them braw.

There are twa hens into the crib,
   Ha'e fed this month and mair,
Mak haste and thraw their necks about,
   That Colin weil may fare.
My turkey slippers I 'll put on,
   My stockins pearl-blue—
It 's a' to pleasure our guidman,
   For he 's baith leal and true.

Sae sweet his voice, sae smooth his tongue ;
   His breath 's like cauler air ;
His very fit has music in 't,
   As he comes up the stair.
And will I see his face again ?
   And will I hear him speak ?
I 'm downricht dizzy wi' the thoucht :
   In troth I 'm like to greet.

THE BOATIE ROWS.

This beautiful song of the domestic affections, which Burns thought nearly equal to *There's nae Luck about the House*, was stated by him to have been the composition of 'a Mr Ewen of Aberdeen,' and the statement has never been contradicted. The person referred to appears to have been Mr John Ewen, a dealer in hardware in Aberdeen, who died on the 21st of October 1821, at the age of eighty. He was a native of Montrose, and at his death he destined his entire fortune, of about £16,000, for the founding of a hospital for the nurture and education of poor children in that burgh. It will be learned with surprise, that in this destination he overlooked a daughter who had married, as he probably thought, imprudently—a strange comment of fact upon the sentiment so touchingly indicated in the song. The will, however, was set aside by a decision of the House of Lords.

O weel may the boat-ie row, And bet-ter may she speed! And weel may the boat-ie row, That wins the bairns' bread! The boat-ie rows, the boat-ie rows, The boat-ie rows in-

deed; And   hap - py   be   the   lot   of   a'   That

wish - es   her   to   speed!

O weel may the boatie row,
    And better may she speed !
And weel may the boatie row,
    That wins the bairns' bread !
The boatie rows, the boatie rows,
    The boatie rows indeed ;
And happy be the lot of a'
    That wishes her to speed !

I cuist my line in Largo Bay,
    And fishes I caught nine ;
There 's three to boil, and three to fry,
    And three to bait the line.
The boatie rows, the boatie rows,
    The boatie rows indeed ;
And happy be the lot of a'
    That wishes her to speed !

O weel may the boatie row,
    That fills a heavy creel,
And cleads us a' frae head to feet,
    And buys our parritch-meal.
The boatie rows, the boatie rows,
    The boatie rows indeed ;
And happy be the lot of a'
    That wish the boatie speed.

When Jamie vow'd he would be mine,
　　And wan frae me my heart,
O muckle lighter grew my creel!
　　He swore we 'd never part.
The boatie rows, the boatie rows,
　　The boatie rows fu' weel;
And muckle lighter is the lade,
　　When love bears up the creel.

My kurch I put upon my head,
　　And dress'd mysel fu' braw;
I trow my heart was douf and wae,
　　When Jamie gaed awa':
But weel may the boatie row,
　　And lucky be her part;
And lightsome be the lassie's care
　　That yields an honest heart!

When Sawnie, Jock, and Janetie,
　　Are up, and gotten lear,
They 'll help to gar the boatie row,
　　And lighten a' our care.
The boatie rows, the boatie rows,
　　The boatie rows fu' weel;
And lightsome be her heart that bears
　　The murlain and the creel!

And when wi' age we 're worn down,
　　And hirpling round the door,
They 'll row to keep us hale and warm,
　　As we did them before:
Then, weel may the boatie row,
　　That wins the bairns' bread;
And happy be the lot of a'
　　That wish the boat to speed![1]

[1] From Johnson's *Scots Musical Museum*, vol. v., published *circa* 1796.
It is customary to abridge this song when sung, by giving only the first,
second, and sixth verses.

This fine modern air is the genuine tune of the ballad. Some years ago it was arranged as a glee, for three voices, by Mr William Knyvett of London, and has deservedly become very popular.

AULD ROBIN GRAY.

This king of all the Scotch ballads had a curious and interesting history. There was an old song of popular extraction, known by its *refrain*, 'The bridegroom grat [that is, wept] when the sun gaed down;' very foolish, but furnished with a pleasing air. An eccentric masculine lady, of great note in Scottish society, named Sophy Johnstone, sang this song to the youthful family of the Earl of Balcarres at Balcarres House, in Fife, and impressed Lady Anne in particular with a deep sense of the beauty of the melody. Soon after the close of the year 1771, Lady Anne, finding herself much alone in the paternal mansion, and rather melancholy, bethought herself of attempting, with such power of verse as she possessed, to compose, to the plaintive tones which had pleased her so much, some little history of virtuous distress in humble life such as might suit them. Taking the name of the old cow-herd of her father's home-farm—Robin Gray—she represented a young maiden as obliged by family misfortunes to accept him for a lover, and as being soon after overwhelmed with grief on the discovery that a youthful sweetheart, supposed to be dead, was still alive. It would appear from a recital of her own, that the ballad did not at first take fully the shape it afterwards bore, for she said one day to her little sister (subsequently Countess of Hardwicke), 'My dear, I have been writing a ballad—I am oppressing my heroine with many misfortunes—I have already sent her Jamie to sea, and broken her father's arm, and made her mother fall sick, and given her auld Robin Gray for a lover; but I wish to load her with a fifth sorrow in the four lines, poor thing! help me to one, I pray.' 'Steal the cow, sister Anne!' said the little Elizabeth. So the cow was immediately *lifted*, and the ballad completed. It soon got into circulation, without the name of the fair author, which was long a matter of mystery.

Balcarres.

Lady Anne survived to 1825, and only acknowledged the author-ship near the close of her life. She had, in 1793, married Sir Andrew Bernard, librarian to George III., who died in 1807.

Cordial as the reception of this fine song was from the beginning, it could not be said to experience the enthusiastic admiration which it now enjoys, till it was accommodated with a superior melody by the Rev. William Leeves, Rector of Wrington, in Somersetshire, the melody to which it is now invariably sung.

Mr Leeves's melody, not being Scottish, is, of course, only admitted here by sufferance, or for convenience. It seems

Mr Leeves's Cottage, Weston-super-mare.

proper that the original Scottish air should be added. It is here transcribed from Johnson's *Museum:*

When the sheep are in the fauld, and the
kye at hame, And a' the warld to
sleep are gane; The waes o' my heart fa' in
showers frae my e'e, When my guid-man lies
sound by me.

When the sheep are in the fauld, and the kye at hame,
And a' the warld to sleep are gane;
The waes o' my heart fa' in showers frae my e'e,
When my guidman lies sound by me.

Young Jam - ie loo'd me weil, and

socht me for his bride; But sav - ing a croun, he had

naething else be - side: To mak that croun a pund, young

Jam - ie gaed to sea; And the croun and the pund were

baith for me. He had - na been a - wa' a

week but on - ly twa, When my mother she fell sick, and the

cow was stown a - wa'; My father brak his arm, and young

Jam - ie   at   the   sea,   And   auld Rob - in   Gray   cam a-

court - in'   me.

Young Jamie loo'd me weil, and socht me for his bride;
But saving a croun, he had naething else beside:
To mak that croun a pund, young Jamie gaed to sea;
And the croun and the pund were baith for me.

He hadna been awa' a week but only twa,
When my mother she fell sick, and the cow was stown awa';
My father brak his arm, and young Jamie at the sea,
And auld Robin Gray cam a-courtin' me.

My father couldna work, and my mother couldna spin;
I toil'd day and nicht, but their bread I couldna win;
Auld Rob maintain'd them baith, and, wi' tears in his e'e,
Said, Jennie, for their sakes, oh, marry me!

My heart it said nay, for I look'd for Jamie back;
But the wind it blew high, and the ship it was a wreck:
The ship it was a wreck—why didna Jamie dee?
Or why do I live to say, Wae 's me?

My father argued sair: my mother didna speak;
But she lookit in my face till my heart was like to break:
Sae they gied him my hand, though my heart was in the sea;
And auld Robin Gray was guidman to me.

I hadna been a wife a week but only four,
When, sitting sae mournfully at the door,
I saw my Jamie's wraith, for I couldna think it he,
Till he said, I 'm come back for to marry thee.

Oh, sair did we greet, and mickle did we say;
We took but ae kiss, and we tore ourselves away:

I wish I were deid ! but I'm no like to dee ;
And why do I live to say, Wae's me !

I gang like a ghaist, and I carena to spin ;
I daurna think on Jamie, for that wad be a sin ;
But I'll do my best a guid wife to be,
For auld Robin Gray is kind unto me.

ROY'S WIFE OF ALDIVALLOCH.

This pretty, lively song was the composition of a lady of

Mrs Grant of Carron.

family, named Grant, born at Aberlour on Speyside, Banffshire,

2 B

about 1745—who married in succession her cousin, Mr Grant of Carron, near Elchies, and a Dr Murray, physician in Bath, where she died about 1814. A portrait of her, representing her as a handsome middle-aged lady in a beautiful dress of the last century, was brought forward in the remarkable museum of local antiquities and other objects of interest which graced the meeting of the British Association at Aberdeen in 1859.

Roy's wife of Al - di - val - loch,

Roy's wife of Al - di - val - loch,

Wat ye how she cheat - ed me, As

I cam o'er the braes o' Bal - loch.

She vowed, she swore, she wad be mine, She

said she lo'ed me best of on - y; But

oh! the fic - kle, faith - less quean, She's

ta'en the carle, and left her John - ie.

Roy's wife of Al - di - val - loch,

Roy's wife of Al - di - val - loch,

Wat ye how she cheat - ed me, As

I cam o'er the braes o' Bal - loch.

Roy's wife of Aldivalloch,
Roy's wife of Aldivalloch,
Wat ye how she cheated me,
As I cam o'er the braes o' Balloch.

She vowed, she swore, she wad be mine,
She said she lo'ed me best of ony;
But oh! the fickle, faithless quean,
She's ta'en the carle, and left her Johnie.
Roy's wife of Aldivalloch, &c.

O, she was a canty quean,
Weel could she dance the Highland walloch;
How happy I had she been mine,
Or I been Roy of Aldivalloch!
Roy's wife of Aldivalloch, &c.

> Her face sae fair, her een sae clear,
>   Her wee bit mou' sae sweet and bonnie ;
> To me she ever will be dear,
>   Though she 's for ever left her Johnie.
>   Roy's wife of Aldivalloch, &c.

It is one of the cases where a kind of immortality has been achieved by the writing of one successful song—for no other composition of Mrs Grant has ever come before the world. It is also one of those cases where a person of refinement has taken up and successfully purified an old vulgar song. It appears that there was a real Roy of Aldivalloch. 'On the 21st February 1727, John Roy, lawful son to Thomas Roy in Aldivalloch, was married to Isabel daughter of Alister Stewart, sometime resident in Cabrach [Highlands of Aberdeenshire].'[1] It is to be feared that the marriage was not a fitting or a happy one, for Mr Peter Buchan has preserved a homely ballad, from which it can be gathered that Roy was an old man, and that 'Tibbie' on one occasion was induced to leave her husband's house with a certain 'Davie Gordon in Kirktown,' but was pursued by Roy, and brought back, after an escape over the braes of Balloch.

> Silly body, Aldivalloch,
> Puir body, Aldivalloch ;
> He lost his hose and baith his shoon,
> Coming through the braes of Balloch.[2]

On the basis of this rough rustic ditty, Mrs Grant of Elchies produced the canzonet of disappointed love here for the hundredth time printed.

---

[1] Robert Carruthers in *Inverness Courier*. The *Banffshire Journal*, in January 1860, recorded the death of Margaret Roy, aged seventy-four, at Aldivalloch, in the Cabrach, Banffshire, the last descendant of the Roys of Aldivalloch.

[2] The entire ballad is presented in Mackay's *Book of Scottish Songs*, p. 65. The *Banffshire Journal*, in recording the death of Margaret Roy, states that an old lady who died in the Cabrach some years ago recollected the Roy of the ballad, which she said was the composition of a shoemaker residing in the neighbourhood of Aldivalloch.

LOCH ERROCH SIDE.

The melody of this song—than which there is scarcely any in greater popular favour, or more deserving of it—was long known as a dancing tune. The song here given in connection with it being that from which it takes its ordinary name, was written for it by a singular genius recognised in Edinburgh as *Balloon* Tytler, from an attempt he made in the art of aërostation about the time of its invention in France. Old Alister Campbell, who remembered the affair, described it to me a great many years ago in brief terms: 'Tytler's baloon,' said he, 'rose over a dyke, and then quietly settled on a midden.' It was a type of most of his ventures in life. I have seen a periodical work of which he was the author, but which he could not be said to have written, the truth being that he composed it at the printer's case from his own thoughts, without the usual intervention of manuscript. In him, some singular mental gifts were clouded by poverty and depressing family cares, and at length, having adopted the views of the Friends of the People, he was compelled to make an abrupt flight to America. He died, while editor of a newspaper, at Salem, Massachusetts, in the year 1805, aged fifty-eight.

As I cam by Loch Er - roch side, The lof - ty hills sur - vey - ing, The wat - er clear, the

heather blooms Their　fra - grance sweet con - vey - ing;

I　met, un - sought, my　love - ly maid,　I

found her like May　morn - ing; With　graces sweet, and

charms so rare, Her　per - son　all　a - dorn - ing.

As I cam by Loch Erroch side,
　The lofty hills surveying,
The water clear, the heather blooms
　Their fragrance sweet conveying ;
I met, unsought, my lovely maid,
　I found her like May morning ;
With graces sweet, and charms so rare,
　Her person all adorning.

How kind her looks, how blest was I,
　While in my arms I prest her !
And she her wishes scarce conceal'd,
　As fondly I caress'd her :
She said, If that your heart be true,
　If constantly you 'll love me,
I heed not care nor fortune's frowns,
　For nought but death shall move me.

But faithful, loving, true, and kind,
    For ever thou shalt find me ;
And of our meeting here so sweet,
    Loch Erroch sweet shall mind me.
Enraptured then, My lovely lass,
    I cried, no more we'll tarry !
We'll leave the fair Loch Erroch side,
    For lovers soon should marry.

To this delightful air Burns afterwards composed his song, *O stay, sweet warbling woodlark, stay;* but both have been thrown into the shade in our own time, as far as popularity is concerned, by a song called *The Lass o' Gowrie*, of which the following seems the best version :

'Twas on a summer afternoon,
A wee before the sun gaed down,
My lassie, wi' her braw new gown,
    Cam o'er the hills to Gowrie.
The rosebud wet wi' morning shower,
Blooms fresh within the sunny bower,
But Katie was the fairest flower
    That ever bloomed in Gowrie.

I praised her beauty, loud and lang,
Around her waist my arms I flang,
And said, My dearie, will ye gang
    To see the Carse o' Gowrie.
I'll tak ye to my father's ha',
In yon green field beside the shaw,
I'll mak ye lady o' them a',
    The brawest wife in Gowrie.

Saft kisses on her lips I laid,
The blush upon her cheeks soon spread,
She whispered modestly and said,
    I'll gang wi' you to Gowrie.
The auld folks soon gave their consent,
Syne for Mess John they quickly sent,
Wha tied us to our hearts' content,
    And now she's Lady Gowrie.

OWER THE MUIR AMANG THE HEATHER.

Com - in' through the Craigs o' Kyle, A-

mang the bon - nie bloom - ing heath - er,

There I met a bon - nie lass - ie,

Keep - in' a' her ewes the - gith - er.

Chorus.

Ower the muir a - mang the heath - er,

Ower the muir a - mang the heath - er,

There I met a bon - nie lass - ie,

Keep - in' a' her ewes the - gith - er.

Comin' through the Craigs o' Kyle,
   Amang the bonnie blooming heather,
There I met a bonnie lassie,
   Keepin' a' her ewes thegither.

    Ower the muir amang the heather,
    Ower the muir amang the heather,
    There I met a bonnie lassie,
    Keepin' a' her ewes thegither.

Says I, My dear, where is thy hame,
   In muir or dale, pray tell me whether?
She said, I tent the fleecy flocks,
   That feed amang the blooming heather.

We sat us down upon a bank,
   Sae warm and sunny was the weather;
She left her flocks at large to rove,
   Amang the bonnie blooming heather.

While thus we sat, she sang a sang,
   Till Echo rang a mile and further,
And aye the burden o' the sang,
   Was, Ower the muir amang the heather.

She charmed my heart, and aye sin' syne,
   I couldna think on ony ither:
By sea and sky she shall be mine,
   The bonnie lass amang the heather!

The above song is said to have been the composition of a woman named Jean Glover, who, strange to say, had deserted respectable, humble Scotch life, to accompany a very poor band of strolling-players. Burns tells us, 'I took the song down from her singing, as she was wandering through the country with a sleight-of-hand blackguard.'

O GIN MY LOVE WERE YON RED ROSE.

O gin my love were yon red rose,
    That grows upon the castle-wa',
And I mysel a drap o' dew,
    Into her bonnie breast to fa' !
Oh there beyond expression blest,
    I 'd feast on beauty a' the night,
Sealed on her silk-saft faulds to rest,
    Till fleyed awa' by Phœbus' light.

O were my love yon lilac fair,
    Wi' purple blossoms to the spring ;
And I a bird to shelter there,
    When wearied on my little wing ;
How I wad mourn when it was torn
    By autumn wild, and winter rude !
How I wad sing on wanton wing
    When youthfu' May its bloom renewed.

The first half of this song was published by Herd ; the second was afterwards added by Burns. In truth, only the first four lines are of any considerable age. They form the beginning of a simple old ditty, which had the following as a refrain :

My love 's bonnie, bonnie, bonnie,
    My love 's bonnie and fair to see ;
And aye when I think on her weel-faured face,
    Then in her company I would be.

The song, as completed by Burns, has been set to more than one air ; but the original and proper one, taking in the above refrain, is as follows :

Oh gin my love were yon red rose, That
grows up-on the cas-tle wa', And I my-sel a
drap o' dew, In-to her bon-nie breast to fa'!
My love's bon-nie, bon-nie, bon-nie, My love's bon-nie and
fair to see; And aye when I think on her
weel-faured face, Then in her com-pan-y I would be.

Oh gin my love were yon red rose
That grows upon the castle wa',
And I mysel a drap o' dew,
Into her bonnie breast to fa' !
My love's bonnie, bonnie, bonnie,
My love's bonnie and fair to see ;
And aye when I think on her weel-faured face,
Then in her company I would be.

FALSE LOVE, AND HA'E YOU PLAYED ME THIS?

False love, and ha'e you played me this, In sim-mer, 'mid the flow-ers? I sall re-pay thee back a-gain, In win-ter, 'mid the show-ers.

> False love, and ha'e you played me this,
>   In simmer, 'mid the flowers?
> I sall repay thee back again,
>   In winter, 'mid the showers.
>
> But again, dear love, and again, dear love,
>   Will ye not turn again?
> As ye look to other women,
>   Shall I to other men.

This romantic fragment appears in Herd's Collection. In Mr Kinloch's *Ancient Scottish Ballads* (1827) there is one entitled *The Gardener*, in which a young man of that profession entreats the love of a young lady by promising her a dress made of his best flowers. Her answer is as follows:

O, fare ye weil, young man, she says,
  Fareweil, and I bid adieu ;
Gin ye 've provided a weed for me
  Amang the simmer flowers,
I 've provided another for you
  Amang the winter showers.

The new-fawn snaw to be your smock,
  It becomes your bodie best ;
Your heid sall be wrapt in the blae cast wind,
  And the cauld rain on your breist.

CAN YE SEW CUSHIONS?

O can ye sew cush - ions, Or can ye sew
sheets, Or can ye sing Ba - loo - loo, When the bairnie
greets? And hee and ba - bird - ie, And hee and ba -
lamb, And hee and ba - bird - ie, My bon - nie wee
lamb. Hee - o, wee - o, what would I do wi' you?

Black's the life that I lead wi' you. O'er mon-y o' you,

lit - tle for to gi'e you, Hee - o, wee - o,

what would I do wi' you?

O can ye sew cushions,
   Or can ye sew sheets,
Or can ye sing Ba-loo-loo,
   When the bairnie greets ?
And hee and ba-birdie,
   And hee and ba-lamb,
And hee and ba-birdie,
   My bonnie wee lamb.
     Hee-o, wee-o, what would I do wi' you ?
     Black 's the life that I lead wi' you.
     O'er mony o' you, little for to gi'e you,
     Hee-o, wee-o, what would I do wi' you ?

I 've placed my cradle
   On yon holly top,
And aye, as the wind blew,
   My cradle did rock.
And hush-a-ba, baby,
   O ba-lilly-loo,
And hee and ba-birdie,
   My bonnie wee doo !
     Hee-o, wee-o, what would I do wi' you ? &c.

   This touching little nursery-song or lullaby appeared in
Johnson's *Museum*.

THE SILLER CROUN.

And ye sall walk in silk at - tire, And
sil - ler ha'e to spare, Gin ye 'll con - sent to
be his bride, Nor think o' Don - ald mair.
Oh, wha wad buy a silk - en goun, Wi'
a puir brok - en heart? Or what's to me a
sil - ler croun, Gin frae my love I part?

And ye sall walk in silk attire,
And siller ha'e to spare,
Gin ye 'll consent to be his bride,
Nor think o' Donald mair.

Oh, wha wad buy a silken goun,
    Wi' a puir broken heart ?
Or what 's to me a siller croun,
    Gin frae my love I part ?

The mind whase every wish is pure,
    Far dearer is to me ;
And ere I 'm forced to break my faith,
    I 'll lay me doun and dee ;
For I ha'e pledged my virgin troth,
    Brave Donald's fate to share,
And he has gi'en to me his heart,
    Wi' a' its virtues rare.

His gentle manners wan my heart,
    He gratefu' took the gift ;
Could I but think to seek it back,
    It wad be waur than theft.
For langest life can ne'er repay
    The love he bears to me ;
And ere I 'm forced to break my troth,
    I 'll lay me doun and dee.

This beautiful song, with its air, was printed in a sheet about
1780, and the name or names of author and composer have never
come to the knowledge of the world.

* * *

MARY'S DREAM.

The moon had climbed the high - est hill, Which
ris - es o'er the source of Dee, And from the eastern

summit shed Her sil - ver light on tower and tree:

When Mar - y laid her down to sleep, Her thoughts on Sandy

far at sea; When soft and low a voice was heard, Say,

Mar - y, weep no more for me.

The moon had climbed the highest hill,
  Which rises o'er the source of Dee,
And from the eastern summit shed
  Her silver light on tower and tree :
When Mary laid her down to sleep,
  Her thoughts on Sandy far at sea ;
When soft and low a voice was heard,
  Say, Mary, weep no more for me.

She from her pillow gently raised
  Her head to ask, who there might be ;
She saw young Sandy shiv'ring stand,
  With visage pale and hollow eye.
O Mary dear, cold is my clay,
  It lies beneath a stormy sea ;
Far, far from thee, I sleep in death ;
  So, Mary, weep no more for me.

Three stormy nights and stormy days
    We tossed upon the raging main ;
And long we strove our bark to save,
    But all our striving was in vain.
Ev'n then, when horror chilled my blood,
    My heart was filled with love for thee ;
The storm is past, and I at rest ;
    So, Mary, weep no more for me.

O maiden dear, thyself prepare,
    We soon shall meet upon that shore
Where love is free from doubt and care,
    And thou and I shall part no more.
Loud crowed the cock, the shadow fled,
    No more of Sandy could she see ;
But soft the passing spirit said,
    Sweet Mary, weep no more for me !

This elegant ballad was the composition of a young man, named
Alexander Low, of humble extraction in Galloway, but who
obtained a learned education, and became tutor in the family of
Mr M'Ghie of Airds, an amiable country gentleman, who had a
number of beautiful daughters.   While he resided at the Airds,
about 1771, the lover of one of the young ladies was lost at sea ;
and upon this incident the ballad was composed.   The young
poet emigrated to America, where he kept an academy for some
years, and died in 1798, aged about forty-eight.

LOGAN WATER.

By   Lo - gan's streams that   rin   sae deep, Fu'

aft wi' glee I 've herd - ed sheep;   Herded sheep or

gath - er'd slaes, Wi' my dear lad, on Lo - gan braes:

But, wae's my heart! thae days are gane, And,

fu' o' grief, I herd my lane; While my dear lad maun

face his faes, Far, far frae me and Lo - gan braes!

By Logan's streams that rin sae deep,
Fu' aft wi' glee I've herded sheep ;
Herded sheep or gather'd slaes,
Wi' my dear lad, on Logan braes :
But, wae's my heart! thae days are gane,
And, fu' o' grief, I herd my lane ;
While my dear lad maun face his faes,
Far, far frae me and Logan braes !

Nae mair at Logan kirk will he,
Atween the preachings, meet wi' me,
Meet wi' me, or, when its mirk,
Convoy me hame frae Logan kirk.
I weel may sing—thae days are gane !
Frae kirk and fair I come alane,
While my dear lad maun face his faes,
Far, far frae me and Logan braes !

This song, to the old tune of *Logan Water*, came before the public about 1783, being the composition of a young journeyman

printer, named John Mayne, a native of Glasgow, who died at
an advanced age in 1836. The air, to which there was a song of
old date and little refinement, is inserted in Mrs Crocket's
manuscript Music-book, 1709.[1] It was printed in the *Orpheus
Caledonius*, with the verses by James Thomson, beginning 'For
ever, Fortune, wilt thou prove.' Burns, having heard Mayne's
song, and being fond of the air, composed a song for the melody,
in which he unconsciously borrowed one of Mayne's couplets,
being the conclusion of the first stanza. It may be greatly
doubted if the Ayrshire bard, on this occasion, excelled the
Glasgow one.

GAE TO THE KYE WI' ME, JOHNIE.

O gae to the kye wi' me, John - ie,

O gae to the kye wi' me; O

gae to the kye wi' me, John - ie,

[1] In the Roxburghe Collection of Broadside Ballads in the British
Museum, there is one called *The Bonny Scottish Lad and the Yielding
Lass*, to an excellent new tune, much in request, called *The Liggan
Waters*. One of the verses may be given, as a specimen:

> Bonny lass, I love thee well,
>   Bonny lad, I love thee better;
> Wilt thou pull off thy hose and shoon,
>   And wend with me to Liggan Water?

And I 'll be mer - ry wi' thee. And

was - na she word - y o' kiss - es, And

was - na she word - y o' three, And

was - na she word - y o' kiss - es, That

Chorus.

gaed to the kye wi' me ? O

gae to the kye wi' me, John - ie, &c.

O gae to the kye wi' me, Johnie,
O gae to the kye wi' me ;
O gae to the kye wi' me, Johnie,
And I 'll be merry wi' thee.

And wasna she wordy o' kisses,
And wasna she wordy o' three,
And wasna she wordy o' kisses,
That gaed to the kye wi' me ?

I have a house a biggin,
  [And siller to mak it braw ;
I have a lass to bring hame till 't,
  That pleases me best of a'.

And if there be a wee bairnie,
  As I trow there may be,
I have a canny auld mother,
  Will doudle 't upon her knee.]

This song, in its full original form, was one of the old rustic chants of the people. It appeared first in Herd's Collection ; afterwards, with its lively air, in Johnson's *Museum*. Having a claim to a place in this work by the attractive character of the melody, it has been unavoidably subjected to some modification in the parts within brackets.

WILL YE GO TO FLANDERS?

Will ye go to Flanders, my Mal - ly O?

Will ye go to Flanders, my bon - nie Mal - ly O? There

we 'll get wine and bran - dy, And sack and su - gar can - dy;

Will ye go to Flan - ders, my Mal - ly O?

Will ye go to Flanders, my Mally O ?
Will ye go to Flanders, my bonnie Mally O ?
　There we 'll get wine and brandy,
　And sack and sugar-candy ;
Will ye go to Flanders, my Mally O ?

Will ye go to Flanders, my Mally O ?
And see the chief commanders, my Mally O ?
　You 'll see the bullets fly,
　And the soldiers how they die,
And the ladies loudly cry, my Mally O ?

This song is from Herd's Collection, and the air from Ritson's (1794).

SUPPLEMENT.

AIR OF THE EWE-BUCHTIN'S BONNIE.

[In connection with this song at page 313, it was stated that Mr Charles Kirkpatrick Sharpe published it with an air which had been composed for it by his father at a surprisingly early period of life. With some difficulty a copy of this rare sheet has been recovered. It bears the title of 'Absence : the words by Lady Grizell Baillie . . . . the air composed for the flageolet by the late Charles Sharpe of Hoddam, Esq., when seven years old: Edinburgh, 1838.' The beauty and suitableness of the air, apart from the singularity attending its composition, recommend it for being reprinted in this collection.]

O, the ewe-bucht-in's bon-nie, baith

e'en-ing and morn, When our blithe shepherds play on the

bog-reed and horn; While we're milking, they're lilting, baith

pleas-ant and clear—But my heart's like to break when I

think on my dear. O the shepherds take pleasure to

blow on the horn, To raise up their flocks o' sheep

soon i' the morn; On the bon-nie green banks they feed

pleas-ant and free, But, a - las, my dear heart, all my

sigh - ing's for thee!

INDEX TO THE FIRST LINES OF THE SONGS.

Edinburgh :
Printed by W. and R. Chambers.

www.ingramcontent.com/pod-product-compliance
Lightning Source LLC
Chambersburg PA
CBHW031823270326
41932CB00008B/525